Small Time Operator

How to Start Your Own Business, Keep Your Books, Pay Your Taxes And Stay Out of Trouble!

by Bernard B. Kamoroff, C.P.A.

BELL SPRINGS Publishing

Laytonville & Willits, California

Please Read:

I have done my very best to give you useful and accurate information in this book, but I cannot guarantee that the information is correct or will be appropriate to your particular situation. Laws, procedures and regulations change frequently and are subject to differing interpretations. It is your responsibility to verify all information and all laws discussed in this book before relying on them. Nothing in this book can substitute for legal advice and cannot be considered as making it unnecessary to obtain such advice. In all situations involving local, state or federal law, obtain specific information from the appropriate government agency or a competent person.

You Can Keep This Book Up To Date:

This edition of Small Time Operator is current as of the date shown below. Every January, we publish a one-page Update Sheet for Small Time Operator, listing changes in tax laws and other government regulations, referenced to the corresponding pages in the book. If you would like a copy of the Update Sheet, send a self-addressed, stamped #10 envelope (business size) and $1.00 to Small Time Operator Update, Box 1240, Willits, CA 95490.

Published by
BELL SPRINGS PUBLISHING
Box 1240, Willits, California 95490
telephone 707/459-6372   fax 707/459-8614
www.bellsprings.com
e-mail: publisher@bellsprings.com

**29th Edition (8th Trade Edition)
60th Printing, April, 2004**
Library of Congress Catalog Number 2004105365
ISBN: 0-917510-22-4

Printed by Consolidated Printers, Berkeley, Ca.
Cover illustration by Bruce McCloskey Design, Ukiah, Ca.
Cover layout by Jeanne H. Koelle, Koelle & Gillette, Willits, Ca.
Illustrations, cartoons and song lyrics used with permission
of copyright holders.

Small Time Operator and the man and cart
are trademarks of Bell Springs Publishing.

BE YOUR OWN BOSS

You can be your own boss. All it really requires is a good idea, some hard work, and a little knowledge.

"A little knowledge" is what this book is all about. *Small Time Operator* will show you how to start and operate your own business.

Small Time Operator is also written for anyone who is self-employed: professionals, freelancers, artists, consultants, independent contractors. You may not consider your occupation a "business," but the laws, the rules, procedures, bookkeeping, taxes, and most everything else you need to know to be successful, are pretty much the same.

And *Small Time Operator* is, hopefully, the road map to your success.

Small Time Operator is a technical manual, a step-by-step guide to help you set up the machinery of your business, the "business end" of your business, and keep it lubricated and well maintained. It is written in everyday English so anyone can understand it. You will not need a business education or an accounting dictionary to grasp the concepts or do the work.

Many people think that businessmen and businesswomen all come out of business school, kind of like Chevys coming out of a G.M. assembly plant. This just isn't true. I know many people in business, and most of them had no formal business education, and little or no experience.

Some new small business owners are people who just got tired of the "nine to five" life, tired of working for someone else, and who decided to go into business for themselves.

Some are people—hard working, talented people—who lost their jobs due to corporate downsizing and outsourcing.

Many new business people are still holding onto their regular jobs, but starting a part-time, sideline business, probably at home, to bring in some extra income, or to make a little money at something that started out as a hobby, or to experiment with their business ideas and learn the ropes before going at it full-time.

And just as many people start their own businesses because they are the kind of individuals who want to control their own destiny, to find independence, to succeed on their own terms.

Small Time Operator comes out of my experience during the past twenty years as a consultant and accountant for small businesses, and from operating two of my own small businesses. I've learned from successes and I've learned from mistakes, my own and others'. Now I hope to teach you what I've learned.

Small Time Operator will show you things to do and things not to do. But like any book, it can't do more than that. You've got to go ahead and do it yourself. Bilbo Baggins said, "One should always begin at the beginning." That's where you are now. Other people, many others, now run their own small businesses.

You can too.

The journey of a thousand miles begins with a single step.
—*Lao Tsu*

Contents

Section One
GETTING STARTED

Trying seems to be a start for getting things done
You get to know the right way by doing it wrong
And when you cross a bridge over shallow water
Does it always mean you're afraid to get wet
When you ought to?

—Barbara Pack

A Small Time Operator: A True Story

When I first met Joe Campbell several years ago, he was working as a switchman for Union Pacific. He liked working on the railroad. Didn't love it, but it was a job.

Joe's hobby and one of his great pleasures in life was electronics. He especially enjoyed assembling electrical gadgets from kits, repairing stereos, playing with anything that had wires and resistors. In the process of building and experimenting, Joe acquired a good theoretical and technical knowledge of electronics. It was not long before he'd built himself a few test meters and started repairing the neighbors' TVs. He used to offer to fix my stereo for free, just to get the experience.

Gradually, Joe's hobby developed into a business. He moved slowly at first, a step at a time. He set up a small workshop in a spare bedroom and began taking in paying business on evenings and weekends. Joe was a good repairman, he didn't charge much, and he gave his customers fast service. And Joe's business grew. He soon found himself with more business than he could handle in his spare time. He started working less hours for the railroad, then quit altogether and set up a small repair shop of his own.

Joe is a success, but not just because he makes his own living. Joe has shaped his life around his interests. He enjoys his work, and his customers recognize and appreciate the personal interest he takes in what he's doing. Joe "made it" because he worked hard to develop his interests and because he had the ambition to learn his trade. It *never* just comes naturally. Prior experience? He had none. A business background? None. Money? He saved a few hundred dollars to spend on test gear and parts, not much more.

The most important lesson to learn from Joe, I feel, is that you can start out easily and simply. You don't have to make the Big Plunge, selling everything you own and going into debt. More than two-thirds of all new businesses are started as part-time or weekend ventures, started by people still holding onto a job while they experiment with their new business. So, start slowly, try it out and learn as you go. You'll get there.

Things worked well for Joe. But if they had not—if he really did not have it in him to be in business for himself, or if he just picked the wrong thing at the wrong time—he could easily have stopped anywhere along the way with little or no loss. And maybe try it again sometime.

What Kind of Business?

Joe's repair shop is an example of what is commonly called a "service" business. He *does* something for his customers and they pay him for his services. You can also support yourself by selling something (sales) or by making something (manufacturing). Many businesses combine several of these aspects, such as sales and service.

A service business is the easiest to set up. It requires the smallest initial investment and the simplest bookkeeping. It is also the easiest kind of business to operate out of your home. On the other hand, you will have to be competent at the service you offer. More than any other business, a service business will require some experience. A service business is more likely to be subject to state licenses and regulations.

If you do something well—fixing things, painting or decorating, writing or editing, cutting hair, programming computers—these are but a few possibilities for your own service business. And if you are good at something, you might consider teaching those skills to others, as a self employed seminar leader or consultant. Be imaginative. Don't ignore your own resources.

Find a need and fill it.
—*Lettered on a cement truck, Oakland, Ca.*

A sales business can take many different forms: retail, wholesale, storefront, mail order, direct sales, network marketing, Internet sales, or some other approach.

Your own sales business allows you to select and handle merchandise that reflects your own interests and tastes, and the interests and needs of your community. Most sales businesses will require inventory (stock on hand) which means a bigger investment than a service business. You may need a storefront or showroom to display your goods and attract customers. You will have to keep inventory records. Bookkeeping is a little more complex.

Sales businesses, however, offer more flexibility than service. Service people are often limited by their training and experience. With sales, as your interests change and as the fashions change, it is easy for your sales business to change with them.

Manufacturing, for many small businesses, means crafts: leather, clothing, pottery, jewelry and furniture to name a few. Crafts offer, probably more than any other business, an opportunity for the craftsperson to do what he or she enjoys for its own pleasure, and get paid for it, too. But again, you have to be good at what you're doing. Nobody wants an ugly necklace or a chair that falls apart. And more than with a sales or service business, you may have a harder time finding a steady and reliable market for your product. But if you have imagination and talent, you might discover that what you think of as your hobby can become your source of income.

Conventional manufacturing often requires a large investment in machinery. But you would be surprised how many successful manufacturing businesses started out in some inventor's garage with homemade, experimental equipment, on a surplus-store budget.

Mike Madsen owns Mike Madsen Leather, manufacturer and seller of hand-made leather goods: "Look around, figure out what you want to do, and then try to sum up your business in one sentence or a paragraph at the most. No more than that or you haven't done it. And then concentrate on doing just that. Realize that business is just like life in a lot of ways, and you take things step by step. You don't become a big business overnight. You build it little by little every day you walk into the building. You get started through your own will and determination and have a little fun at it.

"You can learn a lot by observation. If you own a business, try to visit other people who are in similar businesses. When I was in Argentina I went to seven leather factories. They're very willing to show you something when you're not in direct competition, and they're pleased to show off their business. But if you and I lived in the same city, you might be less willing to show your manufacturing process to a future competitor.

"Small business is the backbone of this country. Big businesses provide main-line products, but it's small business that provides all the little things that make your life interesting. I think it's also the kind of people who are in small business, those of a pioneering spirit. We built a country on pioneering spirit. That's just what being in a small business is, being a pioneer."

Business Failure Rate

The well-known statistics often spouted by the Small Business Administration and other business organizations, that 60% of all new businesses fail the first year, is totally misleading. First of all, I think it is a flawed statistic. Nobody, not even the Internal Revenue Service, has been able to come up with a failure rate for businesses. They can't even determine how many businesses actually exist in the United States.

But even if the failure figures are accurate, just because 60% of new businesses fail, this does not mean your own business has a 60% chance of failure. There are some businesses, businesses that just weren't well thought out, that are virtually guaranteed to fail. There are some businesses, ones that were well thought out and planned, that have an almost 100% chance of success.

Your chance of success or failure has a lot to do with the kind of business you are starting, your ability to find and keep customers, your talent at running a business, and how well you prepare yourself for this new venture.

The Successful Business "Triangle"

There are many, many factors that make a business a success, or a failure. But there are three major points, three major keys to success, that every business should have.

You might think of it as a triangle. If you remember your high school physics, the triangle is the strongest structure that human beings can create. The same applies to business, and the strength comes from all three corners of that triangle.

One corner, and the most obvious, is the product or service you are offering. The more quality and the more value you offer your customers, the more likely you will stand out from the crowd. Offer a product or service that's better, more reliable, more useful, and more appreciated than the cheap products in this mass produced world of ours.

The second corner of your business triangle, and possibly the biggest one, is marketing and promotion: spreading the word about your business, finding and keeping customers. Marketing can take many different approaches, and is often trial and error, finding what works for you. Many business owner devote as much as half their working hours to marketing. And for many business owners, it's a real challenge. But without marketing, no customers. Without customers, no business.

The third corner of your business is the "business end" of the business: the legal and tax issues, the permits and licenses, the office work and bookkeeping that's required of every business, every self-employed individual. It's the grease that keeps the machinery running, the glue that keeps it all from coming apart at the seams. It's the least loved part of business, yet not difficult to learn and manage. After reading this book and spending a few months at it, the "business end" of your business should become almost second nature.

Can You Do It?

There is another important factor in the success of your venture. You. Can you do it?

You don't have to be an expert in the line of business that you're thinking of going into, but you do have to be willing to learn. There are people who actually try to start a certain business because it's a "sure thing," a "guaranteed" big seller, and they know absolutely nothing about the field. Some of these people are, of course, real hustlers, but there are a lot of honest

dopes in this group. They think that a little money and some good intentions are all they need to get started. And most of them soon wind up with neither their money nor any intention of ever being in business again.

I've known a lot of people in business, some who made it, some who didn't. And while nobody has a guaranteed secret for success, I believe that there are a few basic characteristics that you've got to have or be willing to develop if you're going to start a business, *any* business.

Organization: The first and most important characteristic, I feel, is a clear head and the ability to organize your mind and your life. The "absent-minded professor" may be a genius, but he will never keep a business together.

In running a small business, you are going to have to deal with many different people, keep schedules, meet deadlines, organize paperwork, pay bills, and the list goes on. It's all part of every business. So if balancing your checkbook is too much for you, or you just burned up your car engine because you forgot to check the oil, maybe you're not cut out for business. If you are someone who can never find your keys, or your tools, or important documents, you may find running a business more of a struggle. The work in a small business is rarely complicated, but it has to be done and done on time. Remember, this is going to be *your* business. It's all up to you. Being organized is your key to sanity.

Reading Carefully: A second important characteristic is the ability to read carefully. Most of your business transactions will be handled on paper or computer, and if you don't pay attention to what you're doing, you could miss out. You may receive special orders for your product. You will be billed by suppliers in all kinds of ways, sometimes offering discounts if you are prompt in paying. You will have to fill out a lot of government forms. Government agencies cannot exist without forms, and the instructions for these forms are sometimes tricky. If you mess up, these agencies have the most aggravating way of telling you that you have to do it all over again.

Numbers: A third important trait is, if not a "head for numbers," at least a lack of fear of numbers. Tax accountants get rich off of people who look at a column of six numbers and panic. It doesn't have to be that way. The math involved in running a small business is mostly simple arithmetic, addition, subtraction, some multiplication.

Personality: If you plan to operate a retail store, a service business, or any other business where you will be in regular contact with the public, you should be a person who likes to deal with people.

Are you friendly and outgoing, pleased to talk about your products—and the weather, the ball scores, and the latest neighborhood gossip? Do you like selling, solving people's problems, listening to complaints, answering the same questions over and over again? Do you look forward to running a store five, six or even seven days a week, keeping regular hours, stocking shelves, doing repetitive tasks every day?

There are many fine people, potentially excellent business people, who are not the outgoing type, who would never survive behind the counter, and who certainly shouldn't be running a retail operation. And fortunately, there are many businesses that don't require these personality traits. Mail-order, Internet businesses, manufacturing, some service businesses, businesses where you don't face the public every day, businesses where you know all your customers, businesses where you do custom work for only a few people: these businesses do not rely so much on your personality, and they won't require that you constantly act and dress a certain way.

One More Key To Success...

Pay your bills on time. In fact, pay your bills early. Your suppliers, your landlord, your bank, everyone you do business with will love you. They'll go out of their way to help you. You'll be "one of our best customers," and you'll get priority treatment.

What's more, if you pay your bills as soon as you get them, you don't have to keep an unpaid bills file, you don't have to remember that a bill is due. It's one less chore to worry about.

Whether you think you can, or whether you think you can't, you're right.
—Mary Kay Ash, founder, Mary Kay Cosmetics

Get Some Help

Is all of this too much for you? Still feel you have a good product or a good service to sell but, Oh! all this paperwork...

If you are alone in your venture, short of hiring a bookkeeper or finding a partner, there is no alternative. You just have to learn to do it. Very often, however, the future business owner with no business moxie is blessed with a wife, husband, partner or friend who has all those fine traits and is just itchin' to be part of it all.

Mike Madsen, Mike Madsen Leather: "You talk to people who are working on a salary, they don't understand what being in business is all about. They're not risk takers. They're not striving to make a whole number of things work simultaneously. They go to work in the morning and have a prescribed routine and they get off at five o'clock, and they go home and their business is done. But if you're in business for yourself, you don't turn off the switch when you go home. You're constantly thinking about it."

YOUR IDEA—and the Market

Every person who has ever started a business, I imagine, thought he or she had a good idea. It's the smart person, and the rare person, who tries to find out the most important thing: do other people think it's a good idea? The majority of new businesses fail because the majority of new business owners never looked past their own desires and dreams, gave no real forethought to their ventures—no "market research," which is just a fancy term for "look before you leap."

Do people really want what you have to sell? Can you find these people and convince them that they should buy from you instead of from someone else—someone else who may have a better product, a better price, a better location, a good reputation?

No matter how good your business idea is, you still must have a market—someone who is willing to buy your product or pay for your services. Talk to your friends; they're consumers. How many of them would buy what you have to sell? Then look around your community. Does your product or service fit the social, economic and ethnic make-up of the area? Will your product appeal to these people? Can they afford it?

How many other businesses in the area are doing the same thing? How well are they doing? Is there room for one more business of this type? Can you improve upon what's already out there?

As important as it is to do research, don't let it stand in the way of trying things out. Instead of spending the next six months researching the market, you could begin to spread the word, run a few ads, set up a small web site, and know more about your market and whether you have a viable business, than any research will be tell you. You'll know whether you have something people want and are actually willing to pay for.

Mike Simon, Metric Motors Auto Repair: "There are some people who want to work for themselves, and they're not going to be happy working for anybody else. And then other people don't like the responsibility. They want to go in and work their 9 to 5 and not have to worry about it when they go home. It takes a certain kind of person to run your own business, to accept the responsibilities and be thinking abut it all the time. The first two years I worked, I worked seven days a week from 7 in the morning until 7 at night. And now I take Sundays off. But I wouldn't have it any other way. I could have made more money working for somebody else, but I'm happy with the way it is. And I think in the future it will be to my advantage. As for the guy who's working 9 to 5, I'll be better off than he is. Of course, he thinks he's better off than I am."

BUSINESS LOCATION

For retail stores, retail service businesses, restaurants, and other businesses where customers come to you, location is critical. A bad neighborhood, a street that's hard to find, a location away from other shops, a location where it's difficult to park, a store too far away from the kind of customer you seek—any of these factors can easily lead to business failure, quickly. Do not underestimate the importance of the business location. Do not settle for a poor location. Do not compromise.

Is the location in a good business area? How many people shop nearby? Is there adequate parking? Do the neighboring businesses attract the kind of customers you are looking for?

Before you rent a storefront, find out why it's vacant. Try to locate the former tenant and ask him why he moved. Talk to other shopkeepers in the area and learn as much as you can about the area and its shoppers. A nearby supermarket or discount store is usually a plus because it will draw a lot of people to the area.

Be wary if there are several unoccupied buildings for rent. Besides being a general sign of a poor business area, vacant buildings make poor neighbors. Shoppers tend to stay away from them, and from you.

Spend a full day or two observing the area. A steady stream of pedestrians passing your door is the biggest single help a store can get. Avoid side streets, even if they are right around the corner from a main shopping street. Most shoppers will not go out of their way, even a few feet, to check you out. And get a first floor location. Second floor shops are less accessible, less visible, and less inviting. Customers who don't know you will not make that commitment, will not walk up a flight of stairs.

A location on a street that many people use going to and from work will make you even more visible, especially a street with a slow speed limit. If people are whizzing by at 55 mph, you're just a blur in the rear view mirror. Being close to a well known landmark will help because it is a point of reference people can easily remember.

Mall Businesses

Renting space in a busy mall, or inside another much larger business (such as a coffee shop in a

WalMart) will guarantee the customer traffic you want, but the lease payments may be high, and sometimes you must pay a percentage of your sales. You probably will have to conform to rules regarding signage and appearance, and you will not be able to keep your own hours.

Non-Retail Businesses

For businesses that don't rely on customers coming to the door—manufacturers, wholesalers, workshops, mail-order, Internet, many service businesses—the location is no longer of critical concern. You can find a place suitable to your own needs: close to home, inexpensive, close proximity to your suppliers and the services you require, easy access for deliveries and pick-ups.

In many cities, small businesses are finding excellent facilities in old and formerly run-down industrial areas of town. Real estate developers are buying abandoned commercial buildings, fixing them up, dividing them into smaller offices, shops, and warehouse spaces; and renting at prices much lower than the busy shopping areas.

Business Incubators

Some developers are creating what they call "business incubators" (also known as executive suites, business centers, and serviced offices). These facilities provide, in addition to a location, shared support services such as secretaries, management counselors, conference rooms, office equipment, truck docks, and other amenities.

As the term implies, incubators are often first-step locations for new businesses. After a few years, you no longer need nor care to pay for many of the support services. You are ready to be on your own. You've been hatched, so to speak.

Some incubators are simply a rental situation: you rent space and shared services. Some incubators are also investment financing. The individual or company providing the incubator invests in your business, participates in management, takes part ownership of your business, shares in—and sometimes takes most of—the profits.

The Building

Before you sign a rental agreement, be sure the building is right for you. Is it large enough, or is it perhaps too large? Measure the square

footage yourself. Landlords often give out incorrect square footage information.

Will the building require extensive remodeling? Make sure the roof doesn't leak. Test the heating and air conditioning. Do you control your own heating and air conditioning? How expensive will it be to heat and cool the building? Are your utilities on a separate meter from other tenants in the building? Check out exterior lighting around sidewalks and parking areas. How good is the building security?

Learn all you can about the other tenants. If their behavior and activities annoy your customers, you may lose business. Ask neighbors how they feel about the location. Are people hanging out on the corner? How will that affect your business?

Have the store examined by the local building inspector and, if you plan to serve food, by the health inspector. You don't want to learn after you've moved in that you have to spend a thousand bucks to bring the premises up to code. Don't rely on the previous tenant or the landlord for this information. Building violations are often ignored or just not noticed by the inspectors, until a new business moves in.

Is the building wheelchair accessible? Many businesses must comply with the Americans with Disabilities Act (ADA). Find out if you might be required to redesign the entrance.

Zoning

Before you sign a lease, check with the local zoning department to make sure the building is zoned for your use. Find out if there are any special requirements, such as off-street parking or sign limitations. Again, don't rely on the landlord for this information. Even if a similar business previously occupied the same building without zoning problems, it is no guarantee you'll have no problems. The old business may have been there before current zoning laws were in effect (called "grandfathering"), or the former business may have had a variance, one that may or may not be transferred to you.

If there are zoning problems, don't give up right away. Zoning officials often have authority to negotiate variances, to make exceptions to the rules. Be sure to get any variance in writing.

The Lease

Can you get a suitable lease? Without a lease, the landlord can, with little or no notice, evict you or arbitrarily raise the rent to any amount he pleases. Don't count on oral agreements with a landlord. Get a written lease that covers all the details, options, and who's responsible for what. Never assume *anything*.

There is no such thing as a standard lease. Every provision in a lease is negotiable, and you should read and understand every word. You may have to live with it for years.

How many years will the lease run? Is it renewable, will the rent increase, and by how much? Can you get out of the lease if your business fails or if you want to move? Can you sublet? If you sell the business, can you transfer the lease to the new owner? If the landlord sells the building, will you be at the mercy of the new owner, or will the old lease legally be binding on the new owner? Can you get a protection clause in which the landlord agrees not to rent adjacent space to a competitor? Can you get first refusal if adjacent space becomes available?

Who is responsible for repairs, maintenance, janitorial and garbage? How quickly will a problem be fixed? Who is responsible for damage due to fire, or a broken water pipe or any other calamity? Do you have to pay rent if you are forced to close temporarily due to damage to the building? Are there restrictions on parking, or signs, or hours of use? Can the landlord enter your premises without your permission?

Most leases require tenants to have liability insurance, naming the landlord as additionally insured, to protect the landlord in case one of your customers is injured at your business. Many leases require you to have property insurance on the landlord's building and insurance covering other tenants in the building.

Home Based Businesses

Over 50% of all small businesses in the U.S. are operated out of the owners' homes. Depending on the kind of business you operate, the kind of customers, size of the business, and possible problems with zoning, neighbors, parking, delivery, and other issues, your home may be the ideal location to start a new business. See the section "Home Based Businesses."

"As far as I'm concerned, location is everything." Lara Stonebraker owns Cunningham's Coffee, a retail store: "That can make or break a business. If you don't already have an established reputation, nobody will go looking for you in some obscure place. You have to be where there is a lot of foot traffic, and you have to be located next to some other established business that already has a clientele you can draw on.

"The corner is the best choice, and you usually have to pay more rent for it. The middle of the block is less desirable because there isn't as much visibility or parking. Parking can be a great problem. I've known a lot of fine businesses to fail because people would just get exasperated not being able to find a parking space and never go in them.

"One of the things we did at every location we looked at was spend a day just sitting around, hanging around, and watching the traffic flow, the patterns of the way people walk, where they stopped, and how many people came in and out of different stores in order to assess the desirability of that location.

"Talk to the building inspector and the health inspector and find out what the building and health codes are for your particular business. We made the mistake of seeing them after we signed the lease and then discovered that we had to put in a load of improvements that rightfully should not have been our responsibility. That was a large amount of money that was just lost. The inspectors don't check old businesses, but they check every new one. You apply for a permit, you have to get a business license, then they know what kind of business it is and they send out their people. If you're doing any construction inside, any electrical work, the plumber has to get a permit, the electrician has to get a permit—you can't get away from it."

Joe Campbell owns Resistance Repair, a stereo repair shop. He recently moved his shop *away* from a high foot traffic area to a more remote part of town:

"In a service business, especially a technical service business, customers don't have the slightest idea how to determine even the most rudimentary things about their equipment. If it doesn't work, they don't have the means of determining what is wrong. So you get an incredible amount of people who come in and just go on and on, like an old Kenmore on the spin cycle, about some problem which is extremely minor and usually is a hookup problem. They've just got it hooked up wrong, which means they didn't read their instruction book. But it's hard to convince them of that, and they all want detailed explanations.

"If you're in a high foot traffic area, you get the guy who's going to the restaurant next door for lunch, and as he walks out he thinks, 'Ah, there's a stereo repair shop. I'll stop in here and ask this guy about my problem...' and he comes in and there's 20 minutes gone. You get people who come in and say, 'I need your recommendation of the 15 best stereos you can buy, and why.' Just enormous time and energy sinks. Those people don't spend money. The kind of people who spend money are the people who walk in the door with stereos under their arms, and say, 'Fix this mother, it doesn't work, and call me when it's ready.'

"My traffic was never off the street. It was from referrals from other stereo shops. I took around cards and there was such a big demand for a reasonable, good repair shop that they'd send people by.

"You don't need those twerks who walk in off the street. You need the people who have the confidence in you and, by reputation, know that they can dump it in your hands. Now, when somebody walks through that door they've either got a stereo under their arm or they're picking one up. If they're there to pick it up, that means when they leave you're going to have money in the cash register. If they're coming in the door with one, that means two weeks later you're going to have money in the cash register. Those are the only two reasons you want that front door to open."

Rural Businesses

It's a dream many people have, to move to the peace and quiet of the countryside and start a relaxed, prosperous little business. Unfortunately, a large percentage of these rural shops fail. The main reason? There are not enough people and there is not enough money in rural communities to support anything but the most basic businesses.

A tropical fish store is not going to survive in West Pork Chop, Oklahoma. Nor will an art gallery or a leather crafts workshop. The business just isn't there.

Service businesses, repair shops, trades, have the best chance of survival in a rural area. But even these will have to compete with established locals who know everyone in town and have all the business.

When you have a particular area in mind, get to know the area and its residents first before you try to set up a business that caters to them. Ideally, you should live in the area awhile, and then try to judge what product or service the people need. Most country people are not wealthy; they don't spend money on things they have no use for.

Many successful rural businesses do not depend on local customers. They "export" their products and services out of the area. Manufacturing and crafts businesses have retail accounts in nearby metropolitan areas. Mail order businesses, Internet businesses, publishers, designers, and some professionals and consultants can do all their business via the mail, phone, fax and computer.

FINANCING: How Much Do You Need?

How much money you need depends a lot on the type of business you are starting and the type of person you are. If you are willing to work hard, to make a few sacrifices, to live on canned beans for a while, you can start a successful business for little or no investment.

Every service business I know started with almost no money. I started my accounting practice with my computer, an adding machine, and 500 business cards. My friend Joe Campbell started Resistance Repair with $500 worth of test equipment. Another friend's computer programming service was started with $50 in supplies. Self-employed carpenters, mechanics and repair people often start with their box of tools, period.

If you start a crafts business, you will need, besides your tools, materials to make your product. But you do not have to stock a large supply of inventory, and if you hunt around you can always find good deals on remnants and close-out materials. All of the craft business owners interviewed for this book started their businesses with less than $2,000 initial investment.

A retail store requires a good stock of inventory, which will cost at least a few thousand dollars, often a good deal more. A retail business can sometimes save on initial inventory costs by taking goods on consignment, as in a custom dress shop, or by having only samples on hand (or on your web site) and taking orders for the goods.

In addition to the money you need to get started, you will need "working capital" (day to day expenses) to operate the business until it becomes profitable. The money *always* seems to keep going out long before it starts coming in.

Mike Simon owns Metric Motors, a repair shop: "I started with basically nothing and built from that. I had a box of hand tools and some jacks, nothing very impressive. If I had to have a tool, I'd buy it and then I'd have it. I have about $5,000 worth of equipment now. A lot of garage owners buy $20,000 worth of equipment right at the start and don't have the clientele to pay it off. I'd say starting out small would be a smart thing to do. Find some place that's not expensive to rent, like this place. Don't put a lot of money into tools or inventory and try to keep your costs down to a minimum until you can build your business up."

Lara Stonebraker's coffee store: "The worst thing you can do is start a retail business on a shoestring. If you're undercapitalized, your store will not be impressive when you open because it will be empty. There's nothing worse than walking into an empty store. It's bound to fail because it embarrasses people. If you don't have your shelves just crammed with stuff, and if you don't have an attractive, prosperous looking store, you might as well forget it. And you really ought to have not only enough money to open the doors, but enough to run the business for the first six months, because you'll be running it at a loss for sure."

START-UP CAPITAL:
Financing A New Business

There are three typical financing arrangements for new businesses: (1) Self-financing: you put up your own money. (2) Debt financing: you borrow money. (3) Equity financing: you take on a partner or a stockholder, an individual who acquires an ownership interest in your business in exchange for start-up money.

Self-Financing

Just about every new business is at least partly self-financed, and many are 100% self financed. A lot of new business owners cannot find anyone to loan them money or to invest in their untested and obviously risky ventures.

Many new business owners self finance simply because they do not *want* outside financing and the risk and pressure of having to pay off a loan, and do not want to worry about, or share the profits with, a partner or co-owner.

Debt Financing (Loans)

When someone lends you money, you promise to pay it back, usually with interest. Most business loans are personal loans: you, the owner of the business, personally guarantee the loan, and you must repay the loan whether your business succeeds or not, out of your personal non-business assets if necessary. This is quite different from "equity financing" where you acquire a partner or an investor who only gets paid back if the business succeeds.

Most loans to new businesses come from relatives, friends, and acquaintances. Conventional bank loans are difficult to get for first-time business people. People who know you, and possibly people they know, are much more likely to help finance your venture than an extra-cautious, policy-laden bank. Quite often, someone you know or someone you can be introduced to has some extra money, and might be willing to take a chance on your business, if they like you and your idea and the terms of the financing.

There are no real standards when it comes to this kind of informal financing. People lending money will most likely want a better interest rate than they would get at a bank. Often they already have a good idea of the rate they would like to get. The repayment terms are entirely between you and the lender.

Private loans should be in writing and should include the names and addresses of the lender and borrower, the amount, the date the loan was given, the interest rate, and the pay-back terms, and signed by both parties. This is especially important for loans from relatives, so it is clear that this is a loan and not a gift. If you are unable to repay the loan, the lenders can take a bad-debt tax write-off without risk that the IRS will try to say the loan wasn't really a loan, but a non-deductible family gift.

Most loans are paid back over a period of months or years, with equal periodic payments. Some loans are repaid all at once at the end of the loan period. The terms are entirely up to the lender and borrower. You may want a clause allowing you to pay off the loan early without penalty if you, the borrower, so desire.

If the loan agreement is kept simple, you can write it up yourself. If the agreement gets complicated, with late-payment penalties, collateral, provisions for death of one of the parties, etc., you will probably want professional help drafting the agreement.

Find out if your state requires a notary's endorsement, filing or registering the loan papers, or other requirements. Your state's Secretary of State office or the county clerk can probably give you information.

When the loan is paid off, have the lender write "Paid in full" on all copies, sign and date them, and return them to you. If the loan is filed with the state or county, the final pay-off (or "reconveyance") should be recorded.

Bank Loans

For new businesses, bank loans are hard to get. The banks are less willing than ever to take chances on new and untested businesses and new and untested entrepreneurs. Many new businesses are looking for very small loans (small, that is, by bank standards) and banks don't make any money on those. It's a lot of time and paperwork, not to mention the risk, for little return.

Banks, however, do sometimes make small business loans, and a bank just may make one to you—if you can convince the bank that your business has a good potential for success, that you are competent and reliable, and that you have a good plan to repay the loan.

Not all banks are alike, so try several. A young progressive bank is more likely to be interested in you and your needs than staid old First Conservative, Est. 1833. The bank's advertising may indicate its willingness to do business with you.

If you have done business with or obtained a loan from a particular bank, that bank is a good place to start. When a bank knows you, knows something of your willingness and capability to repay a loan, it will be more willing to give serious consideration to your ideas. If you know influential people in the community, have them put in a word for you. "It's who you know" goes a long way in *all* business dealings.

When you meet a banker, come well prepared. Bring a resume that includes your general and educational background and your prior experi-

ence. Read the chapter on business plans at the end of this section, and create one. Bring a personal financial statement and a statement projecting income and expenses of your business for the first six months or year. The chapter "Profit And Loss Statements" in the Bookkeeping section will help you prepare the projections.

The bank will expect you to have some of your own money invested in your business, typically a third to half of the starting capital.

You will most likely need collateral, security to give the bank. The bank may want a mortgage on equipment or even a second mortgage on your home. This is called a "secured" loan, the only kind usually available to new businesses. "Unsecured" loans, ones that don't require collateral, are usually available only to successful, proven businesses who are long time bank customers.

But stop! Are you ready to risk your home or other valuables on your new business? When you borrow money for your business, you are *personally* liable to pay it back. If the business fails, you will be required to repay the loan from your personal funds. In taking out a loan, you are making a big personal commitment. Be sure you are not getting yourself in over your head.

When you get a loan, read the fine print. Look out for loan fees (points), closing costs, late-payment charges, and prepayment penalties.

Other Possible Loan Sources

A surprising number of people finance their new businesses with their personal credit cards. This of course is an expensive method, given the high interest rates most cards charge.

If there is a credit union where you work, they may be more receptive than a bank. Commercial finance companies lend to small businesses, although at high interest rates. If you own stocks and bonds, ask your broker about borrowing against the securities. If you have a retirement plan from a job or another business, you may be able to borrow from the plan or get the funds out of the plan. If you own a life insurance policy, you can borrow on the "cash value" the policy.

If you open them all the same day, they'll all be approved.
—*Karen Behnke, Pacific Wellness Co, on using 17 credit cards to finance her new business.*

If you buy equipment, most equipment dealers have financing plans and installment sales.

Your wholesalers or suppliers may extend short-term credit. But a new business may have to operate C.O.D. (cash on delivery) with your suppliers until you are better established.

Some communities have "revolving loan" or "seed loan" funds for local businesses. Check with the Chamber of Commerce or City Hall.

Small Business Administration (SBA) Loans

The U.S. Small Business Administration has several loan programs for new and expanding "small" businesses. But by government definition, a "small" business is one with as much as $30 million in yearly sales and as many as 1,500 employees! There are a lot of big businesses in these small business programs.

The SBA itself makes no loans to businesses. Regular banks and commercial finance companies make SBA loans, and the SBA guarantees these loans. If you have an SBA guaranteed loan that you cannot repay, the SBA reimburses the lender for most of its loss. The SBA does not give any grants: no free money.

To get an SBA guaranteed loan, you do not apply to the SBA. You apply to a bank or finance company that handles SBA loans. It is up to both the lender and the SBA to decide if you'll get the loan. You will have to convince the SBA and the lender that you have the ability to operate a business successfully and that the loan can be repaid from the business earnings. Most SBA loans will require you to put up collateral, usually equipment or real estate. The bank sets the term of the loan and the interest rate, within SBA limits. Most SBA loans have a 2-3% loan fee.

SBA loans come with strings attached. The agency has a set of operating guidelines you must follow. The SBA may periodically audit your books, which can be both a help and a nuisance.

SBA's current loan programs include:

7(a) Program. The SBA's largest loan program is called the 7(a) Program, the Loan Guarantee Plan. Only about 30% of these loan funds go to new businesses. The bulk of the 7(a) money is lent to existing and expanding small businesses. The maximum 7(a) loan is $2 million, with a 7 to 10-year payback period (25 years for real estate).

LowDoc and SBA Express. Two loan guarantee programs for very small businesses. Up to $150,000 for LowDoc, up to $2 million for SBA Express. LowDoc stands for low documentation.

Micro-Loan Program. For new and very small businesses, the Micro-Loan Program is administered by SBA-approved non-profit organizations. This program provides loans from a few hundred dollars up to $35,000, with up to six year terms. Loan recipients must take a training course.

504 Programs/CDC Loans. The 504 Programs, also known as Certified Development Company (CDC) Loans, make loans to businesses in economically depressed areas, to purchase land, buildings or equipment, but only if the loans are used primarily to create jobs.

CAPLines Loans up to $1.3 million are available to successful businesses needing short-term funds for working capital (not for start-up).

Export Express Program makes loans up to $250,000 to businesses at least one year old who are exporters or want to use the money to expand into exporting.

International Trade Loan Program and the *Export Working Capital Program* make loans up to $1.25 million to export businesses.

Community Express Loans up to $250,000 are available in some low income areas.

Community Adjustment Investment Program (CAIP) loans up to $150,000 are available to businesses in communities that have suffered job losses due to NAFTA.

Loan Programs for Women, Minorities, and Low Income Individuals. Most of the SBA's "targeted" loan programs are part of the Micro-Loan Program. When you talk to the SBA or to a lender, ask if you are eligible for these or other special loan programs.

If you're determined to succeed, you can find a way around any obstacle, even money.
—Nancy Ridge, Ridge Tech Co.

You can get help and more information on SBA loan programs from any SBA office or from a Small Business Development Center. SBDCs work closely with the SBA and are usually affiliated with colleges and universities. Write the Small Business Administration, Washington DC 20416; or call toll-free 1-800-U-ASK-SBA; or visit their web site at www.sba.gov.

Pat Ellington, Kipple Antiques: "There's no point in even going to a bank unless you can say, 'Well, we've been operating now for two years, and we've established a track record, and we want to expand. We've got our books, our balance sheets, we've got good references, some people do extend us credit.' I know that from my own experience. If you go there armed with a certain amount of paperwork, a certain kind of history, you'll have fewer problems dealing with them.

"I have mixed feelings about SBA loans. Sometimes they can be gotten easily, but it's sort of like by magic. And other times, no matter what you give them, no matter what sound business approach you give them, it seems they're deaf to you. That's discouraging. It's like grantsmanship. There's a whole lot to applying, and if you don't have the art, you don't get the loan."

Loans To Yourself

For tax and bookkeeping purposes, there is no such thing as a loan to yourself (except for corporations). Any of your own money that you put into your business is considered personal funds. It is not taxable income, the repayment is not a tax deduction, you cannot pay yourself interest on the funds. As far as the IRS is concerned, loaning money to your own business is the same as taking money out of your right pocket and putting it in your left pocket. The reasoning behind this law will make more sense after you read the chapter "Sole Proprietorship." Partners in partnerships and owners of Limited Liability Companies (LLCs) come under the same law.

Corporations: If you incorporate your business, you can loan your business money and treat it as a regular loan. But be careful: Most states require corporations to have some amount of equity capital, called minimum capitalization, money that you the owner invest in the corporation. Before you loan money to your corpora-

tion, make sure you aren't going to run afoul of your state's capitalization requirements.

Equity Financing

"Equity" means ownership. "Equity financing" is money put up by the owner or owners of the business. Self-financing is, in fact, equity financing, even though I gave it a separate category in this chapter.

Equity financing usually involves an investor who buys into your business. The investor is taking a risk on your business, just as you are. Like the typical lender, the typical investor is usually a friend, acquaintance or relative. Unlike a lender, however, the investor gets his or her money back only if the business succeeds. The owner of the business is not obligated to repay the investor out of personal non-business funds.

How the investor and the business owner share in the profits is negotiable. A 50-50 split is common. I've known investors to accept as little as 30-35% of the profits; some may want a much bigger cut. Investments can be for a specified, limited time or for the life of the business.

Investments can be set up in a variety of ways, depending on how much the investor will or will not participate in the actual running of the business, how much liability exposure the investor wants, and how the business and the investment are legally structured. The investor might become a full partner in a regular partnership, a limited partner in a limited partnership, a stockholder in a corporation, or a member of a Limited Liability Company (LLC). Most states have laws regulating investments and how to set them up. You will most likely need professional help.

Limited Partnerships

Limited partners are not partners in the usual sense of the word. They are investors only, with little or no involvement in the operation of the business. Their liability is limited to the amount of their investment.

Don't confuse a limited partner with a regular business partner who invests money in the business. Limited partnerships are very different from regular (general) partnerships and are subject to much greater government scrutiny. Limited partnerships are registered with the county or the state. A limited partnership must have at least one general partner (you, the owner) with full personal liability just like a sole proprietorship or general partnership.

Limited partnerships should not be confused with Limited Liability Partnerships (LLPs), yet another form of business, described in the Growing Up section.

Limited Liability Company (LLC)

Due to the many restrictions on limited partnerships, businesses wanting the kind of financing limited partnerships offer, are instead setting up Limited Liability Companies. LLCs are not as tightly regulated as limited partnerships, and they offer greater liability protection. Limited Liability Companies are covered in the Growing Up section.

Venture Capital

Venture capital refers to money invested in young, high-potential companies, by investors called venture capitalists.

Venture capitalists are a different breed of investor than the people who typically help finance small businesses, such as friends, relatives and people in the community with some money to invest. Venture capitalists make their living as investors. Venture capitalists are usually only interested in businesses that have potential for huge growth and big profits within a few years, businesses on the cutting-edge of new technology, businesses that are likely to "go public" (make a public stock offering). The typical small sales or service business will not be of interest to venture capitalists.

When you get financing from a venture capitalist you will be taking on a partner who not only wants a percent of the profits but may even want ownership control (51% interest) of your business. You may be able to locate a venture capitalist through referral. Talk to other business people, your banker or an accountant.

Venture capital is also available from Community (or Certified) Development Corporations (CDCs). Many CDCs are non-profit, community sponsored and operated organizations, and many receive government grants. Their goal, in addition to making money on their investments, is to encourage small-scale local enterprises and to expand local job markets. To locate a CDC,

contact a regional Community Action Agency, SBA office, or state office of community affairs. On the Internet: www.sba.gov.

Venture capital is also available from Small Business Investment Companies (SBICs). SBICs are licensed by the Small Business Administration but they are privately organized and privately managed firms; they set their own policies and make their own investment decisions. The Small Business Administration often makes loans to SBICs so they can turn around and invest the money in your business. The SBA publishes a National Directory of SBICs. Write the SBA, Washington, D.C., 20416. www.sba.gov.

A final suggestion for financing your business: Start with the most unlikely prospects first. So when you say the wrong things, discover the holes in your plan, you won't have blown your chances with your best prospects.

LEGAL STRUCTURE

Every new business must decide if it will start as a sole proprietorship, partnership, corporation or Limited Liability Company (LLC).

Sole Proprietorship

Most new one-person businesses and self-employed individuals start as sole proprietors, simply because sole proprietorships are the quickest, easiest and least expensive form of business to start.

If you don't incorporate or set up an LLC, and if you don't have a partner, you are *automatically* a sole proprietor. The simple act of starting a business or becoming self-employed legally makes you a sole proprietor. It does not matter whether you filed any forms, gotten any permits or licenses, notified any government agency, or filed a tax return. Sole proprietorships are discussed below.

Partnership

If you have one or more partners and if you don't incorporate or set up an LLC, you have legally started a partnership. It's automatic, just like a sole proprietorship. Partnerships are covered in the Growing Up section.

The chapter "Husband and Wife Partnerships" in the Your Business section explains the options for setting up a husband and wife partnership.

Corporation or LLC

To become a corporation, nothing is automatic. You file incorporation papers with your state department of corporations, prepare articles of incorporation and bylaws, issue state-approved stock certificates, and pay registration fees and corporate franchise taxes.

A Limited Liability Company (LLC) is similar to a corporation, but with different ownership requirements and taxed differently. To set up an LLC, you register and file special LLC forms with your state. Corporations and LLCs are covered in the Growing Up section.

A business can start as a sole proprietorship or a partnership and incorporate (or become an LLC) at any later date. In fact, most small corporations started as unincorporated businesses and incorporated after they were successful and found a real need to incorporate.

SOLE PROPRIETORSHIP:
The Traditional One-Person Business

A one-person business that has not incorporated is known as a sole proprietorship. There are over 20 million small businesses in this country, and most of them are sole proprietorships. This form of business has flourished because of the opportunities it offers to be boss, run the business, make the decisions, and keep the profits. A sole proprietorship is the easiest form of business to start up. Despite all the regulations, it is the least regulated of all businesses.

Sole proprietors may call themselves business men, business women, shop keepers, entrepreneurs, self employed, artists, craftspeople, artisans, trades people, network or multi-level marketers, direct sellers, drop shippers, sales reps, manufacturers, inventors, employers, moonlighters, full-time, part-time, sideline, you name it. Legally, if you don't incorporate or form a partnership or an LLC, you are a sole proprietor; your business is a sole proprietorship.

Self-employed consultants, professionals, freelancers, outside and independent contractors, free agents, and people who are doing contract work for businesses (sometimes called outsourced work, virtual assistants or external service providers) should understand that they are also sole proprietors. I can't tell you how many times someone has come up to me and said, "I don't have a business, I'm an independent consultant." It doesn't matter what you call yourself. Unless you are on someone else's payroll as an employee, with tax withholding and W-2 wage statements, you *do* have a business, you are a sole proprietor.

You, the owner of the business, the sole proprietor, are your own boss. You make or break your business, which may sound singularly appealing to those of you instilled with the entrepreneurial, pioneering spirit. But you have sole responsibility as well as sole control.

Legal Liability of the Sole Proprietorship

Legally, a sole proprietor (the owner of the business) and the sole proprietorship (the business itself) are one and the same. All business debts and obligations are the personal responsibility of the owner. Lawsuits brought against the business can be taken from the personal assets of the owner. Claims against the owner of the business, personal claims having nothing to do with the business, can be taken from business assets. In other words, a sole proprietor is fully and personally 100% liable for everything that happens to the business.

You should be fully aware of these legal aspects of the sole proprietorship. If you get your business into legal trouble or too far into debt, not only could you lose your business, you could lose your shirt.

The only way to avoid the unlimited personal liability of the sole proprietor is to incorporate or set up an LLC. Generally speaking, the debts of corporations and LLCs are limited to the assets of the business and are not the personal responsibility of the owner or owners. LLCs and corporations are covered in the Growing Up section.

Taxable Profit of the Sole Proprietorship

The sole proprietorship itself does not pay income taxes. The owner, the sole proprietor, pays personal income taxes and pays self-employment

(Social Security/Medicare) taxes based on the profit from the business. The income from the business (sales, fees) less the deductible expenses equals the taxable profit.

The sole proprietorship itself does not file income tax returns or pay income taxes. You file a Schedule C, "Profit or Loss From Business," (or for some small businesses, a Schedule C-EZ) with your 1040 return, and pay personal income taxes on the profit. You also pay self-employment tax, which is Social Security/Medicare tax, in addition to income taxes. These taxes are covered in detail in the Tax section.

Paying Yourself a Wage

You, as the owner of a sole proprietorship, cannot hire yourself as an employee. This is a point of law often misunderstood by new business people. You cannot put yourself on the payroll. You cannot pay yourself a wage and deduct it as a business expense. You may withdraw (that is, pay yourself) as much or as little money as you want, but this "draw" is not a wage, you do not pay payroll taxes on it, and you cannot claim a business deduction for it. The profit of your business, which is computed without regard to your draws, is your "wage" and is included on your personal income tax return.

For example, if your business made a $40,000 profit last year, you personally owe taxes on $40,000. If you withdrew (paid yourself) less than $40,000—or, for that matter, if you didn't even take a penny out of the business—you still pay taxes on $40,000. If you withdrew more than $40,000, you still pay taxes only on $40,000. Owner's draw is covered in more detail in the Bookkeeping section.

CHOOSING A BUSINESS NAME

Thinking up a name for your business can be a lot of fun, an opportunity to let your creativity and your imagination take charge.

Business names can be descriptive (Computer Cave, Pinball Resource) or vague (Facets, Natural Choice), can be cute (We Be Stylin') or professional (Julia Kaye Designs). Business names can be totally made-up words (Verizon, Intel) or real words whose meaning has nothing to do with what your business actually does (Apple) or a family name (J.C. Penney). Or your business name can be downright uncommunicative: "Acme Enterprises" tells people absolutely nothing.

Here are some considerations:

1. Choose a name that is pleasant, easy to pronounce, easy to spell, easy to remember. If your customers choke or stumble on your name every time they mention it, fewer people will hear about you.

2. Customers who hear your name once, or see it listed in the Yellow Pages, form an immediate impression of who you are. Think like a customer. Does your name sound like a company a customer would want to contact?

3. If you want people to connect the business with you personally, using your own name as the company name may be the best choice.

4. Be wary of cute names and current popular expressions: they get stale over time. Be wary of intentionally misspelled words. "Kute Kids Klothes" may seem to be a clever name for a business except for customers who spell it wrong and can't find you in the phone book.

5. Avoid a name that's similar to another business. Customers will confuse you with them. The town I live in has two local print shops, one called Printing Plus and one called Printing Xpress (and both owners have the same first name!); I can never remember which is which.

6. If you will be doing business overseas, investigate whether your name may be offensive or otherwise embarrassing when translated or spoken in another country.

7. Avoid names beginning with articles, that can result in your business being listed under "The" or "An."

8. If customers are likely to look for you in a directory, there may be an advantage to being close to the beginning of the alphabet. Customers go to the Yellow Pages and start calling with the A's, and stop when they find what they want.

9. Don't be trapped by a name that may limit future growth or change. What happens when Main Street Music moves to State Street? Or when The Silver Jeweler switches to gold or diamonds?

10. If you plan to have a web site, and if you want your domain name to be the same as your business name, you should check first to see if the name is already taken. For more information about domain names, see the "Internet" chapter in the Your Business section.

11. Your state may restrict use of certain words in business names. In many states, you cannot use words such as "Real Estate" or "Construction" or "Psychologist" or even "Barber" unless you are licensed.

Registering A Business Name

The next step is to find out if you can legally use the business name you've selected. There are local and state business name registrations, trademark laws, and Internet domain name issues, and they occasionally overlap and conflict.

DBA : Doing Business As
(Fictitious/ Assumed Name Statement)

When a business goes by any name other than the owner's real name, the business is being operated under a "fictitious name" (also known as an "assumed name" or a "DBA"—doing business as). Country Comfort Carpentry, Johnson Plumbing, Ralph's Cleaners are all examples of fictitious names.

People doing business under a fictitious name are required to file a Fictitious Name Statement (or Assumed Name Certificate, or DBA, or whatever it's called in your state). In some states, the Statement is filed with the state; in some states it is filed with the city or county.

Filing a Fictitious Name Statement prevents any other business in the county, or in the entire state (depending on your state's law) from using the same business name—with a few important exceptions covered below.

In addition to filing for the fictitious name, in some states you may be required to publish the Fictitious Name Statement in a local newspaper, the theory being that the public has a right to know with whom they are doing business. The government office that handles Fictitious Names will provide you with a list of acceptable newspapers. Publication costs can be relatively low if your county or state has one of those newspapers that specialize in running legal notices (and little else). If not, small-time newspapers almost always charge less than large-circulation dailies.

In most states, you will be required to renew your fictitious name periodically, usually once every five years. This is something you need to find out and remember. Your state may or may not send you a notice when your renewal is due.

If you fail to renew, someone else can step in and file for your business name, and you will not be able to use it any more.

You usually don't have to register for a fictitious name if you use your real name as your business name, such as "Julia Smith." If, however, you are doing business as "Julia Smith Company" or "Julia Smith, Attorney at Law" or "Julia Smith's Bookstore," some (not all) states consider this to be a fictitious name, subject to regular fictitious name rules.

Corporations and Limited Liability Companies (LLCs): Unless you are operating under a name other than the legal name of the business, you do not usually need to file a Fictitious Name Statement. But you should verify this, as local rules vary from state to state.

Partnerships: Partnerships must file a Fictitious Name Statement unless operating under the full names of all the partners

When you pick a name or several names you like, go to the county or state office that handles fictitious names (assumed names, DBAs) and ask to see their alphabetical list of all names. The list may also be on the agency's web site.

If you live in a large urban area, you may find that your first, second *and* third choices are all already taken. You can try to contact the person who owns the business name and find out if the business is still in existence. If it isn't, and if the owner of the name consents, an Abandonment Statement can be filed, whereby the prior owner gives up all rights to the name. You may simultaneously file a DBA or Fictitious Name Statement for the name. The former owner will probably want you to pay the cost of filing the statement of abandonment and may even want you to pay him a fee for his trouble.

You should be aware of possible trouble if you select a business name that is already being used by an out-of-county or even an out-of-state business. Corporations are usually granted exclusive statewide use of a business name, assuming they were the first in the state to choose the name. Some states grant state-wide trade-name protection to businesses. Your state's Secretary of State maintains a list of business names claimed by corporations and other businesses licensed by the state.

Trademarks

Just because the county or the state approved your DBA or the state approved your corporate name, doesn't mean some other company can't stop you from using it if that company has filed a trademark on the name.

Most large businesses, and many small businesses, obtain federal trademarks. Trademark law is covered in the Your Business section, but generally, a business with a federally registered trademark usually has exclusive use of that name throughout the U.S.

Locate a copy of the Federal Trademark Register (try your library) and look up your proposed business name. You can do a trademark search on the Internet at the U.S. Trademark Office's web site, www.uspto.gov. This search is free.

If your business name is the same as or similar to a trademarked name, you may have problems, particularly if your goods or services are similar to those carrying the trademark and if you are selling in the same part of the country.

What happens if you start your business and find out later that some other business has prior claim to your business name? You will probably get a "cease and desist" letter from some lawyer telling you that you are in violation of the law and that you must cease using that business name, or else they'll take you to court, seek damages, etc. and etc. At that point you can decide if you really are in the wrong, and right or wrong, do you want to fight it in court? There are few clear-cut answers in this area of law. Often, unfortunately, it comes down to who has the most money for lawyers.

Another suggestion: check local telephone directories and national trade directories for your type of business. Trademark or no trademark, avoid a business name already in use.

Robert Haft, founder, Crown Books: We went out and did something like a Nielsen survey. We asked people which names they thought would be best for a bookstore. That narrowed it down to four or five. Then we took those four or five names and did another survey, asking people which of these bookstores they'd been in. 20% of the people said they'd been in a Crown Books store—and that was before we opened. So we said if 20% of the people think they've already been there, that's the name.

LICENSES and PERMITS

The Lord's Prayer contains 56 words. Lincoln's Gettysburg Address, 268 words. The Declaration of Independence, 1,322 words. Federal regulations governing the sale of cabbage, 26,911 words.

When you open a new business, every government agency that can claim jurisdiction over you wants to get into the act. There are forms to file, permits and licenses to obtain, regulations and restrictions to heed. And—always—fees to pay.

Why all the government regulations? Why does water flow downhill? It's just the nature of government to regulate, license, permitize, officialize, "fees, fines and forms" you to death.

Some of the laws were passed to protect the consumer public from unscrupulous or incompetent business people. Some laws were created solely to provide additional revenues to the government. Some...well, who knows.

Most business licenses and permits are required and administered by local governments: the city if you live within city limits; possibly the county. Some businesses must also have state and federal licenses. This chapter will describe the different licenses and permits typically required by states and municipalities and those currently required by the federal government.

Regulations vary from city to city and state to state, and they are changing all the time. You should contact state and local government agencies (anonymously if you prefer) to learn the current requirements and restrictions.

All states, and many cities and counties, have their legal requirements for businesses posted online. Many local and state government agencies let you file forms and get permits online.

To visit your state's main web site, go to www.state.[your state's two-letter abbreviation].gov. For specific state agencies or for your city or county, type in the name of the agency, city, or county in a search engine. Just be sure you are getting your information directly from the government agency and not from another source, which may be inaccurate or out of date.

Local Business Licenses

A local business license, if required, is merely a permit to do business locally. Most business licenses are simply a revenue-raising tax imposed on business, offering no benefits to the business (other than that nice looking piece of paper you get to thumbtack on the wall).

Some states, counties and/or cities require all businesses to get a business license. In many states, no licenses are required at all. Some localities require licenses only for certain types or sizes of businesses. Some cities require "home occupation permits" or similar special licenses only for home-based businesses.

Local business licenses can cost anywhere from $25 or $30 to as much as several hundred dollars, and must be renewed monthly, quarterly, or annually depending on local requirements. The size and the type of business, and the amount of income, sometimes determine how much the license will cost. Ask about the fee structure, and see if you can define your business so it will fit into the least expensive category.

A few large cities issue "Business Registration Certificates" in addition to a business license, charging for both.

In some states, the business license is a combined license, DBA, and sales tax permit.

Bob Matthews, owner of Country Comfort Carpentry: "I never filed a DBA. I liked the name, and right on the checks and letterheads it says 'Country Comfort Carpentry' with my name immediately under it. I felt that's good enough. I never got a business license. I'm in a rural area, twenty miles from town. I feel that business licenses are a tax on people who work in town, to make them conform."

Other Local Permits

Your business may be required to conform to local zoning laws, building codes, health requirements, fire and police regulations. You may be required to get a "use permit" to operate your business in a new location.

I suggest that you contact your local government *before* you open your doors. If you do not get the proper permits or meet the local building codes, the city or county can shut you down.

Help From Local Government

Many cities, particularly smaller ones in eco-nomically depressed areas, are eager to help new businesses locate in their jurisdiction, especially businesses that will be hiring local people. The city will help you through the red tape, and they are likely to help if you have minor zoning or building code problems. Some cities even have a grant or loan fund to help local businesses. Ask at City Hall if they have any kind of economic development program or assistance.

Key Dickason is a partner in Major Dickason's Blend, a coffee store: "My partner is an honest, law-abiding person, and he wanted everything A-OK. Then he found out that what the health inspectors required would cost $2,000: a 3-compartment sink, molding all around the bottom of the restrooms. The sink could not be where we wanted it, it had to be in the storage room, the storage room had to be re-painted.

The reason? Well it's my opinion that the regulatory agencies are loaded with 'genus-clerks' and the only thing that they can see is the letter of the law.

"Genus is Latin for family. It's a biological term. I say it's a sub-species of homo sapiens, and you run across this type of person all the time. When they come in and you're serving coffee in paper cups, they look it up in their book and they say, 'Oh, serving beverages. It's a restaurant.' Then they say that you have to comply with this regulation, and they cite book-and-verse.

"We've been in business a year and haven't done any of the things they demanded. We didn't have the money. When the health inspector comes, he looks around, he says, 'The place is clean, it's nice.' That's it. There's no pressure to comply with the written directive. If they plan to shut us down, then they'd say, `You have 30 days to comply.' Well, then you do it.

Jim McFeely, interviewed in Inc. Magazine: "When my partner and I asked the city of Grand Rapids what was needed to open a business, we were told we needed only two things: a business license and a sales tax license. We obtained the licenses and opened a downtown flea market. We advertised our grand opening, offering nail polish for 25¢ and a package of noodles for 25¢.

"On opening day we got nailed by city licensing for not having a license to sell paint (nail polish), by grocer licensing for not having a day-old variance, and by the fire marshall for not having $900 in fire extinguishers. Two men showed up and demanded to inspect the freight elevator, which hadn't run since 1935. Inspection fee: $285. We were deluged with forms for business activity taxes, interim business taxes and inventory taxes. When we hired a woman to mind the store, we got this huge form from the unemployment office that looked like a wallpaper sample book.

"There were just the two of us. We closed our business forever. One week later we were cited for failure to get a going-out-of-business license. A week after that, the mayor appeared on TV saying, "We have to seek new ways to attract business to Grand Rapids."

State Licenses

Most sales and manufacturing businesses (except those that sell alcoholic beverages) and many service businesses do not need state licenses.

States have traditionally licensed doctors, nurses, lawyers, accountants, architects, engineers, contractors, real estate and insurance agents, and other professionals. Many states license auto mechanics, stereo, TV and computer repair shops, marriage counselors, psychologists, pharmacists, barbers, bill collectors, funeral directors, pest control businesses, private investigators, plumbers, travel agents, caterers, day care centers, tour operators, even dry cleaners, to name a few.

These occupational licenses are usually issued for one or two year periods and, as always, for a fee. Some of the occupational licenses require the licensee to pass a test. Some have education and experience requirements. Contact your state's agency for consumer affairs to inquire about possible licensing of your business. State offices are located at the state capital and usually in the larger cities around the state. Most state licensing agencies are on the Internet.

SALES TAX

Unless you live in a state that does not have a sales tax, you will be required to collect sales tax from your customers and remit the tax to the state (in-state sales only; see below for out-of-state sales). States, counties and cities may all have a sales tax, but usually it is all reported on one combined sales tax return.

Some states have different names for their sales tax: sales and service tax; general excise tax (which should not be confused with federal excise taxes); retailers' occupation tax; transaction privilege tax; gross receipts tax (not to be confused with a different tax imposed by some states that is also called a gross receipts tax—covered in the Tax section).

Generally—and every state is different—retail goods (goods sold to the public; and goods sold to businesses for their own use, not for resale or manufacture) are subject to sales tax. Wholesale goods are exempt from sales tax (except for the State of Hawaii, which has a sales tax on wholesale goods).

Special note: Don't confuse "wholesale" with "discount." Wholesale refers to goods that are sold by one business to another, to re-sell or to go into a manufactured product. The ads in the papers that say "Wholesale to the Public," "Wholesale—Factory To You," or some other misuse of the word are actually referring to discount retail sales, subject to sales tax.

Goods used for samples, demonstration or display are considered resale (non-taxable) by many states. Some states, however, tax them.

Services (as opposed to goods) such as repairs or construction, professional services, and labor charges, are taxed in some states, exempt in others. The time you or your employees put into manufacturing, fabricating or assembling a product is not considered a service. It is part of the cost of the product.

Many states tax prepared food (restaurants, etc.) but exempt groceries. Some states exempt shipping and handling charges, newspapers, magazines, prescription drugs, clothing, manufacturing equipment and printing. Many states tax leased property and rentals. Sales to state and local government agencies are taxable in some states. Sales to U.S. government agencies are exempt from sales tax in all states.

Some states require that the price tag on taxable items include the words "plus tax" or a similar statement.

If you pay sales tax on goods you then re-sell, you still charge sales tax to your customers. You can claim a credit on your sales tax return for the duplicate sales tax paid.

You've probably seen advertisements saying something like "This Month Only: No Sales

Tax." Well, there actually is sales tax, but the seller is absorbing it, paying it out of his own pocket. Some states, however, disallow this practice. To get around this law, some sellers sell goods "sales tax included." A subtle difference to circumvent a silly law.

Depending on the dollar volume of business, you will have to prepare monthly, quarterly or annual sales tax returns, to report your sales and pay the taxes collected. Many states let you keep a portion of the sales tax you collect as a payment for the cost of collecting it. Some states require you to report sales tax on the accrual basis, even if you are on a cash basis for income taxes (explained in the Bookkeeping section).

Building Contractors: In some states, sales tax paid on materials can vary—dramatically—depending on whether you have a "lump sum" contract or a "time and materials" contract. You should get information from your state sales tax department. The right wording may save you and your customers a lot of money.

Seller's (Reseller's) Permits

Every state that collects a sales tax issues seller's permits (also called a reseller's permit, resale number, resale license, sales tax certificate, certificate of authority, or something similar), and every in-state business that sells goods, parts, or taxable services must have one.

Some states will require a security deposit from you before issuing you a seller's permit, which is the state's way of guaranteeing that you will file your sales tax returns and pay what is owed. After a year, paying your sales tax on time, you usually get your deposit back. In lieu of a deposit, most states will let you purchase a sales tax bond from an insurance company.

When a new business applies for a seller's permit, the sales tax people may ask you to estimate your taxable sales, and base the deposit on your estimate. Since you have no idea what your sales will be, no law requires you to be overly optimistic. Keep your sales estimate low, and you may avoid a deposit altogether.

Besides registering you as a seller, a seller's permit gives you the right to buy goods for resale, both finished products and the "raw materials" that go into products you manufacture, without paying sales tax to your supplier.

Only goods that will be resold or manufactured in the normal course of business can be purchased tax-free (except in Hawaii, which taxes wholesale goods). You may not use your seller's permit to make tax-free purchases of office supplies, furniture, equipment, or goods for personal, non-business purposes.

Businesses that sell wholesale goods to other businesses without charging sales tax must keep a record of all customers who make tax-free purchases. Your customers must give you their resale numbers before you can sell to them tax-free. States often provide forms, called Exemption Certificates, for this purpose, or you can buy blank forms from a stationery store.

Usually, you only have to get one Exemption Certificate from each customer, the first time you sell to that customer. You keep your customers' resale numbers and the Exemption Certificates on file. You don't send them to the county or state.

Some states require you to verify your customers' resale numbers, by calling a toll free number, before selling to them.

In states where services are exempt from sales tax, some businesses have problems over the definition of what is a service (not taxable) as opposed to a product (taxable). For example, is an expensive custom-designed computer program a taxable product or a non-taxable service? The same question applies to the work of freelance artists, graphic designers, typesetters, and the like. Find out if your work is subject to sales tax. Sometimes the people in the sales tax office are unsure, so ask to see the rules in writing. A carefully worded contract or invoice that separately bills taxable and non-taxable items may be needed.

Sales Tax Rates

Within your state, different counties and cities often have different sale tax rates. If you are selling goods locally, to a customer who lives in your city or who comes to your business in person to purchase goods, you charge the local sales tax rate.

If you are shipping goods within your state but outside of your local jurisdiction, what rate you charge depends on your state's rules. In many states, you charge your local sales tax rate, even though you may be shipping goods to a location with a different sales tax rate. Some states, however, require you to collect the tax at the rate where the goods are sent.

Out of State Sales

You are not required to collect sales tax on orders shipped out-of-state: mail orders, telephone and fax sales, Internet sales. You do not need a sales tax permit from any state except your own.

If you have an office, warehouse or store in another state, or if you or your employees are regularly travelling through and selling or servicing your goods in another state (what's called "nexus," a physical presence) you must abide by that state's sales tax laws, and you must file sales tax returns in that state, for all retail sales made to that state.

Seminars and Trade Shows: If you sell only occasionally in another state, such as at a seminar or trade show, it is not considered nexus. But you do have to collect sales tax on the taxable sales made at those shows or seminars, and remit the tax to that state (not to your home state).

Out-of-State Deliveries: If you deliver goods to a customer in another state using your own trucks (not UPS, FedEx, or common carriers), some states consider this nexus.

Drop Shipping: Another "nexus" problem involves what's commonly called "drop shipping": when you contract with another business to warehouse and ship products for you. If the business that is warehousing and shipping goods for you is in another state, does such an arrangement constitutes nexus? That is, will the state where the contracting business is located require you to collect sales tax from customers in that state? Your drop-shipper may know the answer, or you may have to contact the taxing agencies in the states involved. This is a different situation than renting and staffing a warehouse and shipping facility of your own, which clearly is a physical presence, and subject to the state's sales tax laws.

Internet Sales

Internet sales are governed by the same sales tax laws that apply to mail order, telephone and catalog sales. The so-called "tax free Internet" does not apply to sales tax. You collect sales tax from customers in your own state. You do not collect sales tax from out-of-state customers.

But with the growth of the Internet, states are trying to redefine "nexus," trying to legally determine when—or if—an Internet site has a physical presence in a given state; and if a state other than your own state can require you to collect sales tax.

The fact that your web site can be viewed and downloaded by someone in another state does not create nexus; there is no physical presence. However, several states claim that if your web server is in their state, you have a physical presence in that state, and therefore subject to that state's sales tax laws, even though your business is located entirely in another state. If your web server is in a state making such a claim, you may want to discuss this problem with your web server or your accountant, or you may want to find a new web server in your own state. So far, I have not heard about any small business being required to pay sales tax to a state over web site or web server locations.

Some large businesses, particularly businesses with stores and warehouses in several states, are setting up separate corporations just to run their Internet operations. These businesses are locating their Internet-only subsidiaries in tax friendly states, in an attempt to avoid collecting sales tax on Internet transactions. The businesses claim they have found a legal loophole to get out of sales tax obligations. The affected states quite obviously smell a rat, and are challenging the businesses in court.

Sales Tax on Downloaded Products

Are digital "products" such as downloaded music, books, and software, subject to sales tax? Some states do tax downloaded items, and some states do not. You should contact your state's sales tax department to find out the laws. (And get them in writing).

If your state does tax downloaded items, you collect the sales tax only from Internet customers who reside in your state. That is assuming you can determine that your customer is in fact in your state. How do you really know, since many Internet sales do not require physical addresses? If your customer says he is not in your state, that's about all you can do; no tax.

Use Tax

Although a seller does not collect sales tax on out-of-state sales, in most states the buyer is supposed to *pay* sales tax on purchases from out-of-state vendors—not to the seller, but directly to the state where the buyer resides (unless the purchases are for resale).

No, I'm not kidding. When you buy a computer or office supplies from an out of state company, your own state wants you to pay sales tax on the purchase. It is called a "use tax" (sometimes called a "compensating tax"). Use tax applies to Internet purchases, mail order, phone, etc. This is not a well-known law, and, as you can imagine, it is not easy to enforce. Several state income tax returns include a line where you estimate the use tax you owe and pay it along with your state income taxes.

Purchases originally made for resale (purchased tax free) but used for another purpose, such as personal use, are subject to the use tax. Your sales tax return has a line where you calculate the use tax you owe on these purchases, and pay it with the sales tax you collected from your customers.

Other State Regulations

To find out about other state requirements, contact the Secretary of State or Consumer Affairs office. Many states publish a booklet of state requirements. Every state has a web site with business regulations. Look up your state at www.state.[your state's two-letter abbreviation].us.

Here are a few common regulations:

States regulate finance charges imposed on customers. Some states regulate shipping and handling charges billed to customers.

States have privacy laws protecting customer information, including information stored online.

Truckers, taxi cab operators, bus lines, and household movers must register with the Public Utilities Commission.

Businesses operating factories or other potential air and water polluting equipment must meet state air and water quality requirements.

Repair shops may need bonds or proof of solvency. Sellers of meat products, fire arms, and alcoholic beverages may require state registration and permits. Many professionals and most financial services are licensed by the states. Many states require telephone marketers to be registered (I personally think they ought to be jailed).

Employers may be subject to state wage and hour laws and occupational safety and health laws. State employment laws are covered in the Growing Up section.

States have the legal right to restrict sales of regulated products (such as firearms, alcohol, and tobacco) to state residents, regardless of where the seller is located. For example, a small winery in California may be prohibited from selling and shipping a bottle of wine to a customer in New York. If your business sells products that might be regulated, you may have to research and abide by the laws in all fifty states.

Federal Identification Numbers

Your business will be required to identify itself on tax forms and licenses by either of two numbers: your Social Security number or a Federal Employer Identification Number (called "FEIN" or, more often, "EIN").

Sole proprietors can use their Social Security number as their business identifying number, unless required to get an EIN.

You must get an Employer Identification Number if:

1. You hire employees.

2. Your business is a partnership, corporation, or LLC.

3. You are required to file an excise tax return (covered in the Tax section).

4. You set up a Qualified Retirement Plan (covered in the Tax Section).

5. You purchase or inherit an existing business.

6. Your state or other government agency, a vendor or customer, your bank, or your insurance company requires you to have an EIN.

As you can see, although the federal identification number is called an "Employer" Identification Number, the EIN is used by any business that needs a federal ID number, whether the business has employees or not.

Many sole proprietors get EINs, even when not required, because the sole proprietors do not want to give out their Social Security number to customers and vendors.

Federal Licenses

Most small businesses do not need any federal licenses. The federal government licenses all businesses engaged in common-carrier transportation, radio and television station construction, manufacture of drugs, alcohol or tobacco products, preparation of meat products, manufacture or sale of firearms, and investment counseling. Contact the Federal Trade Commission, Washington, D.C. 20580. Online: www.ftc.gov.

Federal Agencies:
Business Regulations

The Federal Trade Commission and a dozen other federal agencies have laws affecting all kinds of businesses. The federal agencies publish free booklets and list their business regulations on their web sites. For general information, try businesslaw.gov (do not include the www prefix) or, for the Federal Trade Commission, go to www.ftc.gov (include the www prefix). Or type in the name of the law or agency in a search engine. But as I warn elsewhere, be sure you are getting information directly from the government agency and not from a commercial web site that may be inaccurate or out of date.

A few of the more important regulations:

Guarantees and warranties must comply with the Consumer Products Warranty Law. A warranty refers to the product itself: it will perform as promised for a given period of time. A guarantee is a promise of customer satisfaction: the customer can get an exchange or refund even if the product lives up to its warranty.

You are not required by law to offer a guarantee or a warranty. But if you do, you are required to honor it. Some warranties must be made available to customers before they buy.

Mail order, telephone, fax, and Internet sales businesses must comply with the Mail Order and Telephone Merchandise Rule (also known as the 30-Day Rule): Sellers must ship merchandise within their stated time, or if no time is stated, within 30 days. If there is a delay, the seller must notify the buyer of the delay, and give the buyer a cost-free option (a toll-free number, postage-paid reply card, or e-mail) to cancel the order and receive a full refund within seven days.

To
You c
EIN
www.
over t
829-4
If y
emplo
Line
paid"
Line
ees, and will automatically
returns that you must fill out and return.

Be careful how you fill out Line 13 (number of employees). If you have none, write "NONE" or "0." Remember, you are not an employee of your own business unless you incorporate. If you will have employees but don't know how many, estimate on the low side to avoid an avalanche of unnecessary IRS forms. One employee is enough.

You get one EIN per business, even if the business has more than one location. You keep the same EIN for as long as you own the business, even if you move. If you have more than one business, you should have separate EINs for each business.

Door-to-door sales businesses, and businesses that make face-to-face sales to consumers away from a regular business location (such as presentations at people's homes or at conventions), must give buyers three business days to change their minds and cancel their order. This is called the Cooling Off Rule.

This rule does not apply to mail order or Internet sales, sales to businesses, sales under $25, emergencies, vehicles, real estate, securities investments, or crafts sold at craft shows.

Telephone and fax marketers must comply with the Telemarketing and Consumer Fraud and Abuse Prevention Act, the Telemarketing Sales Rule, and the Telephone Consumer Protection Act.

Unsolicited faxes are prohibited unless you have an established business relationship.

Unsolicited telephone marketing is prohibited if people have signed up for the Federal Do-Not-Call list and during certain times of the day. Telemarketers must comply with many FTC restrictions. We all just *love* telemarketers...

Packages and labels must conform to the Federal Fair Packaging and Labeling Act. Basically, a label must identify the product, list the manufacturer, packer, or distributor, and show the net quantity, both inch/pound and metric. The Act specifies how the label must be printed and where on the goods it must appear.

Textiles, fabric, wool, furs and clothing must be labeled according to a variety of FTC rules. Generally, a label must state (1) the fiber composition of the fabric, (2) country of origin, (3) names or registered identification numbers of the manufacturer and the business marketing the fabric, and (4) care and cleaning instructions.

Warning labels are required on certain products that can injure people, or that may be unsuitable for children, or may cause damage. The U.S. Consumer Products Safety Commission (www.cpsc.gov) has a list of products that require warning labels.

Even if a warning label is not required by law, you may want to include such a label, if your product might cause harm or damage, to protect your customers (and possibly protect yourself in case of a lawsuit).

Advertising, product offers, and claims are regulated by the Federal Trade Commission. Advertising may not be deceptive or misleading (I am just quoting the law. It seems that at least half the advertising I've ever seen is deceptive or misleading). You must have a reasonable basis for all advertising claims. You must have evidence to support your claims. If your advertising says that "studies show…" or "experts prefer…" you are required by law to have copies of the studies and documented statements from the experts.

Environmental benefits cannot be exaggerated. If you say its free, it must be free. Misleading mailings such as facsimile checks and envelopes made to look like they came from government agencies are restricted. Sweepstakes are regulated.

Be especially careful about medical and health claims, as the government tends to crack down on these advertisements the hardest.

Private mail boxes rented from commercial mail receiving agencies (CMRAs, mail box stores) must be labeled with "PMB" or "#" next to the mail box number. You may not use the term "suite" to designate a PMB.

Transportation safety regulations, administered by the Department of Transportation (www.dot.gov) are imposed on truckers, transportation companies, commercial marine businesses, railroads, and aviation businesses.

Environmental protection regulations, administered by the Environmental Protection Agency (www.epa.gov), are imposed on auto repair, metal finishing, printing, painting, chemical, agricultural, electronics and transportation businesses.

Manufacturers and sellers of fresh squeezed juices must put warning labels on unpasteurized products.

Privacy policies, both in print and on web sites, are required of financial institutions and investment businesses, but generally not required of most businesses. However, if you do print or post a privacy policy, you are required by law to adhere to it.

Web sites are prohibited from collecting personal information from children under the age of thirteen without their parent's permission.

Commercial e-mail is regulated by the CAN-SPAM Act. Among other requirements, unsolicited e-mail advertisements sent to someone you do not already have a relationship with, must (1) state that it is an advertisement; (2) have a legitimate e-mail return address; (3) have an honest subject heading; (4) have an opt-out; (5) include your physical postal address. Harvesting e-mail addresses from web sites is prohibited.

Although all businesses are subject to these federal regulations, enforcement is directed primarily at large companies that, due to their size, can and do take advantage of many, many people. Federal agencies usually ignore small businesses unless the agencies get a complaint.

INSURANCE

If you bought all the different kinds of business insurance available to you, you'd be broke before you made your first sale. So you should first determine what insurance is required by law, what insurance is extremely important, what insurance is required by your landlord or by someone lending you money, and what insurance you can do without.

Basic Fire Insurance. Covers fire and lightning losses to your building, equipment, and inventory. Fire premiums vary widely and are based upon the location of your property, the degree of fire protection in your community, the type of construction of the building, the nature of your business and the nature of neighboring businesses. If you move into a building next to a woodworking or dry cleaning shop, your fire premiums will be high even if your business is a low fire risk. A sprinkler system in your building will sharply reduce your premium.

Although your computer may be covered under a fire insurance policy, the data in your computer is usually excluded from coverage.

Extended Coverage. Protects against storms, most explosions, smoke damage, riot, and damage caused by aircraft or vehicles.

Extended coverage sometimes includes vandalism, though this usually requires a separate policy. Vandalism policies cover physical damage to your business premises, but do not usually cover vandalism to web sites or computer files.

Liability Insurance. Pays for claims brought against your business because of bodily injury. A customer, or a delivery person, slips and falls, breaks a leg and files a $50,000 lawsuit; it's not uncommon.

Liability coverage is required by law in only a few states, but I consider liability insurance essential for any retail business. Most leases and rental agreements require you to have liability insurance.

Premiums for merchants usually are based upon the store's square footage. The bigger the store, the higher the premium. For manufacturers and contractors, premiums increase as payroll increases.

You can also purchase Umbrella Insurance, which provides additional liability coverage if a claim exceeds your regular liability limit.

Liability insurance does not cover you, the owner, nor any of your employees, though it would normally cover an outside contractor. It does not cover injuries caused by vehicles or by defective products.

Fire Legal Liability. Covers fire damage to your landlord's building—the portion you occupy only. The rest of the building would be covered by Property Damage Liability. Even if the landlord has fire insurance on the building, you may still be liable if your business caused the fire.

Property Damage Liability. Provides coverage for damage to property of others. There are two types of property damage liability. The first type is damage to property that is not under your control or in your custody. For example, a fire starts in your small office. The damage is minimal but smoke and water destroyed $30,000 worth of Persian rugs in the business next door. Property damage liability covers this situation.

The second type of property damage liability is damage to others' property that is under your control or in your custody, such as property leased or rented to you, and—especially important for repair businesses—property that belongs to your customers.

Products Liability. Covers products designed, manufactured or sold by the insured once the product leaves the business' hands. It covers the business in case the user of the product sues for injury or property damage. The courts generally hold manufacturers strictly liable for any injury caused by their product, sometimes even when the product has not been used correctly.

Distributors, wholesalers, and retail stores can sometimes be liable for products they sell, though not usually. If the products are in their original packages, and if the retailer provides no assembly or advice, the risk is greatly reduced. Some manufacturers will indemnify retailers against product liability claims (sometimes called a "vendors endorsement").

Building contractors and tradespeople often get Completed Operations insurance, a form of product liability insurance that protects you if someone is injured as a result of your work.

Malpractice. Also known as "errors and omissions" and "professional liability." Protects you from lawsuits and losses from professional, ah, "mistakes." This insurance is often expensive and hard to find. Sometimes available from professional societies or trade associations.

Internet "malpractice," someone suing you over the contents of your web site, is covered under some, but not all, malpractice policies.

Bonds. "Surety" bonds guarantee the performance of a job. If you do not complete a job, for any reason, your surety company must do so. Surety bonds are most often used in the construction industry and are always required on public construction projects. Surety bonds are difficult to obtain unless you have $30,000 or more in liquid assets such as cash and inventory.

"Fidelity" bonds are placed on employees, insuring the employer against theft or embezzlement by the bonded employees.

Theft Coverage. Covers burglary (theft from a closed business) and robbery (theft using force or threat of violence). The cost depends on the type of merchandise you stock, your location, and the theft protection on your premises: alarms, bars on the windows, dead bolts, etc. An investment in some security is certainly as important as buying theft insurance. Find out if coverage includes inventory and equipment away from your business premises, such as at a trade show, or in transit to a customer.

Theft coverage does not include fraud or losses due to customers who bounce checks or don't pay their bills.

Theft insurance does not include lost data inside a stolen computer, nor does the insurance cover data "stolen" from your web site by a malicious hacker.

Business Interruption. If your business closes due to fire or other insurable building damage, business interruption insurance will pay you approximately what you would have earned.

You can also purchase "extra expense" insurance, which pays the extra cost of keeping a business operating (such as renting temporary quarters) after a fire or other building damage. Overhead insurance pays you for business overhead expenses you incur during long periods of disability. Similar insurance, called disability or income insurance, provides coverage if you are hospitalized or disabled and have to shut down.

Business interruption insurance does not cover you if your web site goes down. It does not pay for loss of income if your computer is infected with a virus, or crashes.

Business interruption insurance may seem to be something of a luxury. But if you have a fire or other disaster, it might be months before you are back on your feet, even with fire insurance. Most small businesses are not prepared to handle such a calamity, and many never reopen.

For tax purposes, some business interruption premiums are deductible, and some are not. The proceeds from an insurance claim may or may not be taxable to you, depending on what the insurance is actually covering. Your insurance agent should have complete tax information.

Workers Compensation Insurance. Provides disability and death benefits to employees injured or killed on the job, or who become ill due to workplace conditions, regardless of who is at fault. Most (but not all) states require employers to carry workers' comp insurance for all employees, even if they are occasional or part-time. You, the employer, must pay for your employees' workers compensation insurance.

Although a few states do not require workers comp insurance, the employer is still legally liable for injuries an employee incurs on the job. Legally required or not, workers comp insurance is essential to any business with employees.

You are not required to carry workers' comp for independent contractors. However, if an independent contractor is injured while working for you, you may possibly be liable for the injury. Liability insurance usually covers this situation. If your independent contractor hires employees, verify that the contractor has purchased workers' compensation insurance for his employees. Do not let your contractor's employees come to your business if they are not insured by the contractor. If an employee gets hurt, you could be sued.

Some states allow businesses to self-insure rather than purchase a workers' comp policy; but for most small businesses, the required bonds or cash reserves are prohibitively expensive.

You, the owner of the business, may or may not be subject to workers' compensation insurance, depending on your state's laws. In many states, sole proprietors, partners in partnerships, owner/employees of small corporations, and owners of Limited Liability Companies are exempt from workers' comp insurance. Some states make it an option; you decide if you want workers' compensation insurance for yourself.

If you have personal health insurance, check with your health insurance company about on-the-job coverage. Some health insurance policies do not cover any on-the-job injuries.

Workers' compensation premiums for your employees is fully deductible. Workers' comp for yourself is deductible only if your state requires you to have workers comp insurance on yourself. If the coverage is voluntary, the premiums are not deductible (except for corporations).

The minimum premium to obtain a workers' compensation policy, even for one part-time employee, can cost several hundred dollars a year. The high cost of workers compensation insurance is a major reason so many one-person businesses struggle along doing everything themselves instead of hiring someone to help.

Premiums increase as your payroll increases (giving an employee a raise may increase your premium), and vary dramatically with the occupation. Workers' compensation premiums for a roofer are about thirty times higher than for clerical employee. So be sure the insurance company doesn't misclassify you in a high-risk, high-premium category.

You can keep your initial premium at or near the minimum, particularly for part-time and hourly employees, by giving the insurance company a low payroll estimate, since you really don't know how many hours your employees will be working. Once or twice a year, the insurance company will examine your payroll records, comparing your actual payroll to your original estimate. Your premium will be adjusted retroactively. Some insurance companies pay dividends (refunds) after the end of the year if you have a clean record (no claims).

Some states offer workers' compensation insurance through a state-operated insurance fund or risk-sharing pool. In some states, the rates are comparable to or lower than rates from regular insurance companies, particularly if you are hiring only one or two employees. In other states, the state fund is insurance of last resort, for businesses who cannot get coverage from a regular insurance company, and the state coverage may be more expensive. To locate the state-operated insurance fund, look in the Yellow Pages under Insurance or contact the State Employment or Human Resources Department.

A special warning if your employees will be working at their own homes (not at the employer's home): Your workers' comp premium will probably be triple the normal rate. The insurance companies view this as a high risk situation because the employee is at the workplace 24 hours a day and can too-easily claim that any injury at home is work related.

Building contractors: If you hire subcontractors, some states hold you responsible for the subcontractor's workers comp coverage if the subcontractor does not have the insurance. Ask to see a Certificate of Insurance from each subcontractor.

Vehicle Insurance. Liability coverage on all business vehicles is mandatory in most states. If you use your personal vehicle for business, check with your insurance company to make sure you have coverage that includes business use.

If your employees will be driving your vehicles, make sure their liability is included on your policy. If your employees will be driving their own vehicles on your company's business, you should have what's called "non-owned" auto liability insurance, which protects you if one of your employees injures someone or damages someone's property. This non-owned coverage does not protect the employee, who should have his or her own insurance as well.

Personal or business property inside a vehicle, such as merchandise you are delivering, is not usually covered by vehicle insurance.

Environmental Impairment and Pollution Liability. Required by federal law for all gas stations and for businesses located at former gas station sites if the tanks are still in the ground. Other businesses that are at risk for pollution problems, such as quick lubes and even dry cleaners, sometimes purchase this insurance.

Computer and Internet Insurance. Most business insurance policies exclude coverage for Internet and computer related problems. Regular business insurance policies often cover the physical damage, destruction, or theft of a computer, but these policies do not cover lost data, the consequences of lost data, or any problems your computer causes for customers, suppliers or people browsing your web site due to breach of security or stolen personal data. Insurance is available (sometimes called a "net secure" policy) for many of these Internet problems.

Coverage may include reimbursement for computer mishaps, glitches, outages, systems failures, loss or theft or corruption of data, fraud, and breaches of security on the Internet. Some policies protect you from liability, similar to malpractice insurance, should you accidently spread a virus or cause other damage or loss to people accessing your site or using your service, or if you are sued over privacy issues. Some policies cover loss of income due to Internet-related mishaps, similar to business-interruption insurance. None of the Internet or computer insurance is required by law, and truth to tell, some of it is so expensive, and deductibles so high, that most businesses just do without.

Insurance for Home-Based Businesses. Home businesses have special insurance needs and are subject to restrictions on some insurance policies. This is covered in the section on Home-Based Business.

Is there more? Of course. There's Vandalism and Malicious Mischief coverage. Patent Owners insurance. Key Person Life insurance. Boiler and Machinery coverage for equipment failures. Credit insurance for your accounts receivable. Damaged or Destroyed Records insurance. Specialized insurance (unusual kinds of coverage) for specific types of businesses and industries. Fiduciary insurance. Directors and Officers insurance. Wrongful Accounting insurance if you get sued by a shareholder for misstating your financial records (unintentionally, of course). Audit insurance if you get in trouble with the IRS—due to an honest mistake (there is no insurance if you get caught cheating). Copyright insurance. Export insurance. Employment Practices Liability coverage if you are sued by an employee for wrongful treatment. There's even Bad Weather insurance, which covers losses if the weather ruins an outdoor event.

It's just this sort of narrow focus that seems to be a key to a successful business person. The historians and philosophers have the grand sweeping views, but the ones who get rich are people of action who set themselves to a task and do it.
—Don Cusic, Middle Tennessee State Univ.

Purchasing Insurance

Where do you begin? Check with the state, your landlord, and your bank if you are getting a bank loan, to find out what insurance you must carry.

Most leases require tenants to carry liability, property damage and fire legal liability. Banks usually require you to insure property purchased with loan money. Bank loans sometimes require you to carry life insurance naming the bank as beneficiary. Car and equipment leasing firms often require you to obtain liability and/or property insurance on leased equipment.

Over and above any mandatory insurance, liability coverage is the most important to any business where customers, clients, or delivery people come to your door. One lawsuit by an injured customer can wipe you out: your business, and you personally. Make sure the coverage pays attorneys and legal fees as well as any claims.

Beyond liability and mandatory coverage, how much insurance you have or don't have is entirely up to you. How much can you afford? How much do you *want* to afford? How much of a risk are you willing to take, and how comfortable do you feel with that risk?

Most insurance companies offer a Business Owner's Policy ("BOP") or All Risk Insurance, combining many of the above coverages in one policy.

Some insurance companies offer "industry specific" policies, offering special coverage to certain types of businesses. In fact, you might want to contact one of the trade associations for your type of business. Trade associations often offer reasonably-priced insurance packages to members. To find a trade association, ask other people who own similar businesses, or ask at a library if they have a directory of associations, or look on the Internet.

Insurance companies are competitive, offering different rates, packages and premium payment plans. Many insurance policies offer much lower premiums if you opt for large deductibles. For property and equipment coverage, find out if the insurance will reimburse your original cost, replacement cost, or current value at time of loss. These can be significantly different amounts. If you have more than one location, have your insurance agent explain the important difference between "blanket" and "scheduled" coverage.

It is a good idea to shop around. Pick an agent or broker who will devote time to your individual needs, who will at no extra cost survey your entire situation and recommend different insurance options, explaining the advantages and disadvantages of each.

Make sure you are dealing with a solvent, reliable company, one with a good reputation for settling claims. Your agent can show you the company's rating, or check with your state's insurance department.

And finally: Read the policy carefully before you pay for it, not after you've suffered a loss you *thought* was covered.

Self Insurance

In an attempt to reduce insurance costs, business owners sometimes attempt self insurance. Basically this means you are not insured at all but have set aside funds to cover possible losses such as fire or theft or a liability claim against the business. Some people call these funds a "reserve." While self insurance certainly saves on insurance premiums, the money set aside or in the reserve is not considered a business expense and is not tax deductible.

At the time you actually sustain a loss or have to pay on a claim or lawsuit, you may or may not have a tax write-off, depending on the nature of the loss. For example, stolen or destroyed furniture and equipment can be written off only to the extent they haven't already been written off or depreciated; inventory is written off as part of cost-of-goods-sold; legal fees are probably fully deductible, but depend on the circumstances. The chapters on Inventory, Cost of Goods Sold, and specific items in the Tax section explain how to deduct different kinds of losses.

Remember, too, that it is unlikely your self insurance reserve will be large enough to cover a large loss or lawsuit. That's why people buy insurance in the first place.

Insurance required by law must be purchased from an insurance company. Self insurance will not suffice.

The less fixed costs you have, the more survivable you are.
—Stewart Pet Products owner Kitson Logue

THE BUSINESS PLAN

Business owners in general think that writing a business plan is a form of punishment. But business planning is essential to your success. I can tell you from first hand experience, from seeing it happen too many times: Most new business failures are due to a lack of foresight, a failure to think things through. A failure to plan.

Although business plans are often created to try to raise money, most business plans are really for your own use. Business planning is a self-learning process. You need to know everything about your business, your industry, your customers, your competition. You especially need to think out how you are going to find customers or clients and how you are going to market your goods or services to your customers.

The greatest benefit of a business plan is that, by writing everything down, you are more likely to see the entire picture, and you are more likely not to forget some important steps to prepare yourself for this huge venture. Launching a business without a business plan is much like building a house without blueprints. You can certainly do it, but when you discover a mistake in the foundation after the roof is shingled, you're really going to kick yourself.

Mission Statement

A good business plan starts with a short written statement of what your business is, what you want to do, and how you intend to get there. Sounds silly? Maybe, but many people wanting to start a business have not thought out their goals at all, and too many of these people quickly lose their direction and their interest. Although a mission statement can easily resemble a promo piece, keep in mind that this mission statement is for you, to help you visualize and vocalize exactly what you are trying to accomplish.

A Basic Plan

If you've read this entire section of *Small Time Operator*, followed through on the suggestions, done your market research, estimated your start-up expenses, tried your hand at the cash-flow guessing game (covered in the Bookkeeping section), and wrote it all down, you would have yourself a respectable business plan.

Such an informal plan will help you organize your thoughts and observations, show you problems that require more thought and analysis, and help you find all the jigsaw pieces and fit them together.

Don't create your plan in a vacuum. If it seems appropriate to you, talk about your plan, and your new business, with as many people as possible. The best way to avoid wishful thinking is to get feedback from potential buyers, clients, prospects. Listen to their answers. If your new business is going to be successful, other people should be excited about it, interested in hiring you or spending their money on your products. By creating a business that will give people what *they* want, a business that is structured to meet *their* needs, you have found the Secret To Success, the difference between an idea and a solid business.

It is important to understand the limits of a business plan, particularly one this early in the game. The ideas are only that, untested ideas. The numbers are guesses, your own inexperienced, optimistic guesses. Don't rely on them too heavily. Proceed with all caution, keep your eyes open, and let experience, not some written plan, be your guide.

Raising Capital

A business plan created just for yourself can be as informal as you like. But if you are trying to raise start-up capital from individuals or a bank, a more structured business plan will help you get your ideas across to prospective lenders and investors.

Someone who is considering putting money into your venture will most likely want to see a written plan, one that includes:

1. Your business idea.
2. Your background, experience, contacts, etc.
3. Where you plan to locate.
4. How you'll obtain or manufacture inventory.
5. How you will find and keep customers, and the status of the competition.
6. How much money you will need to start, and what the money will be used for.
7. How much time and how much of your own money you plan to commit to the business.
8. How much you will pay yourself.
9. How you will repay the loan or investment.

If you are looking for a loan or for investors, you may be asked to include "pro forma" financial statements, which are projections (forecasts) of income and expenses, profit or loss, cash flow, etc. These "projections" should be more honestly labeled "guesses" or even "hopes and dreams," because that's all they really are, and every banker and any savvy investor knows this.

People who are considering putting money into your business are going to be much more interested in your experience, your knowledge, and how much collateral you have. Quite often, they ask for a business plan just to see how good you are at preparing one, how well you understand business concepts.

Business planning is an ongoing process. After you've been in business awhile, you may want to draw up a new plan to help you make some major decision, such as reorganizing or expanding, or trying out some new, bold idea. By then, you will know your business well, and you will be able to create a much more reliable plan.

Business plans can be and often are much more elaborate and detailed than what I've described here. Entire books are dedicated to the many considerations, formulas, options and everything else you can conceivably fit onto graphs, charts, schedules, computer screens, and densely packed pages, to create some mighty impressive plans indeed, some of which are quite valuable and some of which are utterly useless. Sometimes, too much "information" will work against you, unable to see the forest for the trees.

Mary Baechler, founder and CEO of Racing Strollers, Yakima, Wa, talking to Inc. Magazine: "A good business plan will help you get a loan about as much as a nice suit. There's a myth that you need a good plan before launching a business. Many of the people who will tell you to write a plan are consultants that, oh my gosh, make money helping you to write such a plan. When your numbers are good, you don't really need a formal plan. When your numbers are stinko, a business plan doesn't fool anyone. And bankers don't make loans unless there's collateral."

Before you dive into anything, do a little research, write up a business plan, figure out if you're going to pay the mortgage or lose your shirt. Got an idea that is too hot to take the time for all that? Well be prepared to fail.
—Walter Jeffries, Flash Magazine

Research is everything. You've got to find where you fit into the puzzle.
—Mikal Ali, Sidestreet Inc. Greeting Cards

Statistics are no substitute for judgment.
—Henry Clay

The Customer Is Always Right—But Who Cares.

> —sign on the Shady Nook Snack Bar,
> Laytonville, California

There are only two rules in Customer Relations: 1. The Customer Is Always Right. 2. If the customer is ever wrong, re-read rule #1.
> —Business owner Stew Leonard

Customers are often right, and even when they are not, they think they are. We'll pretend they are because it's not worth fighting to prove it to them.
> —Jay Goltz, founder and owner,
> Artists Frame Service

I still go by the old rule that the customer is always right, even when he or she is clearly wrong.   —Consultant Marilyn Ross

The customer is seldom right. But the customer is always in charge.
> —Business owner Larry Taylor

Never tell a customer he's wrong. It's like putting gasoline on a fire.
> —John Tschohl, president,
> Service Quality Institute, Minneapolis

No one ever wins an argument with a customer.
> —Dale Carnegie

Section Two
BOOKKEEPING

The best memory is not so firm
as faded ink.
            —Chinese proverb

"If you take one from three hundred
and sixty-five, what remains?" asked
Humpty Dumpty.
"Three hundred and sixty-four, of
course," said Alice.
Humpty Dumpty looked doubtful. "I'd
rather see that done on paper,"
he said.
            —from Alice in Wonderland

Warming Up to an Unpopular Subject

Bookkeeping seems to be the one aspect of business that so many people dread. Columns upon columns of numbers, streams of adding machine tape, balancing the books (whatever that means), computer printouts that look great but make no sense, and "I'm a shopkeeper, not an accountant."

Whenever I try to explain or defend the paperwork end of business to a new business person, I always feel I have two strikes against me before I even open my mouth. But once a person understands why a business requires a set of ledgers and how these records can be kept with a minimum of time and effort, the fear vanishes, the work *somehow* gets done, and you are left with the satisfaction of seeing the total picture and of having done it yourself. And that's a nice feeling.

Bookkeeping is an integral part of business, of *your* business. To attempt a definition, bookkeeping is a system designed to record, summarize and analyze your financial activity: your sales, purchases, credit accounts, cash, payrolls, inventory, equipment. Your "books" are your ledgers and worksheets, the bound papers or the computer software, on which the bookkeeping activity is recorded or "posted."

Why Keep a Set of Books?

Most new business people think that they must keep books only because the government requires them to. Well, it's true, the IRS does require every business to keep a set of books. (The IRS's basic bookkeeping requirement is, "You must keep records to correctly figure your taxes.") But there is a lot more to bookkeeping than taxes and tax law requirements.

The real reason you'd *want* to keep a set of books, as you will learn soon enough, is because you need the information to run your business. Can you ever expect to make a good decision based on incomplete information? Your books are your only source of complete information about your business. It is virtually impossible to keep all your business information in your head. You may think you know your business like the back of your hand, but you would be surprised to see how much you don't know unless you can see the total financial picture. This is doubly true of a home-based business where personal and business expenses can get intermingled and confused.

Business failures have been blamed, time and again, on a lack of accurate financial records. Bob Willis, former owner of Booknews, a defunct bookstore: "Our biggest mistake was that we didn't keep a regular set of books. Half of our records were on scraps of paper and receipts. We didn't know whether some accounts were paid or not. We thought we were making a profit, but a good set of books would have shown us the truth: we were going broke. And you know, had I realized that, I could have taken steps to change things, to head us in a better direction."

Without a complete set of books, you find yourself trying to evaluate your business by looking at isolated areas, such as cash and inventory—these being the most observable, and also the most misleading. If, for example, you price your product based solely on its cost to you plus some arbitrary markup—a common mistake with beginners—you could be selling at a loss and not even know it. This happened at Booknews: "We knew what the books were costing us, but we didn't have any real idea of what our total overhead was—rent, insurance, supplies, utilities, payroll taxes, the rest. We sold a lot of books because we sold at a discount, and I thought we were doing well. Do you know it took me four months to realize that every single book we sold, we sold at a loss."

A good bookkeeping system will provide you with information essential to the survival of your business. Only with a complete set of books will you be able to evaluate your business and make any needed changes and plans for the future.

Joe Campbell, Resistance Repair: "Everybody who runs a business should sit down and figure out what it costs them to turn the key in that door every morning. Overhead. I never knew until I sat down and calculated exactly what my expenses were, what it costs me to have that place down there. And it's $80 a day! When you walk in there in the morning you know exactly what you gotta do before you start putting bread on the table. You gotta make eighty bucks for the man. And then you start making money for yourself."

Setting Up Your Books

Where do you begin? How much bookkeeping do you need? If your business is a one man, one woman, or a husband-and-wife operation, your records can be kept quite simple. A bank account, a set of income and expenditure ledgers and a few worksheets are about all you will need.

Do you sell on account? You will need records of each credit customer. If you hire employees, you need payroll records for each employee. Manufacturing and sales businesses need inventory records. Partnerships must keep records of each partner's contributions and withdrawals. Limited Liability Companies (LLCs) and corporations have even more requirements.

But let's take things one step at a time. *None of the bookkeeping records need be too complicated for most people to set up, to keep themselves and to understand.*

Computer or Hand Posted Ledgers?

Do you need bookkeeping software or can you use a simple set of hand-posted ledgers?

Computer prepared ledgers are basically identical to hand-posted ledgers. They're faster, cleaner looking, free of mathematical errors, and easier to rearrange and fine-tune to fit your needs. You can enter one payment that is posted to your checkbook and expense ledger, and also to your inventory, payroll, equipment, or other ledgers. You can post income to your bank account and income ledger, and update your record of credit customers. The software can give you daily, weekly, monthly and annual totals in any category you want, and keep track of your bank balance at the same time.

Hand posted ledgers, pencil on paper, have benefits as well. Although they take more time, and you've got to add everything by hand, they are easy to learn and to understand. The simple fact that you have to take time to write things down helps tremendously in learning how ledgers work, how they interrelate, and how to use them.

With hand-posted ledgers you don't need a computer, you don't need to master any software, you don't have to worry about files that disappear, programs that crash, viruses that damage or wipe out your files, and employees

that snoop. You won't have to turn on the computer every time you want to post a check.

The computer industry would like everyone to think that hand-posted ledgers are something from the past, as out of date as horse and buggy transportation. But the truth is that half of all new businesses use hand-posted ledgers the first year, and some never see a need for anything else. The majority of businesses, however, eventually switch to computer bookkeeping.

Spreadsheets

If you use and are comfortable with spreadsheets, a spreadsheet program can easily be set up as a set of ledgers. In fact, the word "spreadsheet" is an old accounting term that originally referred to a piece of ledger paper that had so many columns, it had to be folded over to fit in a binder. Today's computer spreadsheets are not much different.

Most spreadsheet programs come with a ready-to-use bookkeeping template, or you can purchase a template for your spreadsheet. (I helped design a set of spreadsheet ledgers, on a ready-to-run disk, that are set up like the sample ledgers in *Small Time Operator*. Pop the disk in and just add your numbers! *Small Time Operator: The Software* is available from my publisher, toll free 800-515-8050).

Accounting (Bookkeeping) Software

A spreadsheet may be all you need to keep your ledgers. But if you want more elaborate bookkeeping, if you want ledgers that are integrated with other business functions, accounting software offers more options and complexity. Accounting software often includes check writing, bank account balancing, inventory control, payroll, job costing, accounts receivable and payable, individual customer accounts, and other business functions. Some accounting software is for general business use, and some is for specific types of businesses and specific industries.

Accounting software should be fully integrated, able to pass information back and forth between all of its functions, and able to share data with other programs on your computer, so you don't have to enter numbers more than once.

Accounting software comes in many forms and levels of complexity. No one program is right for all businesses. You may have to try out a few programs to find one that meets your business needs and your computer expertise. Fortunately, many software vendors offer free sample versions of their programs that you can download from the Internet and use for a trial period. If you like the program, you can purchase it or sign up to use it online. If you don't pay for the program, at the end of the trial period it stops working, but you will be able to save the work you've already done. Your files will not be deleted.

Accounting software can be a mixed blessing. By eliminating the mechanics of individually posting the ledgers, eliminating the step-by-step think-it-through process, you create the dangerous possibility of ledgers you don't know where all the numbers came from, the possibility that you won't examine the numbers as carefully as you should, missing some important information or failing to catch a serious error.

If your accounting software is producing documents you don't know what to do with, ledgers you do not fully understand, numbers that don't seem right, Stop! Go back to square one, take the time to figure out what you have, take the time to understand your accounting system.

Specialized single-function accounting software is available such as programs for inventory control or job costing. Again, try to find a vendor who will let you "try it before you buy it."

The Bookkeeping

This Bookkeeping section is for all businesses, whether you use a computer or a pencil. The procedures are the same, the results are the same. To show you how to set up and keep your books, I have created a sample set of ledgers that are typical of both hand-posted and software bookkeeping systems.

The Ledger Section includes sample income, expenditure, credit, petty cash, inventory, equipment, depreciation and payroll ledgers, and year-end summaries that you can actually use. If you want a hand-posted system, you may photocopy the sample ledgers or copy them onto blank ledger sheets. If you use a computer, most bookkeeping programs let you choose your own column headings and categories. You can use my sample ledgers as prototypes, you can create your own categories, or you can stay with the default categories that come with your software.

Pencil or computer, bookkeeping is bookkeeping. Whether you arrive at your destination on a bicycle or in a limo, you'll still get there. This Bookkeeping section will show you the route.

Business Bank Account

As soon as you start your business, before you open your doors, go to the bank and open a separate business checking account. Keep your business finances and your personal finances separate. Nothing can be more confusing than mixing business with pleasure, financially.

Many states require you to have a DBA (fictitious name or assumed name statement) before you can open a bank account in your business name. Talk to your bank ahead of time and find out all the requirements. Some banks impose larger service charges and require larger minimum deposits for business accounts.

There are three Important Rules to follow:

Rule One: Avoid paying business bills in cash. Try to pay all business bills by check, or by credit card, or automatic bank deduction, or other electronic transaction. Your expenses are more easily recorded, better documented, and unlikely to be forgotten when paid by a method other than out-of-pocket cash. Some payments, of course, will have to be in cash, but keep them to a minimum (see the "Petty Cash" chapter).

Rule Two: Deposit all your income, checks and cash, into the business bank account. You will have a complete record of your earnings. Deposit checks as soon as possible. Every day you wait increases the chances that the check writer will have emptied or closed the account.

Rule Three: Try not to use the business account to pay personal, non-business expenses. While it is legal for a sole proprietor to mix business and personal funds in the same bank account (unless your bank prohibits it), the bookkeeping can get unnecessarily confusing when business and personal expense are commingled. Partnerships, corporations and LLCs should never combine business funds with the owners' personal funds. This can result in legal and tax complications you definitely want to avoid.

A Few Bank Account Rules-of-Thumb:

1. Balance your bank account every month. It is too easy to make an adding error. You don't want to bounce a check on your most important supplier because you thought you were down to the last $10 when you were really down to the last dime. Never balanced a bank account? A chapter in the Your Business section explains how to do it.

2. Keep bank statements and canceled checks (if your bank returns cancelled checks) at least three years. They are the best documentation you have if you ever need to support your records. Three years is the normal statute of limitations set by the IRS for income tax audits.

3. Try not to write any checks payable to "cash." Checks written to cash leave you no record of how the money was spent.

4. Expenses that are partly personal and partly business, such as automobile expenses, or rent and utilities for a home business, or your credit card bill if it includes business and non-business purchases, are partly deductible: the business portion. These expenses can be handled in one of two ways: (1) Pay these bills from your personal checking account, then post the business portion to your business ledgers (explained in the "Expenditure" chapter); or (2) Pay the bills from your business checking account; post the business portion to its proper column in the expenditure ledger, and post the non- business portion to the "Non-Deductible" column (explained in the "Expenditure" chapter).

Tax & Legal Requirements: Bank Accounts

No federal law requires you to have a bank account. The IRS does not require you to deposit your business income in a bank account. The IRS does require you to report all income, whether deposited in a bank account or not.

Some states require all businesses to deposit all checks payable to the business, in a business bank account. In these states, cashing a business check is prohibited by law. So you may be required by your state law to have a bank account, if your business gets checks.

No law requires you to keep separate business and personal checking accounts (sole proprietors only; all other forms of business must have separate bank accounts). You can pay business bills from a personal checking account, and get a full business deduction. You can deposit business checks into a personal bank account, if your bank's rules don't prohibit such activity.

Most banks, however, will require you to set up a business bank account before they will let you deposit or cash checks made out to a business name. If your business name is the same as your name, your bank will probably let you deposit or cash business checks without setting up a separate business account.

Joe Campbell, Resistance Repair: "My problem was that I would look in our checking account, our one and only checking account, and I'd say, Wow, there's $1,000 in there. Let's buy the new tires we need for the car. The kids need a new pair of shoes, and I buy them a pair of shoes. And I see we still have $700 in the bank, we're in good shape. Then all the parts bills come in, and I owe $800. I have to put creditors off. Having that parts money in a separate account tells you exactly where you are. It's security. Plus it's emergency cash if you have to go in and get it."

Bookkeeping Simplified:
An Introduction to the Single Entry System

The ledgers in *Small Time Operator* and the ledgers in many software systems are simple "single entry" ledgers. For any transaction, only one entry is made, either to income or to expenditure. Single entry bookkeeping keeps the paperwork to a minimum while still providing you with the basic information to manage your business and prepare tax returns.

There are two disadvantages to this simple bookkeeping system. Single entry bookkeeping will provide a record of your income and expenditures but will not automatically provide a complete record of inventory on hand, equipment, outstanding loans or other assets and liabilities.

The other drawback to single entry bookkeeping is the lack of a built-in double check of arithmetical accuracy. These disadvantages are partly offset by the additional asset records that the equipment and inventory ledgers provide, and by the Total columns in the ledgers that provide a partial math double check.

The alternative to single entry bookkeeping, the well known and elaborate system called "double entry" bookkeeping, compares to our single entry system as a fancy stereo compares to a portable CD player. Double entry is a complete bookkeeping system that provides cross checks and automatic balancing of the books, that minimizes errors, and that transforms bookkeeping from a part-time nuisance into a full-time occupation.

In double entry bookkeeping, every transaction requires two separate entries, a "debit" and a "credit." These terms originated in double entry bookkeeping, along with the expression "balancing the books": total debits must equal total credits for the books to be "in balance."

Double entry bookkeeping is a science. It is *the* perfected bookkeeping system, and it requires a full semester in college to master. Simplicity is our goal. I find that most small businesses are better off without the refinements (and the headaches) of a double entry system.

Some bookkeeping software is programmed for full double-entry accounting; but many software systems combine the simplicity of a single-entry system with the additional entries and the math checks lacking in hand-posted ledgers.

Cash Accounting Vs. Accrual

You must choose between two accounting methods: "cash" or "accrual."

"Cash method" (also called "cash basis") does not mean all your transactions are in cash. It refers to how you record your sales and purchases, and how you post your ledgers.

Under the cash method, income is recorded when the money is received, and expenses are recorded when paid, with a few exceptions explained below. (In accounting terminology, the word "cash" refers to checks, money orders and credit card receipts as well as currency).

Credit sales for which you haven't yet been paid, and purchases you haven't yet paid for, do not show on cash-method ledgers.

Accrual accounting, by comparison, records all income and expenses whether paid or not. Credit transactions—money you owe, and money owed to you—do show on accrual ledgers. (Credit transactions refer to credit you extend to your customers, or credit your suppliers extend to you; they do not refer to credit cards, which are treated as cash transactions).

For most small businesses, accrual accounting becomes a factor only at year-end. A sale made in December, for which you aren't paid until January of the new year, is recorded on December's ledgers and becomes taxable income for the old year. When the cash is received in January, it is not part of the new year's income. If you are using the cash method, the sale and the taxable income would be recorded in January when the money came in. You wouldn't pay taxes on it until a full year later.

Under the accrual method, figuring income at year-end can be tricky if you have a contract for a large job that is partially complete at December 31. For tax purposes, the completed part of the contract is reported as December's income, the balance as next year's income. This will probably require some estimating and guess work on your part. Under cash accounting, you would only report payments received by December 31.

If you use the accrual system, expenses that you've incurred but not paid by December 31, become tax deductions for the year just ended, not the year paid. Under the cash system, you would not record, or get a tax deduction, for an expense until you paid for it.

There is, however, an important exception for inventory. Inventory cannot be written off until sold, regardless of when you acquired it or when you paid for it. This is covered in the Tax section, under "Cost of Goods Sold," and you should understand it thoroughly. You cannot run out at December 31, buy a truckload of merchandise, and expect to write it off immediately.

Three more exceptions: (1) Some prepaid expenses are not deductible the year paid. See "Prepaid Expenses" in the Tax Section. (2) Purchases using a bank credit card are deductible the year charged, even if not paid until the following year. See "Credit Card Purchases" in the Bookkeeping Section. (3) If you buy equipment or other business assets on time, making installment payments over several years, you may be able to write off the entire cost the year of purchase, and you will be eligible for the First Year Tax Write Off (explained in the Tax section). You should ask your accountant how to record installment purchases.

Which Method Do You Choose?

Cash accounting is easier to understand and easier to figure than accrual accounting, so most small businesses prefer to use the cash method.

If your gross (total) annual sales are $1 million or less, you can choose either the cash or accrual method. For most new businesses, that's the end of the decision making. Until you hit $1 million a year in sales, you can use cash accounting.

If your annual sales are over $1 million a year, the IRS has the following rules:

1. Sales businesses, general manufacturers, and "information services" (publishers) must use the accrual method.

2. Service businesses, contractors, and custom (special order) manufacturers, where more than 50% of the total income is for services rendered (less than 50% of total income is for parts, materials, goods), can choose either the cash or accrual system—as long as your total annual sales are $10 million or less ($5 million or less if your business is a C corporation).

Bookkeeping

To make things easy for inexperienced bookkeepers, the bookkeeping instructions in this section are exactly the same for both cash and accrual businesses, until year end. The year-end instructions explain how to adjust your ledgers so they are, at your choice, either cash or accrual.

This simplified system will work fine as long as you don't need precise figures at the end of each month. Since you make adjustments only at year-end, at any time during the year the figures may be off slightly.

More Than One Business

If you have more than one business, the IRS requires that you keep a separate set of ledgers for each business. However, instead of actually setting up more than one business, you can have separate "divisions" within one business, which will require only one set of ledgers. See "Multiple Businesses" in the Your Business section.

Defining Income

For bookkeeping and taxes, you must distinguish between "business" income and "non-business" income. Business income is what you earn from selling a product or providing a service. Only your business income is included on your income ledgers. Non-business income is reported and taxes paid on it, but it is kept separate from your business income.

Rental income is considered business income only if you are in the rental business. All other rental income is "non-business income."

Interest income depends on its source. Interest received on loans is not business income unless you are in the business of lending money. Interest received on accounts receivable (interest charges added to money your customers owe you) is business income, to be included here. Interest from a bank account is non-business income, even though the business earned it, and should be reported separately.

The differentiation between business and non-business income is not just academic, not just accounting talk. Although business and non-business income are both subject to income tax, business income is also subject to self-employment tax (covered in the Tax section). Non-business income escapes self-employment tax.

"Gross income" is your total business income before any expenses. "Net income" is the income after expenses have been deducted. The income discussed here is the gross income.

Barter: If you barter or trade goods or services, you include the fair market value of what you receive as part of your business income. This is covered in the Tax section.

Deposits and Advances: If you take deposits or advances from your customers, they are considered income if they are not returnable. Returnable deposits and advances are not recorded as income.

Your Own Money: Any of your own money put into the business, any money others invest in your business, and any loans received are not income to your business. You pay no taxes on this money. Do not include these amounts as part of your income.

When your business is still small, you think of it like a personal checkbook. Money comes in, money goes out, and if there's any left, we go out to dinner.

—*Business owner John Seiffer*

Recording Income: Step One

Income is recorded in two steps. Step One: at the time you make a sale, record the sale on an invoice, cash receipt, or cash register tape. Step Two will be to summarize the sales in your income ledger.

Some software automatically combines Steps One and Two. But it is still best understood as a two-step procedure. I can't overemphasize how important it is that you understand your bookkeeping completely, which means understanding what your software is doing.

Let's examine Step One. How you record each sale depends primarily on your volume of sales.

Low Volume of Sales

If your business has only a few sales each month, you can prepare a custom invoice for each sale. Include your name or business name; address, telephone, etc.; date of sale; customer's name and address; description of sale; amount, showing sales tax separately; a place to indicate when paid. Give the original invoice to your customer and keep a duplicate copy for your records.

Pinball Alley
Box 640, Laytonville CA 95454
We buy old Pinballs—Any Condition
707/984-6746

June 14

INVOICE to:
B. Bear, Laytonville

Repair Gottlieb King Pin, 4 hours	$80.00
2 flipper coils	16.00
set of rubber bands	10.00
bulbs	8.50
sales tax on parts	2.50
Total	$117.00

Depending on your inclination and your finances, your invoices can be prepared on specially printed and custom-designed forms, or you can type the information on plain paper, or you can use your computer to produce the invoices.

Medium Volume of Sales

Businesses with a larger volume of sales often use pre-printed or computer generated invoices. Most everyone is familiar with the cash receipt books and invoices many businesses use to record individual sales: pre-numbered forms, in duplicate, one for the customer, one for you. You can purchase receipt books and invoices with your business name custom-printed at the top, or you can purchase a rubber stamp and mark each receipt individually.

Note: Don't confuse this book of cash receipts with other books labeled "Cash Receipts" that are in fact ledgers for recording income totals.

Throughout *Small Time Operator*, the terms sales slips, sales receipts, cash receipts, bills, and invoices are used interchangeably. They all refer to individual sales records. The term "statement," however, means something else to most businesses. A statement (or statement of account) is a summary of invoices and payments over a period of time. Some businesses issue statements, some don't. Most businesses don't pay from statements, so if your bill says "statement" instead of "invoice," it may not get paid.

The procedure for using cash receipts or invoices is simple. If the receipts are not pre-numbered, number them. Use a separate receipt for each sale. Make a duplicate copy of each receipt. Write the date, amount, and description of the sale. Show any sales tax separately. If this is a credit sale, write CREDIT SALE on the receipt.

Give the original receipt or invoice to your customer. Leave the duplicate in your receipt book. The duplicate copies will be summarized and posted to your income ledger.

If you void any invoice, do not throw it out. Mark it "VOID" and keep it in your receipt book. Although you should not include the voided receipt in your summary total, keep a record of it here, just so you'll know what happened to it.

Instead of a book of cash receipts, you can purchase individual two-part or three-part invoice forms from an office supply store or printer, with your name imprinted on them. These forms are used in the same way as the cash receipts.

Computer accounting and word processing software can easily design and print invoices.

Large Volume of Sales

Businesses with many sales each day, convenience stores, auto parts stores, hardware stores and the like, will need a good cash register to keep track of sales. You can spend a small fortune on a new state-of-the-art cash register, or you may be able to find a good used one. Keep an eye out for businesses that are going out of business. They are often selling *everything*.

Terms of Sale

If you offer return privileges or discounts for prompt payment, these should be spelled out on your invoice. "Net 30" means you expect payment in 30 days. "2%–10, net 30" means if your customers pay within ten days they get a 2% discount. A "P.O." is a purchase order number, which many business customers use for their records. Their P.O. number should appear on your invoice, in addition to your invoice number.

Who pays shipping should be specified. "FOB" stands for Freight on Board. "FOB your-business-location" means your customer pays freight. "FOB the-customer's-location" means you will pay the shipping to your customer.

If you offer credit terms, federal law requires you to disclose, in detail, your credit terms and finance charges. See "Credit Sales" below.

Recording Income, Step Two: The Income Ledger

The income ledger is a summary record of your sales invoices, cash receipts or cash register tapes. It is one of the most important business records you have. It tells you—daily, weekly if you want, monthly, and at year end—how much income you've earned and how much sales tax you've collected. It helps you manage your business by showing you the days and the months that are slow or busy so that you can better plan your expenditures, advertising, sales, even vacations. It is a guide to preparing cash flow infor-

mation (cash flow and financial management are discussed at the end of this section). The income ledger saves you time preparing your sales tax reports and income tax returns.

The sample income ledger can be used as is or adapted to your individual needs and your state's sales tax requirements. Accounting software will have an income ledger that is similar to this one. Use a separate ledger page for each month. Each page has 7 columns:

1. *Date.* You may post daily or periodically. How often you post the income ledger depends on you and the volume of sales you have.

2. *Sales period.* If you are posting daily, use the line corresponding with the date. If you are not posting daily, note the sales period here, such as "June 3-5." This is explained below. You can also use this column for notations you want to make.

3. *Taxable sales,* excluding sales tax. If you do not have to collect sales tax, use this column for total sales and ignore the rest of the columns.

4. *Sales tax collected.*

5 and 6. *Non-taxable sales.* Some states require non-taxable sales to be broken down into categories, such as labor, freight, wholesale, etc.

7. *Total sales amount,* including sales tax. This column serves as a double check on your totals: the sum of the amounts in Columns 3, 4, 5 and 6 should equal the amount in Column 7.

You will be summarizing your individual sales (from Step One of Recording Income) and posting the summary totals to the income ledger.

Daily Posting

If you have a moderate or heavy volume of sales, you probably should post the income ledger daily. Add up your sales for the day and post your totals to the proper columns in the ledger. Compute separate totals for taxable sales (post to Col. 3), sales tax (Col. 4), non-taxable sales (Columns 5 and 6), and total (Column 7). No need to make any entries under Sales Period (Column 2).

After you have posted the ledger, add the daily totals in Columns 3, 4, 5, and 6 together. They should equal the total in Column 7, which is the grand total for the day. If you get a different amount, you will have to locate your adding error. The procedure is a lot simpler in the doing than in the explaining. You really should have no trouble getting the hang of it.

INCODE LEDGER Month of _June_

1 DATE	2 SALES PERIOD	3 TAXABLE SALES	4 SALES TAX	5 NON-TAXABLE SALES Freight	6 w/Sale	7 TOTAL SALES
1		173 24	10 39			183 63
2		217 36	13 04	7 00		237 40
3						
4						
5	3rd – 5th	577 82	34 67	18 00		630 49
6		118 71	7 12			125 83
7	closed					
8		266 94	16 02	14 19	275 00	572 15
9						

Income Ledger   Month of: June

1 Date	2 Sales Period	3 Taxable Sales	4 Sales Tax	5 Freight	6 Wholesale	7 Other	8 Total Sales
			Non-Taxable Sales				
1		$173.24	$10.39				$183.63
2		$217.36	$13.04	$7.00			$237.40
3							
4							
5	3rd - 5th	$577.82	$34.67	$18.00			$630.49
6		$118.71	$7.12				$125.83
7	closed						
8		$266.94	$16.02	$14.19	$275.00		$572.15
9							

Two samples of the same income ledger. The computer version adds all the totals automatically and gives subtotals (daily, weekly, monthly, annually) anytime you want.

Posting Every Few Days or Once a Week

If you have only a few sales each day, you may wish to post the ledger every few days or once a week. Total all your sales for the period, keeping separate totals for taxable sales, sales tax, and non-taxable sales. Enter the totals on the line corresponding with the last day of your sales period. For example, if the sales you are combining are for June 3 through June 5, post your totals on the June 5 line. Under Sales Period (Column Two), note the period: "June 3rd-5th."

Don't feel that you must stick to one method of posting once you have started. If daily posting becomes too tedious, try posting every three days or five days. If you post your income ledger every few days, and a busy time comes along, switch over to daily posting for the busy period.

The posting only becomes a nightmare if the paperwork is allowed to accumulate. All of a sudden there's a three week backlog, all the receipts are mixed up, some billings are missing and, Oh, how I hate bookkeeping! It doesn't have to happen that way if you keep your ledger up to date.

How to Post Sales Returns

Sales returns, both cash and credit, should be handled as if they were negative sales:

1. Prepare a separate credit/return slip for each return, and mark it clearly "RETURN" or "REFUND" or "CREDIT MEMO."

2. Write down all the information that was on the original invoice, including the sales tax.

3. Include the return slip (credit memo, etc.) with your *current* batch of sales receipts.

4. When you add up the current receipts to post to the income ledger, subtract the amounts on the return slips from the total.

End of Month Procedure

No matter how frequently or infrequently you do your posting, run a monthly total at month-end, even though it may not be a full 5 or 7 days since your last regular posting. Don't let a posting period cross months. You will often want, and some tax forms may require, monthly totals. As with your daily or period totals, your monthly totals in Columns 3, 4, 5 and 6 should equal the total in Column 7.

Year-end Procedure

Record the 12 monthly totals on the year-end summary page. Your yearly totals in Columns 3, 4, 5 and 6 should equal the total in Column 7.

If you are keeping books on the accrual method (see the chapter "Cash Accounting Vs. Accrual"), that's all there is to it. No year-end adjustments are needed. You're done until next year.

If you are using the cash method, you adjust your year-end total by subtracting any credit sales that are still unpaid at year end. These are your year-end accounts receivable. Since you haven't been paid yet for these sales, they shouldn't appear on cash ledgers. (If this doesn't make complete sense to you, go back and re-read "Cash Accounting Vs. Accrual").

When the credit sales are paid in the new year, record them in the new year's income ledger.

If these cash method adjustments turn into a headache for you, or you find them too confusing, you can simplify things by not posting *any* credit sales until you receive payment. In this way your income ledger is perpetually on the cash basis, and no year-end adjustment is needed.

Altering The Ledgers

Feel free to alter the income ledger to suit your needs. Many businesses post taxable sales and sales tax (Columns 3 & 4) as one combined figure in one column, and then back off the sales tax from the monthly totals. Some businesses want a separate column for each product or group of products they sell, or for different services they provide. You may not need the non-taxable sales

information (Columns 5 & 6) or you may want to re-title them. And for some businesses, the Total column may be all you want and need, period.

Filing Your Sales Receipts

Keep your sales receipts (and all other business records) at least three years. These are the source documents that support your tax returns. If your invoices are not already bound, batch and bind them monthly (staples, rubber bands, manilla envelopes) before filing them away.

Installment Sales

Installment sales, where you receive periodic payments on account, are handled in one of two ways. If you are on the cash basis, post your income ledger as the payments come in. If you are on the accrual basis, you have the option to (1) record the income as the payments come in, same as cash-basis businesses; or (2) post the entire amount of the sale to your income ledger when you make the sale.

Accrual businesses should get help from an accountant when making this choice. A lot of tax money may be at stake.

Under both above methods, you should set up a record to keep track of each sale: the full amount of the sale, the terms agreed upon, the payments, and the balance owed. This record is kept in addition to your income ledger; installment sales are posted to both.

Return (Bounced) Checks

If a customer's check bounces, your bank will return the check to you with an explanation. "Insufficient funds" means that there is not enough money in the customer's account to pay the check. Often, this is not an intentionally written bad check. Get in touch with your customer and find out when you can redeposit the check (better yet, ask the customer to come back and give you cash). If the check bounces a second time, the bank will not accept it a third time. Your bank will impose a service charge on you if your customer's check bounces, two charges if it bounces twice.

"Account closed" means just that. This is not a good sign. Honest people don't usually write checks on closed accounts. If the check came

back from the bank marked "Stop Payment," the customer deliberately stopped payment. Stop payments are usually used when checks are lost or stolen, but sometimes a customer gets mad or changes his mind after the sale, and stops payment in order to be sure he'll get his money back. In either case, try to contact your customer, find out what happened, and get payment. "Return to maker" is a general term; usually it means the same as "insufficient funds."

One possible way to collect on a bounced check is to "put it in for collection," a procedure that is very effective when you are dealing with well-meaning customers who are always down to their last penny. You give the bounced check back to your bank and request that it be held for collection. Your bank then sends the check back to your customer's bank, which will hold the check for up to a month. If any funds are deposited to the customer's account during this holding period, any checks held for collection will be paid first. Banks usually charge a fee for this service.

If all attempts at collection prove futile, file the bounced check in a folder marked "Bad Debts." Bad debts will be a year-end expenditure entry, explained in the expenditure ledger instructions. Make no entry in your income ledger.

Credit Sales

There is no doubt that offering credit to your customers will increase sales. "Buy Now Pay Later" has virtually replaced "In God We Trust" as America's slogan. Many, many people have come to expect, even demand, that they be allowed to buy on credit. Shoppers may not go out of their way to find a store that offers quality merchandise at low prices, but they will always be on the lookout for a store that will sell to them on credit. And they are often willing to pay higher prices for the privilege: we all know people who buy gasoline only at a station that takes their credit card, even though the gas is 5¢ cheaper at the cash-only station across the street.

There are two ways to extend credit: directly; or via credit cards such as MasterCard and VISA. This chapter is about *direct* credit, credit you extend directly to your customers. Credit cards are covered in a following chapter.

Almost all wholesale businesses extend direct credit to their business customers. Many retail stores and self-employed individuals extend direct credit to regular customers and clients.

Direct credit involves more work and bookkeeping on your part and a much larger expenditure of energy. You decide who you will and will not extend credit to and how flexible or inflexible your credit policy will be. It is a good idea to have a formal, written credit policy that applies to all customers, although you will find, time and again, that each customer is different and may require special handling. Any customer seeking credit should be made aware of your policy, which should clearly state (1) maximum credit allowed, (2) payment timetable, and (3) any finance charges or late charges.

Adding finance charges, late charges or interest to late payments may or may not be a good idea for your business. Customers who are always short of cash tend to give priority to bills that add finance charges. But many customers resent the implied threat, particularly when it comes from a small business where the customer knows you personally. There is something inherently unfriendly about late payment penalties.

There's an old saying, you can catch more bees with honey than with vinegar (or something like that). Rather than threatening a penalty, offer an incentive for prompt or early payment: a small discount, or free shipping, or a "special" gift. Not only will you get a better response, you will generate more goodwill with your customers. *And* you can skip the next chapter.

Federal Laws—Finance Charges

If you impose finance charges, you must abide by the Federal Truth in Lending Act, Fair Credit Billing Act and Equal Credit Opportunity Act.

The Truth in Lending Act requires that all customers be told the full details of the finance charges. Before the first transaction is made on any credit account, the creditor (you, the merchant) must disclose in writing (1) the conditions under which a finance charge may be imposed, (2) method of determining the amount of the finance charge, (3) the minimum periodic payment required, and (4) your customer's legal rights regarding possible errors or questions.

The Fair Credit Billing Act requires you to make prompt correction of a billing mistake.

The Equal Credit Opportunity Act prohibits discrimination against an applicant for credit on the basis of age, sex, marital status, race, religion, etc. If you deny credit, this Act requires you to tell an applicant why credit was denied. You must keep all credit applications for a year.

These Acts specify what information must be presented to the customer, right down to the exact wording and size of the print, and when the information must be made available.

In addition to the above laws, you may have to abide by the Consumer Credit Protection Act, Fair Credit Reporting Act, and Fair Debt Collection Practices Act. You can get information about all of these wonderful laws from the Federal Trade Commission, Washington, D.C. 20580, or on the Internet at www.ftc.gov.

None of the above federal laws regulate what interest you may charge your customers. Most states have usury laws that specify maximum interest, how it is to be calculated, and probably a hundred other details. Contact your state's Department of Consumer Affairs.

Credit Ledger

If you don't have a large number of credit sales, you can easily set up a credit ledger to keep track of unpaid accounts (accounts receivable). The credit ledger is kept in addition to the income ledger. Credit sales are posted to both. You can use the sample credit ledger page as a prototype. The ledger has six columns:

Column One: Date of sale.
Column Two: Customer's name.
Column Three: Invoice number.
Column Four: Total amount of sale (including sales tax).
Column Five: Date paid.
Column Six: Memo (for any notes you want).

Each credit sale should be recorded on a separate line on the credit ledger. Post Columns One through Four from the invoice, either when you make the sale or when you post to your income ledger. (Be sure to write the words "CREDIT

CREDIT LEDGER

1 SALE DATE	2 CUSTOMER	3 INV. NO.	4 TOTAL SALE AMOUNT	5 DATE PAID	6 MEMO
1-18	Brenneman	113	53 12	2-10	
1-23	S. Ross	128	17 92		notice sent 3-1
1-24	Rygh	134	8 82	2.28	
2-12	Miley	186	10 71		

SALE" on the sales receipt when you make the sale.) Post Column Five when you get paid. At any time, you can glance down your credit ledger and, by looking at Column Five, tell who still owes you money. Now, collecting that money—that's another story.

Remember, credit sales are posted to your income ledger as well as to any credit ledger. The income ledger is your only complete record of income from all sales.

An Alternative Credit Record

An alternative to the credit ledger is to make extra copies of credit sales invoices and use them in lieu of a ledger. Print your invoices in three-part, rather than two-part forms, and use the third copy as your record of credit sales. File the third copy of all credit sale invoices in a folder marked "Unpaid."

When you receive payment, pull the copy from the "Unpaid" folder and then either file it in a "Paid" folder or throw it away. Once paid, this "third copy" is an extra. There is no reason to keep it unless you want a record of paid-up customers. This method eliminates the need for a credit ledger, but it involves more pieces of paper (which can be easily lost) and more expensive forms.

If you only have a two-part sales invoice (one for the customer, one for you) you should *not* put your one remaining copy in a credit file. It should stay batched with the rest of the sales receipts. If you start shuffling receipts around, some here, some there, and lose numerical control, you are just asking for trouble. The result of such haphazard bookkeeping is usually an incomplete set of records and insupportable ledgers.

Businesses that regularly make a large number of credit sales will probably need a more elaborate credit system. Stores with regular credit customers often keep a separate file on each customer with a complete record of sales and payments. Such files can be informal or can be part of a complicated system of billings and monthly statements. For you not-so-small-time operators who need to keep close track of credit sales, there are several commercially designed systems available. Most computer bookkeeping systems include a credit ledger.

You and Your Credit Customers

The hardest part of direct credit is trying to collect past-due accounts from slow or non-paying customers. I can think of no single aspect of business that is more upsetting than trying to deal with people who can't or won't pay their bills. You begin to resent the customers and they begin to resent you. Bad and sometimes bitter feelings build up. You decide for yourself where you draw the line, that the money is no longer worth the aggravation.

In fact, extending too much credit can destroy a business. I know a small grocery store, owned by a nice and eager-to-please couple, that offered credit to everyone in the neighborhood. Quite a few customers ran up large bills they couldn't pay, until the shopkeepers finally cut off their credit. The customers, unable or unwilling to face the store owners, not only didn't pay their bills, they stopped coming in the store completely. They bought their groceries elsewhere. The poor couple not only never collected on the old sales, they lost out on new sales as well. The couple went broke and the store folded. A few months later, a brand new but much wiser owner reopened the store. And, lo and behold, all the old deadbeat customers came back to shop! It wasn't the new owner's responsibility to collect the old owner's debts, this was a new business. The new owner extended limited credit to reliable customers and never let the accounts get too high or too far behind. She had the rare talent of being able to look a negligent customer right in the eye, and say, friendly yet firmly, "Pay up." And they did. And she prospered.

Business is easy. You buy low and sell high. Those accountants, marketing experts, engineers and all the rest are just confusing the issues.

—*R. Farmer, Indiana University*

Posting Uncollectible Accounts

At year-end, you should review all unpaid credit sales and determine which are uncollectible. If you keep a credit ledger, write "Uncollectible" and the year in Column Six next to those accounts that are uncollectible. Add up the uncollectible accounts for the year, and record the amount in your Bad Debts folder (see the previous discussion of Return Checks). If you keep the third-part sales receipts instead of a credit ledger, pull out the uncollectible receipts from the unpaid file and mark each "Uncollectible." Add up the sales from all the uncollectible receipts. Staple the uncollectible receipts together, write the total on the front (or attach the adding machine tape), and file in your Bad Debts folder. Bad debts are a business expense computed at year-end. The procedures are explained below in The Expenditure Ledger chapters.

Only include in your list of uncollectible accounts those that you are certain are uncollectible. If you are unsure, let it ride until next year. You can write off a bad debt in any future year that it becomes definitely uncollectible.

Credit Cards

Accepting credit cards such as MasterCard and VISA will eliminate the headaches of direct credit selling. You will not need credit ledgers, you will never have to hound people to pay up. Sales are processed through your regular checking account.

Credit cards are an easy way to handle international sales. You process international sales in U.S. dollars, and you get paid the same amount as though it was a U.S. transaction. No currency conversions to worry about, and no extra fees.

You cannot apply directly to VISA or MasterCard to become a credit-card merchant. You go through a bank or other credit card processor.

Banks also process American Express and Discover cards, but you sign up for these cards directly with American Express and Discover. Your bank can tell you how to contact American Express and Discover.

Banks are very choosy about who they will set up as credit-card merchants. Visible public operations, such as retail stores, usually have no trouble getting credit-card merchant status ("merchant status" is a bank term that means you can accept credit cards). But new mail order, home, and Internet businesses are often turned down. Too many fraudulent scams and here-today-gone-tomorrow entrepreneurs have cost the banks too much money.

If you've been in business a few years or if you have a good relationship with a bank, you are more likely to be approved. Keep in mind that the bank, not the credit card company, decides who gets merchant status. So if one bank turns you down, try another (and *another*).

Some businesses that are turned down by banks try to get credit-card status through third-party service bureaus, sometimes called processing centers or independent sales organizations (ISOs). Some of these operations, however, are excessively expensive or downright fraudulent. Be cautious of these people, especially if they want money up-front to "process" or "evaluate" your application. Find out what bank they represent and check with VISA and MasterCard to find out if the ISO is properly registered.

Credit card processing is offered by some trade and business associations, by Costco and similar "members-only" groups, and by several Internet services (covered below).

Credit Card Fees

Fees for setting you up as a credit card merchant and for processing your transactions, can vary, often dramatically, depending on where you get your merchant status (bank or ISO), dollar volume, and number of transactions a month.

For small accounts, banks typically charge 3% to 5% of the sale amount. Banks charge higher percentages for Internet and mail-order businesses. Some banks and ISOs also have a minimum monthly fee, or a per-transaction fee, in addition to the 3%-5% they deduct from your sales. Once a month, you receive a statement of activity.

Credit Card Terminals

Businesses process credit cards using an electronic terminal. The terminal hooks up to your regular telephone line (no special wiring needed) and processes all credit card transactions electronically, including depositing the money in your bank account. The terminal will automatically reject invalid and stolen cards.

You can purchase a terminal, or you may be required to lease the terminal. Buying a terminal is a lot less expensive than leasing, but ISOs in particular make a lot of their profit from leasing terminals and often refuse to sell them outright.

If you don't have a terminal, you can usually process credit cards over the telephone. You call a number, enter the information, and the transaction is processed much like a transaction using a terminal. Many banks offer software to process credit card sales using your computer.

Credit Card Chargebacks

You usually will not be responsible for stolen or invalid cards, as long as you follow the procedures required by your bank, such as checking signatures and expiration dates, but this applies only to face-to-face transactions.

If you take credit card orders over the telephone, fax, or from the Internet, banks will not accept responsibility for invalid, fraudulent or stolen credit cards that were processed in what they call "card not present" transactions. Even if your credit card terminal accepts the sale and gives you an approval, there is no guarantee that you won't get charged back if there is a problem.

Credit card fraud is a significant problem for some Internet merchants. The ease with which people can hide their identities and use fraudulent credit card numbers is greater on the Internet, because the huge size and anonymous nature of the Internet invites all kinds of scam artists to try their luck.

The fear most people have, that credit card numbers and personal information will be intercepted while traveling across the Internet from your customer's computer to your web site, is very unlikely. It is almost impossible for a thief to catch a credit card number in flight.

The real fraud problem is from criminals who already have stolen or bogus credit card numbers. The problem is not so much for the person whose credit card was fraudulently charged (who rarely if ever has to pay), but for the merchant who accepted the card, who absorbs the loss.

You, as a merchant, should take as many precautions as you can, particularly if a large amount of money is at stake. You can ask for telephone numbers from people who place orders, and call them back to "confirm" the order. A credit card thief is not likely to give you a valid telephone number. You can call your credit card processor's toll free number and verify the card owner's address. If the address your customer gave you is different, that may be a warning flag.

Even when a sale is totally legitimate, it does not guarantee payment if there is a dispute. If your customer refuses to pay your bill for any plausible reason, claiming that the merchandise was never received, or it was damaged, or it was returned, or never even ordered, the bank will side with the customer every time. If the dispute is not resolved to the customer's satisfaction, the bank will charge-back your account, and there is little or nothing you can do about it.

Internet Credit Card Transactions

If you are set up as a credit card merchant, you will be able to accept credit cards from your Internet customers as well as from your in-person, telephone, fax, and mail-order customers.

If you are not set up as a credit card merchant, you can sign up with an Internet-only credit card processing service. These Internet processors can only handle your Internet sales, and only from customers willing to provide their credit card information online. Your customers are billed by the credit card processor, not by your business. In some arrangements, your customers are actually transferred to a separate web site belonging to the processor. The third-party processor then remits payment to you, after deducting their fees. Many web hosts offer credit card processing. So does the popular PayPal service (paypal.com). Or type in "credit card processing" in a search engine.

Web sites that take credit cards claim to offer secure transactions ("secure server"), meaning your customers' credit card information cannot be stolen. How secure "secure" really is depends on a lot of factors including the systems set up by your web server and the determination of a potential thief. This is something to discuss with the company that will be hosting your site or handling your credit card processing. It is important to find out if you will be held liable for fraudulent transactions or stolen information.

If you don't have annoying little problems, you're not in business.
—Shirley Halperin, co-owner, Smug Magazine

Debit Cards / Check Cards

Debit (check) cards are processed exactly the same as credit cards. Credit card terminals and third-party processors accept debit cards. You pay the same fees. ATM cards and debit cards with a PIN (personal identification number) require special terminals and, of course, can only be used in face-to-face transactions.

Lara Stonebraker, Cunningham's Coffee, a retail coffee store: "We thought about having accounts for people in the neighborhood but decided that we didn't want to mess with it. It would take a lot of book work, keeping track of the accounts and what they owe. But we do have MasterCard and VISA. People just don't carry the cash around any more. I think people are more willing to spend money if they can charge it, because they feel they won't be billed for a long time."

Nick Mein, owner of Wallpapers Plus, a neighborhood retail store: "I don't think the credit cards are worth it. We must have had $600 of credit sales at the very most. And they take 3%, which is a lot for a mini-merchant like me. Besides, everybody has a checking account. I'd rather take checks than VISA. In my business it's easy for me to take checks because the kind of people who buy our stuff are usually responsible. We've never had a bounced check."

The Expenditure Ledger

The expenditure ledger is your record of all payments: business expenses, payroll, loan repayments, personal draws (money you pay to yourself), and any other cash outlays.

The most important function of the expenditure ledger is to separate different types of expenditures. The columns in the ledger represent categories, such as inventory, supplies, rent, etc. Each expenditure is posted to its appropriate column. For this reason, you cannot summarize a number of transactions on one line as you can with sales in the income ledger.

There are literally hundreds of different categories of expenditure on which small businesses spend their money. The Tax section of this book lists over 100 of the more typical items. But you certainly don't want to post a ledger with 100 columns, or even with 50 or 25 columns. Visions of green eyeshades, tall stool and columns and columns of numbers. Not necessary. The secret is to use only the categories you need and want.

Some categories of expenditures have their own column because they are required to be shown separately on your income tax return. Other categories should also be listed separately because they are used repeatedly or in large dollar amounts. You will want to know where your big dollars went and so will the IRS. Occasional or small expenses can often be combined under a single "miscellaneous" column.

The sample expenditure ledger in the Ledger Section has 11 categories, specific enough to give you a good idea of how your money was spent and provide information for preparing your income taxes, yet general enough to make the ledgers useful to a large variety of businesses.

Although these ledger categories have worked for many businesses, they may or may not fit your particular business. Feel free to retitle columns, to add or delete columns. If you are using accounting software, the software will include a selection of categories that are similar to mine, that can be kept or changed as you like.

Here is a recommended system of posting:

Payments in currency: Record the expenditure in your ledger when you make the payment. Do not put it off even a few hours; it's too easy to forget. Mark your receipts "posted" (so you'll know later that, yes, you did post them to your ledger) and keep them in a file or envelope.

Payments by check: When you write a check, record the information in your checkbook: check number, date, amount, paid to, and a brief description of what the payment is for.

Try to get an invoice or receipt for every bill you pay. Keep one copy as a record of your payment. Destroy duplicate copies so you won't mistakenly pay an invoice twice. Write the check number on each receipt or invoice before filing it. If there is ever a question about the bill, the check number will tell you that, yes, the bill was paid and here's a record of the check to prove it.

Credit card purchases: When you write a check for payment, post the business purchases to their correct columns. Post the non-business purchases to the Non-Deductible column.

The credit card does not have to be in the business name. If it is a business expense, it is deductible (sole proprietors only).

If you are making partial payments on your credit card bill, you will have to figure out an easy method of allocating those payments. Any system that eventually gets all of your business expenses posted to your ledgers will work.

Purchases made with bank credit cards such as VISA and MasterCard are deducted the year you make the charge, not the year paid, even for cash-basis businesses. So you can post your entire credit card bill each month, whether you pay it or not. This rule does not apply to store credit cards or gasoline company cards.

Electronic payments, automatically deducted from your checking account, often appear only on your monthly bank statement. Probably the easiest system is to post these payments to your expenditure ledger once a month when you get your bank statement. Just don't forget, if your cash is tight, that your bank account wrote itself a check, and there is less money in that account than your checkbook might indicate.

Online payments: Most online payments are credit card or electronic payments, handled as described above. The IRS allows you to keep your receipts on your computer. A "hard copy" is not required, but it is a good idea for backup.

If you are keeping hand-posted ledgers, you copy the information from your checkbook into the expenditure ledger. How often you sit down and copy the information depends on your time schedule and the volume of checks you write. Whatever schedule you choose, stick to it. Don't get behind in the paperwork. If you are using a computer, most accounting programs combine the check writing and the ledger so no recopying is necessary.

You can pay business expenses from your personal account (even if you have a separate business checking account), and you are entitled to a full tax deduction. Post all business expenses to the expenditure ledger, regardless of which checking account you use (sole proprietors only).

Checkbook and Ledger Combined?

Probably some of you are already asking why have both a checkbook and an expenditure ledger? The expenditure ledger provides you with information that your checkbook does not show, such as expenditures paid by cash, and unpaid expenses at year-end. The ledger makes it easy to summarize and review categories of expenditure. Your checkbook cannot readily show you how much you spent on inventory or parts last month, or on office supplies; it doesn't even show the total combined expenditures.

Your checkbook, on the other hand, shows your running bank balance and has space for ticking off the canceled checks, for recording void checks and adding errors, and for posting deposits.

Many computer bookkeeping systems combine the checkbook and ledger functions. You can also buy hand-posted bookkeeping systems (often called "one-write" systems), or you can easily design your own system, that combines the expenditure ledger and checkbook. A lot of small businesses use and like them. I personally find them a bit unwieldy and a little too complicated for people with no bookkeeping experience. The system I describe here takes more time and pencil pushing, but it is easy for a beginner to understand. Once you have mastered bookkeeping and feel comfortable with your ledgers, which will take a few months, you will be in a better position to experiment with different methods.

Posting the Expenditure Ledger

The first column is for the date.

The second column is for the check number. If you pay by currency, write "cash" in this column. If you pay by money order, write "M.O." If the payment was automatically deducted from your bank account, write "electronic" or some other word to indicate the nature of the transaction.

The third column shows to whom the money was paid. This column can also be used to make any notes.

The fourth column shows the total amount of the payment. This column will provide a double check of your monthly and year-end totals. Post all payments to this "Total" column and to one or more of the following detail expenditure columns:

DATE	CHECK NO.	PAYEE	TOTAL	1 INVEN-TORY	2 SUPPLIES, POSTAGE, ETC.	3 OUTSIDE CONTRACTORS	4 EMPLOYEE PAYROLL	5 ADVERTISING	6 RENT	7 UTILITIES	8 TAXES & LICENSES	9	10 MISC.	11 NON-DEDUCT.

Column One—Inventory. If you make or sell a product, this will be your most important column. Record in Column #1 all the goods you purchase for resale or for manufacturing, including any delivery charges. Include all the related materials that go into or are consumed in the process of preparing your product for sale such as a jeweler's solder or a dressmaker's thread. Include packaging materials if they are an integral part of your product.

If your packaging costs are only occasional or incidental, record them in Column #2. Do not include in Column #1 office supplies, tools, equipment or any material purchased for reasons other than resale.

Column Two—Supplies, Postage, Etc. These are expenses incidental to your work. Office supplies, paper, pencils, coffee, small tools that will not last more than a year. Do not include the supplies that become part of your product or are consumed in making your product; such expenses are considered part of inventory, and belong in Column #1. Draws for Petty Cash should also be posted to Column Two. Petty cash is explained later in this chapter.

Column Three—Outside Contractors. For independent contractors, consultants, and other individuals who are not employees on your payroll (see "Hiring Help" in the Growing Up section). Also use this column for professional services such as a bookkeeper and tax accountant.

Column Four—Employee Payroll. You record employee payroll both here in Column #4 and in a separate payroll ledger (discussed in the "Hiring Help" chapter). The separate payroll ledger shows the full detail of the payment: gross pay, amounts withheld, and net pay. Column #4, however, should show only the net pay, the actual amount of the payroll check (the employee's take-home pay).

Payroll taxes that you withhold from your employees are also recorded in Column #4, but only at the time you pay them to the government. Withheld taxes include income, Social Security, Medicare, and possibly state disability.

Don't confuse these withheld payroll taxes with payroll taxes that you, the employer, pay, such as employer's portion of Social Security and Medicare, and federal and state unemployment taxes. Employer-paid payroll taxes are posted to Column #8—Taxes and Licenses. This is a confusing area because the employees' and employer's taxes are reported to the government on the same form and paid with the same check.

Payments to yourself should not be recorded here unless you have incorporated and are an owner-employee of your corporation. As a sole proprietor, a partner in a partnership, or an owner of a Limited Liability Company, your own "wage" is not an expense of your business, and is posted to Column #11—"Non Deductible."

Column Five—Advertising. You can include promotion expenses, such as brochures and business gifts, in this column if you want.

Column Six—Rent. Rent on business property is fully deductible except for some lease-purchase contracts. If you own the building your business occupies, you depreciate the building (covered in the "Tax" section).

Home-based businesses: Rent on an office, workshop, studio or other business space in the home is deductible only if it meets strict IRS requirements, covered in the Home Business section. If you do qualify, you then determine what percentage of your home is used for business. The percentage is based on the amount of space devoted to business. For example, if one room out of five, or 20% of your home, is used for business, 20% of your rent expense can be charged to your business. You can pay your home rent from your personal checking account or from your business checking account; but only the business portion is posted as a business expense in Column #6. The personal portion is not deductible (either post to Column #11 or do not post at all).

Column Seven—Utilities. Power, water, garbage, heating oil or propane, etc. Your telephone expenses can be included in this column or given their own column.

Home-based businesses: The business portion of your utilities is the same percentage as the business portion of your home (see Column #6 above). If you are not eligible for a home office deduction, you cannot deduct home utilities. Home business owners should read "Telephones and Tax Deductions" in the Home Business section. Include the deductible portion of your home business phone here.

Column Eight—Taxes and Licenses. Record any tax payment or license fee here except withheld payroll taxes (see instructions under Column #4). Note in the "Paid To" column what the payment is for; you will need this information for your income tax return.

Regarding sales tax: the only sales tax that should be posted to Column #8 is the amount you remit to the state, collected from your sales. Any sales tax you pay when purchasing supplies, tools or anything else should be included as part of the price of the goods purchased. For example, if your business cards cost $40.00 plus $2.40 sales tax, you should enter $42.40 in Column #2. Nothing should be entered in Column #8.

Column Nine—is blank. I cannot possibly foresee all your needs, so here is one extra untitled column to use or not to use as you see fit.

Column Ten—Miscellaneous. The ol' catch-all. For unusual expenditures and expenditures that do not recur enough to justify their own column. For example, this column might include: Payments for insurance. Dues and organization fees. Out-of-town travel. Education ex-

penses. Minor repairs. Entertainment. Interest (repayment of a loan principal should be posted to Column #11—"Non-Deductible"). A more detailed list of items to post to Column #10 can be found in the Tax section.

Any expense that you are posting to Column #10 that starts to recur regularly should be moved to its own column. Use Column #9 or another column you are not using. Feel free to change the heading of any column in the ledger to suit your needs.

Column Eleven—Non-Deductible. Use for:

1. Personal draws—money you pay yourself.

2. Furniture, tools, equipment, machinery, buildings and other fixed (depreciable) assets. These expenses *are* deductible, but may have to be depreciated over a period of years. Some people post these asset to the Miscellaneous column; some set up a separate column just for fixed assets. Whatever column you use, these purchases should also be recorded on the Depreciation Worksheet/Equipment Ledger in the Ledger Section. Depreciation and the depreciation worksheet are explained in the Tax section.

3. Repayment of business loans—principal only. A loan is not income when received and is not an expense when paid. Any interest paid on a business loan *is* a valid expense and should be posted to Column #10.

4. Fines or penalties for breaking the law, including traffic tickets. These may be "valid" business expenses, but they are not deductible for income taxes. Contractual or other fines or penalties (if you did not violate state or federal law) are deductible.

5. Accounts Payable. This relates to year-end adjustments to bring your ledgers up to full accrual. Explained at the end of this chapter.

6. If you write a check on your business account for personal, non-business expenses, or if you write a check for something that is part personal and part business, the non-business portion is not deductible and should be posted here. The business portion is fully deductible (unless it is one of the exceptions covered here or in the Tax section of the book) and should be posted to its appropriate column.

"Quality Is Not An Option."
  —*Trademark of Crown Petroleum Company*

Uncashed Checks

If a check you write is never cashed, lost in the mail, or stop payment issued, make a negative (bracketed) entry in your expenditure ledger, reducing the expense. Under "Payee" make a note of what you are doing. Also go back to the original entry and note there what happened and the date you posted the negative entry.

Recording Vehicle Expenses

There are two ways to record car and truck expenses. You may keep track of actual expenses, or you can take a Standard Mileage Allowance (also called the Standard Mileage Rate). The "Vehicle Expenses" chapter in the Tax section explains both methods. If you decide to take the Standard Mileage Allowance, you do not have to make any entries in your expenditure ledger until year-end. If you plan to keep track of actual expenses, you should record all vehicle expenses as they are incurred. Use Column #9 in your expenditure ledger to record these expenses. Note that the cost of the vehicle and any major repairs should not be included in Column #9. These costs may have to be depreciated along with other fixed assets (see Column #11 above and the "Depreciation" chapter in the Tax section). If you use the Standard Mileage Allowance, however, you do not depreciate your vehicle.

Monthly Totals

Total all the columns of your expenditure ledger each month. Cross-check the monthly totals to the Total column. Correct any errors.

Do not, however, start a new expenditure ledger page for each new month. If a month ends and only half a page is used, double-underline your total, skip two lines and start the next month on the same page.

Year-End Procedures

You make several year-end ledger entries. None are difficult. The Year-End Expenditure Summary in the ledger section has been designed to help you post the year-end entries.

Step One: Post the monthly totals in their proper columns to the summary sheet.

Step Two: This step is only for people using accrual accounting. People using the cash method of accounting can skip to Step Three. (If you are not sure what I am talking about, re-read the chapter "Cash Accounting Vs. Accrual.")

This step is the adjustment to bring your books up to full accrual. Under accrual accounting, all expenses are recorded whether paid or not. Throughout the year, for ease in posting, only the paid expenses have been recorded. So now you post any unpaid bills to your ledger. List the bills individually, one to a line, and post to the appropriate columns. As you record each unpaid bill, clearly mark it "ACCOUNTS PAYABLE." Any other unpaid expense for the year just ended, such as payroll taxes, should also be recorded on this year-end summary, one to a line, even if you have not received a bill.

Step Three: Add up the Total column and columns #1 through #11. Cross-check your total: the sum of the totals in columns #1 through #11 should equal the total in the Total column.

Step Four: For accrual accounting, total the return (bounced) checks and the uncollectible credit accounts in your Bad Debts folder (discussed earlier in this section) and post in the Total column. If, however, you are using the cash method, include the bounced checks but do not include any unpaid credit sales.

Step Five: If you use the Standard Mileage Allowance for vehicle expenses (covered in the Tax section), calculate vehicle expense on this summary sheet and post to the Total column.

Step Six: If you take depreciation, record the depreciation expense from the depreciation worksheets (discussed in the Tax section) in the Total column. If your accountant figures your depreciation for you, just skip this step.

Step Seven: Purchases made with bank credit cards, such as VISA and MasterCard, are deductible the year charged, not the year paid, even for cash basis taxpayers. Credit card purchases unpaid at December 31 should be added to your ledger for the year (don't deduct them a second time next year when you pay them). This law does not apply to store credit cards, which (for cash basis taxpayers) are deducted when paid.

Accounts Payable

Accounts payable ("payables") are unpaid bills and unpaid accounts that you owe, and expenses you've incurred but haven't yet been billed for.

This Accounts Payable adjustment is for accrual method businesses only. Cash method businesses can skip it.

The accounts payable that you posted to the Year-End Expenditure Summary require special handling when paid next year. These expenses are deductible the year they were incurred, which is the year just ended. They may not be deducted again next year, even though they will be paid next year. When the bills are paid (you will recognize them because you marked them "ACCOUNTS PAYABLE" when you posted them to the summary) they are posted to Column #11—"Non-Deductible".

Altering the Ledgers and Designing Your Own

After a year's experience with these ledgers, learning which categories of expense you need and don't need, you can easily design your own hand or computer ledgers. Do you need the Outside Contractor column, or the Payroll column, or the Advertising column? Instead, you may want a separate column for equipment purchases, or freight charges, or travel, or some other category important to your business. Many small businesses set up their expenditure ledger to exactly match the categories on the income tax forms. For my own business, I try to use as few columns as possible to minimize my book work; and yet I've met business owners who felt they had to have 16 columns to keep their expenditures straight.

If you use hand-posted ledgers, you can create your own ledgers using accounting ledger paper (also called accountants' work sheets), available in any office supply store. The ledger paper usually comes in 50-sheet pads and with anywhere from two to 25 columns, and is designed to go in three-ring binders.

Ledgers get a lot of use and abuse. The loose leaf ledgers do not hold up well, the pages tear out easily. Treat yourself instead to a heavy duty post binder and heavy duty ledger sheets.

And, of course, all varieties of commercial ledgers and prepackaged bookkeeping systems are available from most office supply stores.

Petty Cash

A petty cash fund provides a systematic method for paying and recording out-of-pocket cash payments and payments too small to be made by check. ("Cash" in petty cash refers to currency, *not* to checks; which is just the opposite of my earlier definition. Nobody's perfect.)

I suggest, for starters, that you do not have a petty cash fund. It's more bookkeeping, more paperwork, more procedures to remember. Pay the nickel-and-dime expenditures out of what cash is on hand, and record them directly and immediately in your expenditure ledger. Any

Petty Cash Ledger

1	2	3	4
Date	Payee	Amount	Balance
3/1	(Beginning balance)		$50.00
3/12	Stamps	$12.50	$37.50
3/16	C.O.D. charge	$12.75	$24.75
3/17	Office Supplies	$6.99	$17.76
3/20	donation to Boy Scouts	$4.00	$13.76
3/31	coffee for the machine	$5.29	$8.47

respectable accountant would roll over in his subsidiary ledgers, so to speak, if he heard me say this, because the absence of a petty cash fund can result in poor cash control, increasing the possibility of incomplete records and "misappropriation" (that means theft) of funds. But if yours is a one person business or if you alone have access to the money, the importance of cash control is outweighed, I feel, by the need for a simple set of books.

If a petty cash fund is what you want or need, I have devised a relatively simple system for handling petty cash. It is a compromise between no system at all and a bookkeeper's dream, and it requires you to follow three rules.

1. Keep no more than $50 in the fund (or $20, or whatever seems a reasonable amount to you).

2. Make payments out of the fund only for miscellaneous supplies and postage, expenses that normally would be posted to Column 2 in the expenditure ledger.

3. Use the fund only when there is no practical way to write a check instead.

If you promise to follow those ground rules here is the procedure:

1. Write a check payable to "Petty Cash" for $50 (or $20). Cash the check at your bank and put the money, a piece of accounting worksheet paper and a pencil in a separate cash box or cigar box, whatever is handy and relatively safe.

2. Record the check as an expenditure in your ledger, posting it to Column 11, Non-Deductible.

3. Every time you make a payment from the petty cash fund, record the date, payee and amount on your accounting worksheet, which has just become your petty cash ledger. Get receipts for the payments if possible and put them in the box with the cash.

4. When the fund starts to get low, total the payments recorded on the worksheet, and add up the remaining cash in the box. The worksheet total and the remaining cash should equal the amount that was originally in the fund ($50 or $20). If you are out of balance, you either made an adding error, recorded a payment wrong, failed to record a payment, or else you've been robbed. If you can't find an error, adjust the worksheet total so that your petty cash fund is back in balance. Staple all the petty cash receipts to the worksheet and file it away.

5. Write a check payable to "Petty Cash" or to yourself equal in amount to the total (or the corrected total if there was an error) from the worksheet. Cash the check and put the money in your petty cash box with a new worksheet. Sharpen the pencil.

6. Record the check in the expenditure ledger in Column Two—Supplies, Postage, Etc. Thereafter, whenever your petty cash fund gets low, and also at year-end, repeat steps #4, 5 and 6.

Calculators and Adding Machines

Every business owner probably lives with a pocket calculator. But when it comes to posting ledgers, adding columns of figures, balancing bank accounts or any business activity involving more than just a few numbers, the pocket calculator leaves much to be desired. Most of the calculators are small, and their keyboards are tiny. It is easy, too easy, to make a mistake. Punch a 6, and your finger strays onto the 5. Try this: get out your calculator and add a column of 25 numbers. Note your answer, and then add the numbers a second time. Got two different answers, didn't you? Happens to me all the time. Now, which amount is correct? There is no way to check your figures, no tape to look at.

An adding machine tape is indispensable for checking your totals, locating errors and keeping a record of your calculations. A tape will help you when you are interrupted in the middle of a column of numbers, and what *was* the last number you entered?

Here are some guidelines when shopping for an adding machine:

1. Buy a machine with a large keyboard, well-spaced to accommodate your hand allowing maximum speed and minimum error. Buy a machine with an LED display (real lights, usually green) instead of an LCD or liquid crystal display (the silvery and often dim-looking numbers that are difficult to read in bright light).

2. Adding machines vary in the number of digits they can handle. Select one with at least an eight-digit capacity.

3. Your machine should be able to print negative (minus) numbers and negative balances in red so they will stand out easily.

You can count all the grains of sand on the beach, and still find you're on the wrong beach.
—*Business owner Geoffrey D. Batrouney*

Profit & Loss Statement

Bear Soft Pretzel Company

January through September

	Month of September		Year-to-Date	
Income from ledger		$2,095		$13,724
Beginning inventory	$900		$310	
Purchases	$1,230		$6,710	
	$2,130		$7,020	
Estimated inventory				
30-Sep-1992	($1,000)		($1,000)	
Cost-of-goods-sold		$1,130		$6,020
Gross Profit		**$965**		**$7,704**
Other expenses				
Rent	$50		$450	
Supplies	$13		$74	
Other			$27	
Total Other Expenses		$63		$551
Net Profit		**$902**		**$7,153**

Financial Management: Using Your Ledgers

Your books are more than just a record of your business activity and an aid to preparing income tax forms. They are valuable tools to help you manage your business successfully.

PROFIT-AND-LOSS Statement

Without a schedule of profit and loss, it is difficult for the owner of even the smallest business to determine whether or not the business is making a profit. Your cash balances and the day-to-day cash income and outgo, as important as they are, are not a good indication of profit or loss. Cash flow can, in fact, give you a totally misleading picture of how your business is doing.

Simple profit and loss statements (also called income statements or break-even point statements), prepared monthly from your ledgers, can tell you a great deal about your business. A profit and loss statement is, basically, a schedule showing your income and your expenses and the difference between the two. Here is a procedure for preparing a simple profit and loss statement:

Income. The income on the statement is the monthly income total from your income ledger (Columns #3, #5 and #6). You should exclude sales tax, loan income and any money you put into the business from your own personal funds.

Expenses. Expenses should be separated into two groups: inventory (Column #1 in the expenditure ledger) and all other expenses (Columns #2 through #10). Do not include Column #11.

If you have inventory, you estimate the cost of the inventory on hand at the end of the month. If it is only an insignificant amount, you can ignore it. The inventory on hand at the beginning of the month *plus* the current month's purchases from Column #1, *less* your estimate of inventory on hand at the end of the month gives you your actual current inventory expense. This expense is called "cost-of-goods-sold" and is covered in greater depth in the Tax section.

Estimated Cash Flow Projection Month of June			
	Cash In	**Cash Out**	**Balance**
First of Month			
Cash on hand June 1			$3,000
June 1 rent payment		$600	
June 1 utilities		$150	$2,250
Week #1			
Receipts	$1,000		
Inventory purchases		$2,000	
Supplies		$ 50	$1,200
Week #2			
Receipts	$1,000		
Payroll		$500	$1,700
Week #3			
Receipts	$1,000		
Supplies		$50	$2,650
Week #4			
Receipts	$1,000		
Payroll		$ 500	
Inventory purchases		$1,000	
Personal draw		$ 500	$1,650

"All other expenses" are your operating expenses and include everything in Columns #2 through #10 except sales tax paid (recorded in Column #8—"Taxes and Licenses"). Be sure not to include any expenditures from Column #11—"Non-Deductible."

Your income *less* the cost-of-goods-sold (inventory expense) gives you what is known as "gross profit." Gross profit *less* all the other expenses gives you your "net" profit or loss.

By showing both a gross and a net profit or loss, you can tell more easily how your expenses relate to income. If you are losing money, you can readily determine if it is the cost of the inventory (cost-of-goods-sold) or the other expenses that are responsible for the loss.

A service business that has no inventory does not have to compute cost-of-goods-sold or gross profit. For such a business, income less "all other expenses" equals net profit or loss.

A statement prepared in the above manner will give you profit and loss information for the month just ended. Some business owners like to see a second column in their profit and loss statement that shows the year-to-date activity. The year-to-date column is prepared in almost the same way as the monthly column. Year-to-date income is the sum of all the monthly income totals in Columns #3, #5 and #6 from January 1 to date, including the month just ended.

Cost-of-goods-sold is slightly different. It is the inventory on hand at January 1st, plus the sum of all the monthly totals in expenditure ledger Column #1, less the same ending inventory that you estimated for the monthly column. "All other expenses" is the sum of all the monthly totals in Columns #2 through #10 (again excluding sales tax payments in Column #8).

Your profit and loss statement should look something like the Bear Soft Pretzel Co. illustration. This type of profit and loss statement is only approximate. It does not include unpaid expenses or expenses computed at year-end such as depreciation, and it should not be used for preparing income tax forms.

CASH FLOW

One of the most damaging things that can happen to a business is a cash shortage. Here you are with a successful business, tons of customers, and no cash. Whoa! How did that happen? I know of profitable businesses actually forced to shut down for a lack of immediate cash.

To help avoid a sudden cash squeeze, many businesses prepare monthly cash flow projections: estimates of cash that will be coming in and cash that will be spent during the upcoming month. These projections show approximately how much cash will be on hand during the month and alert you to possible cash shortages.

During the first few months your business is in operation, cash projections will be difficult for you to make. You cannot yet estimate how much income will be coming in nor will you be familiar enough with your regular expense requirements. But the first few months are a critical time for any business. You should make some attempt to estimate and be prepared for cash needs. Here is a way to project your first month's cash flow:

First determine how much cash you will need to get your business off to a good start.

If yours is a sales or manufacturing business or a service business that stocks parts, estimate how much additional inventory you will need during the first month of business.

Next, add expenses that will be paid during the first month, such as supplies and payroll, and those that will be paid by the first of the next month, such as rent and utilities. Be sure to include your own wage or draw. Then add another 20% for unanticipated expenses.

The sum of the above items should give you an estimate of your first month's expenses. Now, how much income do you anticipate during the first month of operation? Obviously, this can only be a guess, but be conservative. And once you've arrived at a good guess, knock it down by 25%. All new business owners are over-optimistic.

Comparing the "guess-timated" income to the projected expenses will give you some idea of your cash needs. It is a rough idea, admittedly; but it is better than no idea at all. Once you have a few months' actual experience behind you, cash flow projections will become easier and more accurate. A good procedure is to estimate income and expenditures week by week, showing the cash on hand at the end of each week.

The main purpose of a cash flow statement is to warn you *in advance* when cash might get dangerously low. If you know of a big cash outlay coming up next month, such as a loan payment or a tax payment, or a predictable seasonal drop in sales, the cash flow statement will show you whether your regular income will provide enough cash to meet expenses.

If the statement predicts a cash shortage, you can plan in advance to avoid the problem. Postpone a payment that is not immediately necessary, or plan a sale to generate more income, or seek a short-term loan. Banks are usually willing to loan short-term funds (usually thirty days or sixty days) to profitable businesses. What's more, the fact that you have actually prepared a cash flow statement indicates to a banker that you are knowledgeable about your business and, therefore, a better risk than someone who has no financial knowledge at all.

INVENTORY CONTROL

Any business that sells or manufactures goods and any service business that stocks parts, needs some sort of inventory control, some way of knowing what has been ordered, what is on hand, and when it's time to reorder. For a very small business or one selling only a small variety of items, the inventory purchase records in your expenditure ledger (Column #1) and your day-to-day observations of the stock on hand will probably provide you with the information you need to maintain adequate inventory control. A periodic count, or "inventory," is the easiest and quickest way to determine what is still on hand and what needs to be reordered. (In business jargon, "inventory" is both a noun and a verb).

Larger businesses and those selling a large selection of merchandise will need more formal procedures for controlling inventory. Such businesses should maintain a record of all stock ordered, received and sold. "Perpetual inventory" records, as they are called, can be kept on index cards, one card for each type of item in stock, or in inventory ledgers, with a ledger page for each different item. Both the cards and the ledgers have the same format. An up-to-date and accurate inventory record can tell you at a glance your balance on hand, what is still on order, and how long it takes to receive an order.

How to Keep an Inventory Record

When you place your order, record the quantity and the date of the order in the Ordered column. When you receive the order, line out the

INVENTORY RECORD

Item #3 Silver Buckle   Supplier L. J. Silver Co.

DATE ORDERED	QUANTITY ORDERED	DATE REC'D.	QUANTITY REC'D.	QUANTITY SOLD	BALANCE ON-HAND
1-31	50				0
		2-13	35		35
				13	22
				4	18
		3-1	15		33
				10	23
3-12	50				23

entry in the Ordered column and enter the information in the Received column. Posting the date received will give you an idea how long it takes your suppliers to send you an ordered item. If you receive only part of your order, record the undelivered back-ordered quantity and the original order date in the Ordered column.

On the sample inventory record, 50 silver buckles were ordered on January 31. A partial shipment of 35 arrived February 13. The back-ordered 15 buckles finally arrived on March 1. The number of items sold should be recorded when the sale is made or at the end of the day, summarized from the day's sales slips.

At least once a year and preferably every six months the perpetual records should be "proven" (verified) by taking a physical count. If there is a discrepancy, the records should be adjusted to agree with the count. If the difference is substantial, you know something is wrong. Either you have not been updating the records correctly, or your inventory is being stolen.

Inventory control, like cash flow, is a management tool only. It is meant to help you run your business. The methods I have described for inventory control are only suggestions. Feel free to alter or ignore them. Any system or non-system that works for you is probably a good one.

Computer Inventory Control Programs

Businesses with large or varied inventories have found computer inventory programs extremely useful; some say essential. Computer inventory records should look similar to the ledgers shown here, and they should provide you with exactly the information you need. Shop around for a program that meets your needs. Computer inventory records should be verified by taking physical counts on a regular basis, just like hand-posted records; a computer record is just as likely to be incorrect.

Larry Campbell, of Ingram Book Company, a book wholesaler whose customers are small bookstores: "One of the quiet, simple programs at Ingram seems to be a step back in time: the 'Card In Book' system. Booksellers pay 3¢ each for cards sent with each shipment, to go in each book. When a retail customer buys a book, the clerk takes the card. At the end of the day, the store can easily reorder sold titles. It's low-tech. If you're a small store, you don't need computer inventory control, but you still need an inventory management program."

Section Three
GROWING UP

Most people would succeed in small things
if they were not troubled with great
ambitions.

—Longfellow

Growing Up

"LEARN the different methods and little known techniques used today in building small companies into Powerful Places in Industry."
—from the cover of another book on starting a business

Well, maybe John D. Rockefeller did start with a two-pump filling station and some spectacular ambitions. After all, bigger and better has been a trademark of this big country of ours for as long as most of us can remember. For years we have associated big business, big industry with prosperity, happiness and the good life.

But today it seems that America's "powerful places in industry" are just too powerful, and they are choking, not helping, our economy. In the last few years we have witnessed huge corporations laying off thousands of employees without warning, and doubling and tripling their prices and their profits, with us powerless to stop them. Bigger is no longer synonymous with better, and big business no longer seems to be able or willing to provide us a good way of life.

Small Time Operator is not going to be much help to the Rockefellers among you with dreams of building your business into "powerful places in industry." I feel that small business can offer you personal satisfaction and a good livelihood. But "small" does not have to mean that you are forever the one person business, unable to grow. Business growth can be successful and profitable, beneficial to you and your customers. Business growth, however, can be mistimed and miscalculated, turning against you and doing you in.

Very often a business expands because a situation presents itself that the owner "just can't pass up": the adjacent store-front becomes vacant, and the landlord offers to knock out the separating partition and rent both stores to you; a competitor is failing and offers to sell his business to you, cheap. Or maybe your customers have been encouraging expansion, suggesting that you offer some related product or service. And as frequent a reason for expansion as any, you're out to catch a bigger fish; success in your present business is tempting you on to bigger and better success (bigger and better?).

You should put in some real thinking time before making a decision about expanding:

1. Just as your present business was slow going at first, the expanded business will take time to get on its own feet. You will probably be making less money for a while, possibly even losing money for a year or two. Are you prepared for a repeat of the early, lean days?

2. Expansion is going to require more capital. It means investing your savings or borrowing. Far and away, the Number One reason successful businesses fail is because they took on debt to finance expansion and could not generate enough additional income to pay it back.

3. If you plan to acquire a second business location, be prepared for a major increase in the amount and type of work you will have to do. Someone must be hired to run one of the stores for you, and suddenly you will find yourself not only buyer, seller, bookkeeper, market analyst and the rest, but manager also. Some real skills are required to manage a multi-store operation, not the least of which is being able to deal with employees: hiring, training, supervising, delegating authority, and sometimes firing.

4. The paperwork will just about double. How well do you handle it now?

5. Your own leisure time away from business will be reduced, possibly eliminated.

6. A re-warning about financial commitments: Legally, you and your unincorporated business are one and the same. Any liabilities of your business are also personal ones.

He is well paid that is well satisfied.
—Shakespeare, from Merchant of Venice

Do successful businesses grow every year? Most do, at least for awhile, slow and steady for some, huge leaps for others. But at some point, all businesses reach their "peak," or their "maturity," where they reach the limit of what they can accomplish within the framework they've created and built. Where they go from there... well, that's the decision every business owner has to make for him and herself.

Hugo said, "Caution is the eldest child of wisdom." Think this decision through. Don't let any outside factors lure you into a move that you aren't ready for. Whether you choose to stay small or take a chance on expansion, be totally satisfied that you have made the right decision.

HIRING HELP: How to Save Time and Money By Not Becoming an Employer

Hiring employees will just about double the amount of your paperwork. As an employer, you must keep payroll records for each employee; withhold income, Social Security, Medicare and state taxes; prepare quarterly and year-end payroll tax returns; pay employer's portion of Social Security and Medicare taxes and unemployment taxes; purchase workers' compensation insurance; and prepare year-end earnings statements for each employee. It's been estimated that the employer's taxes, worker's compensation insurance and paperwork will cost you an additional 30%. In other words, if you pay a wage of $10.00 per hour, it's really costing you about $13.00.

Businesses hiring employees are more closely regulated than one-person businesses. The IRS and the states demand prompt payroll tax returns and require strict adherence to employment laws. If you are late filing your payroll tax return, if you don't pay the employment taxes when due, the IRS is likely to move quickly. Whenever you hear about the IRS padlocking a business and impounding the bank account, it's usually because of unpaid payroll taxes. And the penalties are severe.

Legislators have done their level best to create a legal environment that tempts us, when hiring, to focus on everything but finding the best person for the job.

—George Gendron, Inc. Magazine

Independent (Outside) Contractors

Some small businesses can sometimes get outside help without hiring employees. These businesses often hire independent contractors, also called outside contractors. "Outside" refers to being from outside your business. It has nothing to do with working out of doors. (Free Agent is another term for independent contractor.)

Independent contractors are in business for themselves, people who sell their services to you. When you hire an independent contractor, you pay the contractor his or her fee in full. You do not withhold taxes, pay employment taxes, or file payroll tax returns. You can hire on an as-needed basis, and you don't have to worry about sick pay or vacation time or the trauma of laying off or firing an employee.

Who is an independent contractor? The IRS says, "Generally, people in business for themselves are not employees. [Individuals] in an independent trade in which they offer their services to the public are usually not employees."

A key determining point, as far as the IRS is concerned: Does the person perform service for more than one business? A person working solely for you is usually your employee. A person providing services to several businesses is probably an independent contractor.

Independent contractors usually have DBAs, business licenses, a business bank account, invoice forms, their own office, their own tools and equipment, a set of ledgers, and similar indications of being self-employed. Independent contractors sometimes have employees of their own. Independent contractors are basically small business owners, just like the businesses hiring them.

Who is an employee?

The IRS is likely to consider a person your employee and not an independent contractor if the individual: (1) Uses your tools, materials and equipment instead of his or her own; (2) Receives on-the-job training; (3) Must follow hours that you set; (4) Is told not just what must be done but *how* the work is to be done; (5) Hires or supervises your workers; (6) Receives health insurance, sick pay, vacation pay, or similar employee benefits; (7) Gets a regular paycheck; (8) Can quit at any time without incurring liability.

Two other factors the IRS will consider are (1) how similar workers are treated in other businesses, what the custom is within your industry; and (2) whether or not you filed a 1099-MISC form for the contractor (covered below).

Here are two hypothetical examples to help illustrate employees vs. independent contractors:

Example 1: The Clever Leather Company (that's you) needs help making belts. You want someone to cut the leather into two-inch wide strips so you can devote your talent to the design work. You hire your buddy for $15.00 an hour, sit him down in your shop, and tell him to cut out 250 two-inch wide belts, each three feet long.

The Clever Leather Company has just become a bona-fide employer. When you pay your friend, you withhold income, Social Security and Medicare taxes, send the withheld taxes to the government, pay employer Social Security, Medicare and unemployment taxes, keep payroll ledgers, prepare year-end earnings statements. Ugh.

Example 2: The More Clever Than Ever Leather Company (that's me) needs help making belts. I want someone to cut the leather into two-inch wide strips so I can devote my talent to the design work. I call up the Leather Cutting Company (that's *my* buddy) and order up 250 of his standard 2" wide, 3' long belts. The Leather Cutting Company produces the belts on its own work schedule and delivers the completed order to me.

The More Clever Than Ever Leather Company just conducted business with an independent contractor. More Clever Than Ever Leather wrote a check for the full amount billed and recorded it in the expenditure ledger.

Seriously, it is important that you carefully determine the legal status of your hired help. A person who falls within the definition of an employee is an employee no matter what you call him. It also does not matter how payments are measured or paid, what they are called, or whether the employee works full or part-time.

If you are still unsure how to classify your worker, you can request a "Determination of Employee Work Status" from the IRS on form #SS-8. Not many businesses file this request because the IRS nearly always rules that workers are employees. In fact, many accountants suggest that businesses do not file form SS-8. The ac-

countants warn that, if you have already paid workers as independent contractors, if the IRS rules against you, you will be subject to back taxes and penalties. You may want to talk to your accountant about this.

There is another and much more serious problem if you hire people and treat them as independent contractors when the law says they should be employees. If one of these people gets injured on the job and is not covered by workers' compensation insurance, you could find yourself with medical bills and a large lawsuit.

Contracting With Your Contractor

When hiring someone you plan to pay as an independent contractor, be absolutely sure that the person fully understands what you are doing: that he or she is not your employee, that he considers himself in business for himself, that he is not eligible for employee benefits or sick leave, that he is not covered for workers compensation should he be injured on the job, that he knows he is responsible for his own taxes and insurance and Social Security, and that he will not be eligible for unemployment insurance when the job is finished. I suggest a signed contract with the contractor, clearly defining the work and the legal relationship.

Many small businesses have gotten into expensive trouble with the federal and state government because former "independent contractors" (who really should have been paid as employees) complained to the IRS when they were turned down for unemployment insurance or fined for not paying their own Social Security.

One thing I hate is staff meetings. And, you know, you read all these things about motivating people. I hate doing that. Why do I want to spend my time motivating people? I want to make some deals, make some money, and have a good time.
—Small business owner Sam Leandro.

We prefer the no-frills motivation style for our employees. If they want to do it, they do it. If they don't, I get somebody else, simple as that.
—Kevin Gallagher, partner,
Quicksilver Messenger Service.

9595 ☐ VOID ☐ CORRECTED

PAYER'S name, street address, city, state, and ZIP code		1 Rents	OMB No. 1545-0115	Miscellaneous Income
Monkeywrench Motors 7831 Claremont Berkeley CA 94700		$		
		2 Royalties		
		$	Form 1099-MISC	
		3 Other income	4 Federal income tax withheld	Copy A
		$	$	For Internal Revenue Service Center
PAYER'S Federal identification number	RECIPIENT'S identification number	5 Fishing boat proceeds	6 Medical and health care payments	File with Form 1096.
123-45-6789	987-65-4321	$	$	
RECIPIENT'S name		7 Nonemployee compensation	8 Substitute payments in lieu of dividends or interest	For Privacy Act and Paperwork Reduction Act Notice, see the
Crystal Rosa		$5,650		
		$	$	
Street address (including apt. no.)		9 Payer made direct sales of $5,000 or more of consumer products to a buyer (recipient) for resale ▶ ☐	10 Crop insurance proceeds	General Instructions for Forms 1099, 1098, 5498, and W-2G.
106 State Street			$	
City, state, and ZIP code		11	12	
Santa Cruz CA 95062				
Account number (optional)	2nd TIN not.	13 Excess golden parachute payments	14 Gross proceeds paid to an attorney	
	☐	$	$	
15		16 State tax withheld	17 State/Payer's state no.	18 State income
		$	CA--same	$
		$		$

Form 1099-MISC   Cat. No. 14425J   Department of the Treasury - Internal Revenue Service

File a 1099-MISC for every outside contractor who received $600 or more during the year and for outside sales people who purchased $5,000 or more in goods from you.

Form 1096 must accompany the 1099 forms sent to the IRS.

IRS Forms For Independent Contractors

For each contractor you paid $600 or more during the year, you file form #1099-MISC, "Report of Miscellaneous Income." The form shows the contractor's name, address, Social Security number or Federal Employer Identification Number (EIN) and amount paid. You include your name, address, phone number and ID number as well. One copy of the 1099 goes to the IRS and another to the contractor.

In addition, if your outside contractors are independent sales agents, you report, on Form 1099-MISC, each sales agent who purchased $5,000 or more in goods from you.

The 1099-MISC forms must be given to your contractors no later than January 31 of the new year. The IRS copies of the 1099 forms are accompanied by a Form 1096, "Annual Summary and Transmittal of U.S. Information Returns." The 1096 and 1099's must be filed with the IRS by the last day in February. You can get a 30-day extension to file your 1096 with the IRS by filing electronically or by filing Form 8809. Don't you love all these numbers?

The IRS provides a form W-9 for your independent contractor to fill out, showing his or her name, address, and Social Security number or EIN. By signing the W-9 form, the independent contractor certifies to you that he or she is giving you correct information. You keep the form in your files; it does not get sent to the IRS. This W-9 form is optional. The independent contractor is not required to fill out the form, but he is required to give you his Social Security or EIN. If the contractor refuses, you will probably be required to withhold taxes from his pay.

Incorporated Independent Contractor

Some independent contractors incorporate themselves. When you hire an incorporated independent contractor, you are contracting with a corporation and not an individual. The incorporated contractor is an employee of his or her own company, which means more paperwork and corporate forms and tax returns for the contractor, but makes it much easier and safer for you. You don't have to concern yourself with the contractor vs. employee rules, and you don't have to file 1099 or 1096 forms.

Some independent contractors set up their own one-person corporations, just so that businesses will hire them without having to put them on the payroll and deal with payroll taxes and fringe benefits or any worry that the IRS will step in and rule that the independent contractor is an employee.

"Under the Table"/Off The Books Payments

And now, a word or two about paying a worker "under the table" (off the books). The term means that the worker is not on the payroll as an employee, the payment is usually in cash, and no record is made of the payment. This is usually done to avoid payroll taxes and the expense of workers' comp insurance, which is illegal and can get you in more trouble than it's worth.

If the worker is supposed to be an employee, not only can you get in the same trouble as the independent contractor problems mentioned above, you have no defense whatsoever when you get caught. At least when you are mislabeling employees as independent contractors, you can argue the issue and possibly minimize penalties.

If your "under the table" worker doesn't file taxes, that's fraud, and you could well be implicated. Again, an injury on the job could be disastrous. On top of all this misery, since you don't record the payment, you lose the expense deduction and pay more income taxes. Enough?

Special Situations

Subcontractors. Are subcontractors employees or outside contractors? For IRS purposes, the general rules regarding employees versus outside contractors apply to subcontractors. A subcontractor who is actually in business for himself, offering services to several building contractors, is most likely an outside contractor. Some states require contractors to purchase workers' compensation insurance for subcontractors if the subcontractors do not have the insurance themselves, even if the subcontractor is legally an outside contractor. Some states require subcontractors to be licensed.

Statutory Employees. One strange exception to the above rules applies to people the IRS calls statutory employees: full-time life insurance salespeople; some commission truck drivers who deliver laundry, food or beverages other than milk; certain individuals working from their own homes, on materials supplied by the employer; and traveling sales people working full-time, selling to businesses (not to consumers).

Statutory employees are subject to regular employee Social Security and Medicare taxes, but otherwise are treated as outside contractors. They file Schedule C like a sole proprietor and are entitled to regular business deductions.

This is a confusing area of the law. If you are a statutory employee, or someone employing a statutory employee, you should get more details from the IRS or an accountant.

Statutory Non-Employees. The IRS has another special rule, applying only to certain commission sales people: direct sellers, some delivery people selling consumer goods, licensed real estate agents, and some newspaper vendors. The IRS permits these salespeople, called "statutory non-employees," to be classified as outside contractors, if there is a written agreement stating that they are independent contractors and responsible for their own taxes. The regular employee-versus-contractor tests do not apply.

Out-of-State Residents. If you hire an outside contractor who resides in another state, who comes into your state to work for you, some states require you to withhold state taxes on the contractor. Check with your state's income tax or employment offices.

An entrepreneur is someone who takes a prospective employee out into the country, to a hill overlooking a great estate, points to the mansion, the swimming pool, the stables, the tennis courts, and says, "If you come with me and work your butt off, someday all this will be mine."

—Harvey Mackay, "Swim With The Sharks"

Steps to Becoming an Employer

To meet the legal requirements of becoming an employer, you will have to deal with the federal government and the state government, and you will probably have to obtain workers' comp insurance. These are one-time-only procedures, but they require quite a bit of paperwork. If possible, start these procedures a month before you plan to hire your first employee.

Federal Requirements

1. Contact the IRS and tell them you are about to become an employer. Request Form SS-4, "Application for Employer Identification Number" (you can also fill out an SS-4 form on the Internet at www.irs.gov). Ask for a free copy of Publication #15, "Circular E–Employer's Tax Guide." Publication 15 has detailed instructions for complying with federal requirements and includes federal withholding tables.

2. Ask the IRS for several copies of Form W-4, Employees Withholding Allowance Certificate. Each new employee must fill out a W-4 showing marital status and the number of exemptions claimed. You keep the W-4's in your files (except for employees claiming 11 or more exemptions; or employees claiming to be exempt from withholding whose wages are expected to exceed $200 a week. These W-4's must be sent to the IRS).

3. All employers must comply with Occupational Safety & Health Administration (OSHA)

regulations. If you have more than ten employees, OSHA requires you to keep routine job safety records (some retail businesses with low injury rates are exempt from this requirement). Write OSHA, U.S. Department of Labor, Washington D.C. 20210; www.osha.gov.

4. Most employers are subject to the Fair Labor Standards Act (FSLA). This act sets a minimum wage for certain employees, and sets overtime pay (more than 40 hours per week) at not less than 1½ times the regular rate of pay. Child labor laws, equal pay for men and women, comp time, and other regulations are included in the FLSA. The Act does not require vacation, holiday or sick pay, or fringe benefits. It does not place any limit on number of hours people work. Exempt from the Act are most executives, administrators, professionals, outside sales people, and some amusement park employees, seamen, farm workers, and some computer-related work. Also exempt are unincorporated family businesses that employ only family members. For more details, write the Department of Labor, Washington D.C. 20210, or visit their web site at www.ftc.gov.

5. The Personal Responsibility and Work Opportunity Reconciliation Act (also known as the Welfare Reform Act, and the New Hire Reporting Program) requires employers to fill out a New Hire Report for each new or rehired employee and send the form to your state's employment department, usually within twenty days.

6. The Americans With Disabilities Act prohibits job discrimination against certain disabled people, and requires employers with 15 or more employees to provide reasonable accommodations for disabled employees.

7. If you have 20 or more employees, you must comply with the Age Discrimination in Employment Act, which is administered by OSHA.

State Requirements

1. Contact your state department of employment. Most states assign a state Employer's ID Number, in addition to your Federal EIN. Some states issue federal EINs along with the state ID, saving you the extra step of dealing with the IRS.

Minimum work for minimum pay.
—Minimum wage earner Tim Hanna

2. Every state that has an income tax on wages requires employers to withhold state income tax. The states publish employer's tax guides that include state withholding tables.

3. Most states have employer-paid state unemployment insurance, in addition to federal unemployment insurance (discussed below). The state will require you to submit an application and receive an insurance rating. The rates vary from state to state and from occupation to occupation.

4. Most states require employers to have Worker's Compensation Insurance. See "Insurance" in the Getting Started section.

5. Many states have other payroll taxes for employers and/or employees: disability insurance, employment training taxes, etc.

6. Some states, and even some cities, set their own minimum wage, higher than the federal minimum. Some states or localities may have "living wage" laws, paid family leave laws, required paid vacations, required employee medical insurance (no federal law requires employers to give paid vacations or medical benefits). Be sure you know what's required of you as an employer before hiring your first employee.

Federal Procedures and Taxes for Employers

Below are the basic federal procedures for most employers. These laws do change occasionally. You should get the IRS's "Circular E, Employer's Tax Guide" (Publication 15) to verify these rules. Unlike income taxes, there is no "grey" or questionable area where payroll taxes are involved. There is only one way to do it—their way.

These payroll laws and taxes apply regardless of how you pay your employees. You cannot avoid the taxes by paying in goods and services instead of cash, by bartering or trading, or by paying the money to a third party.

Withholding. The IRS requires that you withhold income tax from each employee's paycheck. The amount is calculated from the tables in Publication 15.

Social Security Tax. The Federal Insurance Contributions Act (FICA) requires employers to withhold Social Security tax (also known as OASDI—old age, survivors, and disability insurance) and Medicare tax (also known as Hospitalization). Social Security tax is 6.2% on each employee's earnings, up to an earnings maximum of $87,900 (2004 maximum—look out, it goes up every year).

The Medicare tax, levied in addition to the Social Security tax, is 1.45% on each employee's earnings, regardless of how much they make; there is no maximum earnings for the Medicare tax. So, the total Social Security/Medicare tax on employees making $87,900 or less is 7.65%.

You are liable for an employer's portion of Social Security and Medicare taxes in addition to the taxes withheld from your employees. This is money you, the employer, pay out of your own pocket on behalf of your employees. The employer's tax is exactly the same as the employee's tax: 6.2% Social Security tax on each employee's earnings up to $87,900; and 1.45% Medicare tax on each employee's earnings, with no maximum.

So, the total employer's tax on employees making $87,900 or less is also 7.65%. Do not confuse this employer's tax with the self-employment tax discussed in the Tax section of the book. They are different taxes.

Earned Income Credit. Many low income employees are eligible for an Earned Income Tax Credit (EIC or EITC), reducing their income taxes. For some employees, the Earned Income Tax Credit is greater than the income tax owed, reducing income tax below zero. In these cases, the credit is "refundable," becoming in effect a negative income tax. If any of your employees are eligible for the "refundable" credit, instead of waiting until they file their tax returns to claim the credit, they can request to receive a part of it in advance, in their paychecks, increasing their take home pay during the year. Employees fill

---

Form W-2 Wage and Tax Statement

a Control number	OMB No. 1545-0008
b Employer identification number 68-1234567	1 Wages, tips, other compensation $4,300.00 — 2 Federal income tax withheld $327.50
c Employer's name, address, and ZIP code Music Photo Service 640 Bell Springs Rd Laytonville CA 95454	3 Social security wages $4,300.00 — 4 Social security tax withheld $267.70
	5 Medicare wages and tips $4,300.00 — 6 Medicare tax withheld $ 62.35
	7 Social security tips — 8 Allocated tips
d Employee's social security number 222-22-2222	9 Advance EIC payment — 10 Dependent care benefits
e Employee's first name and initial Last name Julia P. Rose 106 State Street Laytonville CA 95454	11 Nonqualified plans — 12a
	13 Statutory employee Retirement plan Third-party sick pay — 12b
	14 Other — 12c
	12d
f Employee's address and ZIP code	
15 State Employer's state ID number CA	61444 — 16 State wages, tips, etc. $4,300.00 — 17 State income tax $67.70 — 18 Local wages, tips, etc. — 19 Local income tax — 20 Locality name	

Department of the Treasury—Internal Revenue Service

Form W-3 Transmittal of Wage and Tax Statements

a Control number 33333	For Official Use Only ▶ OMB No. 1545-0008
b Kind of Payer 941 [X] Military 943 Hshld. emp. Medicare govt. emp. Third-party sick pay CT-1	1 Wages, tips, other compensation $ 4,300.00 — 2 Federal income tax withheld $ 327.50
	3 Social security wages $ 4,300.00 — 4 Social security tax withheld $ 267.70
c Total number of Forms W-2 1 — d Establishment number	5 Medicare wages and tips $ 4,300.00 — 6 Medicare tax withheld $ 62.35
e Employer identification number 68-1234567	7 Social security tips $ — 8 Allocated tips $
f Employer's name Music Photo Service 640 Bell Springs Road Laytonville CA 95454	9 Advance EIC payments $ — 10 Dependent care benefits $
	11 Nonqualified plans $ — 12 Deferred compensation $
	13 For third-party sick pay use only
g Employer's address and ZIP code	14 Income tax withheld by payer of third-party sick pay $
h Other EIN used this year	
15 State Employer's state ID number CA	61444	16 State wages, tips, etc. $ 4,300.00 — 17 State income tax $ 67.70
	18 Local wages, tips, etc. $ — 19 Local income tax $
Contact person Sam Leandro	Telephone number (707) 984-7117 — For Official Use Only
E-mail address	Fax number ( )

Under penalties of perjury, I declare that I have examined this return and accompanying documents, and, to the best of my knowledge and belief, they are true, correct, and complete.

Signature ▶ *Sam Leandro* Title ▶ owner Date ▶ January 31,

Department of the Treasury Internal Revenue Service

out a form W-5. Employers increase the take home pay accordingly. IRS Publication #15, "Employer's Tax Guide," has instructions and tables to compute the Advance EITC.

Payroll Tax Returns. Federal Payroll Tax Returns (Form #941) are due quarterly on April 30 for January, February and March; July 31 for April, May and June; October 31 for July, August and September; and January 31 for October, November and December. Taxes reported on Form 941 are taxes withheld from your employees (federal income, Social Security and Medicare), and the employer's portion of employee Social Security and Medicare. Do *not* include self-employment tax.

As long as the total payroll taxes due in any one quarter are less than $2,500, the entire amount can be remitted with the return. If, however, at the end of any month in the quarter, total taxes due (combined employee and employer portions) are $2,500 or more, you must deposit the full amount by the 15th day of the next month. Deposits are reported on yet another form, #8109, "Federal Tax Deposit (FTD) Coupon," and paid to an authorized commercial bank or to a Federal Reserve bank. You can obtain the names of authorized banks at any local bank. Deposits can also be made electronically.

The deposit information is confusing enough to warrant an illustration. (Maybe it's confusing enough to go back and read the chapter, "How Not To Become An Employer.") In January, let's say you withheld from your employees $700 in income tax and $300 in Social Security and Medicare taxes. Your tax liability at the end of January is the $1,000 withheld plus $300 (your employer portion) for a total of $1,300. Since this amount is under $2,500 there is no need to file anything at that time. Okay so far?

Now in February, let's say the same taxes recur: $1,000 withholding and $300 employer's portion, or $1,300. Your total tax liability is now $2,600 for the two months. Since you are now over the $2,500 limit, you must deposit the full $2,600 with an authorized bank by March 15.

Taxes for March, the last month of the quarter, are due when you file the quarterly return on April 30, assuming that March's taxes are less than $2,500. If your payroll jumped in March, and March's taxes alone are $2,500 or more, a deposit of the full amount must be made by April 15. A different and more complicated set of deposit rules apply if your total annual payroll taxes exceed $50,000.

W-2 and W-3 Statements. Ask the IRS to send you several copies of form W-2, "Wage and Tax Statement." You fill out a W-2 form for each employee, annually at year-end. You must mail or give out the W-2 forms by January 31. Three copies of the W-2 are given to the employee, one copy you retain, and one copy is sent to the Social Security Administration (the SSA).

The Social Security Administration copies of the W-2's should be sent with Form W-3, "Transmittal of Income and Tax Statements," no later than February 28. W-3's are available from the IRS. You can get a 30-day extension to file your W-3 by filing Form 8809.

Businesses with ten or fewer employees can file W-2s and W-3s over the Internet at www.ssa.gov/employer.

Unemployment Tax. As an employer, you are subject to Federal Unemployment tax (F.U.T.A.) if during the year you, (a) paid wages of $1,500 or more in any calendar quarter, or (b) had one or more employees for some portion of at least one day during each of twenty different calendar weeks (better re-read that slowly).

Unemployment tax is imposed on you, the employer. It is not deducted from your employee's wages. An annual return is filed on Form #940, or for many small businesses, the simpler Form #940-EZ, Employer's Federal Unemployment Tax Return, on or before January 31 of next year. The rate is 6.2% of the first $7,000 of wages paid to each employee during the year. You may receive credit of up to 5.4% for state unemployment taxes you pay, so your net federal tax could be as low as 0.8%.

Immigration. The Bureau of Citizenship and Immigration Services (CIS, formerly the Immigration and Naturalization Service or INS) Reform and Control Act makes it a crime to "knowingly hire any alien not authorized to work in the U.S." All new employees must have "proof of employment eligibility" such as a Social Security card, military registration card, or immigrant "green card" (which is actually white, not green, and is officially called a Permanent Residence Card, Form I-551). Employers must fill out an Employment Eligibility Verification Form #I-9 for each employee, available from CIS offices, and retain the forms in your files. For more information, see the CIS Publication #M274, "Handbook For Employers." Call the CIS toll free at 800-375-5283, or on the Internet at uscis.gov.

Restaurant and nightclub owners. Employees must report their tips to you, if they are more than $20 a month. You must withhold income and payroll taxes, and pay employer's payroll taxes on the tips, just as you do on wages. Restaurant owners may claim a special tax credit equal to the employer's portion of FICA taxes paid on tips, to the extent tips and wages exceed the minimum wage. If you have more than 10 employees, you must report income and tips-related information on Form #8027.

Agricultural employers come under different federal laws, particularly regarding Social Security and Medicare taxes, minimum wage and overtime pay. See IRS Publication #51, "Agricultural Employer's Tax Guide."

Family Employees

If you plan to hire your husband or wife, the chapter "Husband and Wife Partnerships" in the Your Business section will explain your options and tax consequences. Generally, putting your spouse on the payroll will neither increase nor decrease your combined income or payroll taxes.

You may have a significant tax savings if you hire your children to help out in the business. You can pay each of your children up to $4,850 a year (2004 maximum), and write it off as a business expense. The kids pay no federal income taxes and do not have to file an income tax return. Neither the kids or the parents pay any Social Security, Medicare or federal unemployment taxes. The children are usually exempt from federal minimum wage and child labor requirements.

Here are the rules:

1. Your business must be a sole proprietorship, or a husband-and-wife partnership.

2. Your child must be under the age of 18.

3. The child must perform legitimate work to justify the salary earned. The work has to be business related: You can't hire your 17 year old to baby sit your 3 year old and then take a business deduction. You should document the job, keep time records, write regular paychecks.

4. If the child has bank interest or other "unearned income" it cannot exceed $750.

5. The child's total income from all sources combined cannot exceed $4,850.

If your child is 18 or older, or earns more than the above maximums, you still may be able to hire your child and save on income and payroll taxes. But the rules start changing, with a lot of variables. The IRS's "Circular E, Employer's Tax Guide" (Publication 15) includes a chart that explains what federal payroll taxes are required for children on the payroll.

You should check your state's employment laws before you hire your children. Many states have laws similar to the IRS, and impose no state income or payroll taxes, nor require worker's compensation insurance on your children. Check your state employer's guide. Do not rely on verbal information from state agencies. People who work at state employment departments are often unaware of child employment laws.

If children hire their parents, the parents are considered regular employees, subject to all regular employment and income taxes, except Federal Unemployment Tax (FUTA). Parents are exempt from FUTA tax.

Payroll Ledgers

Every employer must keep a payroll ledger in addition to the expenditure ledger. The payroll ledger shows all the details of every paycheck for every employee. Payroll ledgers can be purchased ready to use or as part of a software program, or you can design your own. The Ledger section includes a sample payroll ledger.

Payroll ledgers should be permanent. Keep them as long as you own the business, longer if possible. Long-gone employees can come back to haunt you years later, usually when there's some problem with Social Security retirement.

Use a separate ledger page for each employee. Head the page with the employee's name, address and Social Security number. Write down the employee's hourly or monthly rate of pay at the top of the page. If the rate changes during

PAYROLL LEDGER

Name								Social Security			
Address								Pay Rate			

1	2	3	4	5	6	7	8	9	10	11	12	13
PAYCHECK DATE	CHECK NO.	PAY PERIOD	HOURS REG	O/T	GROSS	F.I.T.	SOCIAL SECURITY	MEDI-CARE	STATE INCOME	OTHER WITHHOLDING		NET PAY

the year, show the new rate as well as the old and the date of change.

The payroll ledger should have a column for each of the following:

1. Date of paycheck.
2. Check number.
3. Payroll period.
4. Number of regular hours worked.
5. Number of overtime hours worked.
6. Gross pay.
7. Federal income tax withheld.
8. Social Security taxes withheld.
9. Medicare taxes withheld.
10. State income taxes withheld.
11-12. Columns for other withholding: state requirements, retirement, health insurance, etc.
13. Net "take-home" pay.

Remember that the net pay is also posted to your expenditure ledger in Column #4.

Payroll Software

All computer accounting programs include payroll ledgers that are very similar to these hand-posted ledgers. If you have several employees, payroll software will save you many hours of time every month. The software can prepare individual payroll statements for each employee in addition to your payroll ledger. Some software can prepare your payroll tax returns and year-end W-2 statements as well.

Mike Madsen, M. Madsen Leather: "When you're first getting started you don't always hire the best people. You don't know what you are looking for. You might hire somebody who is sympathetic to you or flatters you or somebody who is good looking. But they might not fit the job. You've got to think in terms of what the job is, and hire people for the job, and not hire friends. I'd say it's better to make friends of the people that work for you, but never hire friends."

Nick Mein, Wallpapers Plus: "A person's gotta be happy if he or she is going to work for you. The women working for me were terribly unhappy. This one woman who worked for me, who I really liked, was a great saleswoman. She'd been going to a shrink, and he told her, 'Work's bad for you.' So she called up and said, 'I won't be in.' A lot of jobs depended on her charm; she brought a lot of people in the store. And she just gave up on it. That's irritating. No 'stick-to-it-ivity' my father calls it; no perseverance.

"It's difficult to be nice to your employees because they're going to take advantage of you. They're going to start coming in late. All the people who worked for me are perfect examples. I'd say, 'Get in at 9:30, do what ordering needs to be done, and open the doors at ten. I want you to be ready to sell at ten.' And they do that for a while, but then they say, `I want to get in a little later because there's no ordering to do, there's no backlog.' I say okay. And then eventually, they're coming in at eleven. Because they felt nobody was coming in the shop until 11 or 11:30. If you're not on it everyday, you get screwed. You have to be on it all the time. And then, they leave early.

"If you have somebody working for you you've got to make it absolutely plain that they're being paid for the specified hours. I find that really hard to do, keep people to that, because I'm a little bit like that myself. On a really slow day, I'd say, 'Go ahead, go home early.' Then it always happens: next day some woman would call and say, 'I came by your shop at 5:20 and you weren't there.' That's bad service."

PARTNERSHIPS

Partnerships offer opportunities often not available to the one-person business: more capital, more skills and ideas, the extra energy generated when two or more people are working together. Partnerships are the traditional meeting ground of the "idea" person and the "money" person. Having a partner can relieve the sole proprietor pressures of having to do everything yourself. And, at last, you can take a little vacation without having to shut down the business.

Most partnerships are planned as a long-term relationship, to last the life of the business (hopefully). But many partnerships are temporary arrangements, often on a project-by-project basis. When the project is completed, the partnership dissolves, and you move on to the next venture.

Partnerships have drawbacks as well. The independence and sole decision making that only the sole proprietor has is now shared. There is more paperwork. Inter-personal relations with your partners may require both time and tact. Most important, the legal consequences of having one or more partners can be serious.

Legal Aspects of General Partnerships

Partnership are governed by state law. Every state except Louisiana bases their partnership laws on the Uniform Partnership Act (UPA) or the Revised Uniform Partnership Act (RUPA). Both Acts have the same basic rules, but with two important differences.

Under UPA, a partnership is legally inseparable from the owners, the partners. Under RUPA, a partnership is a separate legal entity from the owners. What does this mean to you?

Under UPA, death or withdrawal of one partner or the addition of a new partner legally terminated a partnership. The partnership could continue, but technically a new business and a new partnership agreement had to be created. Under RUPA, a partnership can continue in existence if a partner leaves or a new partner is added. RUPA makes life a lot easier for partnerships that want or need to switch owners.

Under RUPA, partners can sue their partnerships, and partnerships can sue partners, for misdeeds. This is not allowed under UPA, where the partners and the partnerships were legally one and the same. You couldn't sue yourself. Whether this new provision is a step forward or a step backward is something I prefer not to speculate on.

General Vs. Limited Partnerships

There are three kinds of partnerships. The kind covered in this chapter, the typical business partnership, is called a "general" partnership.

There is also something called a "limited" partnership, which is not a partnership in the usual sense. A limited partnership is an investment financing arrangement, with one general partner who owns and operates the business, with full legal and financial responsibility, much like a sole proprietor; and one or more limited partners, who are investors only. The limited partners have no involvement in the management of the business, and usually have no personal liability beyond their investment. Limited partnerships are covered under "Equity Financing" in the Getting Started section of the book. This chapter is for general partnerships only.

A third kind of partnership, a Limited Liability Partnership, or LLP (not to be confused with a limited partnership), is used almost exclusively by legal and accounting firms. LLPs are covered in the Limited Liability Company chapter.

Should either of the above issues affect your partnership, contact your state and find out whether you are governed by UPA or RUPA.

Most other partnership laws are the same under both Acts, the same in all states. And the most important law is legal liability of partners.

Individual partners can be held personally responsible for the debts and legal obligations of the partnership. Most important: all partners can be held personally, individually liable for the acts of any partner acting on partnership business. If your partner, representing the business, goes out and gets a bank loan, you can be personally responsible to repay the debt, even if you didn't sign the papers yourself, even if you didn't know about the loan. If your partner gets into legal trouble while on partnership business, you may also be in legal trouble.

The only way out of this unlimited liability is to incorporate or set up a Limited Liability Company (LLC). Both are covered in this section.

Like sole proprietors, partners cannot be employees of their partnerships. Partners can draw a "wage," called a "guaranteed payment," or they can merely share in the profits of the partnership, or some combination of the two. Profits and guaranteed payments are taxable to the individual partners. Partners are subject to Self-Employment tax (covered in the Tax section).

Partnerships *can* hire regular employees, but the partners themselves cannot be employees.

A partnership must have a federal identification number, obtained by filing Form SS-4, "Employer's Federal Identification Number" (EIN). If the partnership will have no employees, be sure line 12 on the form, asking about employees, is marked "Not Applicable" (N/A). This will alert the IRS not to send you payroll forms.

Partnerships file a partnership income tax return, on form 1065, although the partnership itself pays no taxes. Each partner pays personal income tax on his or her share of the profits, on Schedule E of the regular 1040 tax return. Each partner is taxed on his or her full share of the profit whether distributed to the partners or not.

Partnerships get the same licenses, permits, DBAs, etc. as any other business. In some states, partnerships must also be registered with the county clerk or a state office.

Husband and wife partnerships are considered general partnerships, but there are additional legal, tax, and personal issues involved. See the chapter "Husband and Wife Partnerships" in the Your Business section.

Partnership Agreements

A partnership agreement is an "understanding" between partners as to how the business will be conducted. Many partnership agreements are nothing more than a handshake and a "Let's do it." Often such agreements turn out to be more of a *mis*understanding than anything else.

A written partnership agreement is not required by law, but if you don't have one, you are asking for nothing but trouble. What's more, without a written agreement, state law, not the partners, will dictate how the partnership is run.

In most states, if you don't have a written agreement, state law says that each partner shares equally in the profits (regardless of the time or money contributed) and has equal voice in the management of the partnership. A partnership with a written agreement is not bound by these laws; you can make your own rules.

Partnership agreements are not binding on outside ("third") parties. A lender or a creditor can go after any and all partners, no matter what the partnership agreement says.

A written partnership agreement should be signed by all the partners and should include:

1. A simple statement of business goals. Long range goals should be included as well. For example, one partner may want a business that will provide a good livelihood for many years; while the other partner may be dreaming of building up the business and when it becomes successful and established, selling it for a big profit. These two partners obviously have a serious conflict of interest. If partners do not agree on the basics, the partnership is doomed from the start.

2. How much each partner is to contribute, in cash, property, and time, and when the contributions are to be made.

All the people we talk to or survey seem to want a partner, until they actually have one.

—*Inc. Magazine*

3. How each partner will share in the profits and losses. The easiest and most common arrangement is an equal division of profits between partners. You may wish, however, to provide for an unequal division of profits to compensate for differences in time or money contributed or for differences in ability and experience.

A partner can draw a wage to reflect actual time spent running the business. The wage is known as a "guaranteed payment to partner." It is not a regular employee wage for tax purposes. There is no withholding, no employee payroll taxes. It is part of the partner's total partnership income. Paying a wage is common when one partner works day-to-day in the business and the other doesn't, or when partners do not put in equal time. After the wage is paid, any remaining profit (or loss) for the year is then divided between the partners according to your agreement. Specify any wage arrangement in the agreement.

4. Who will have authority to sign checks?

5. Procedures for withdrawing funds and paying profits, how much and when, to prevent partners from arbitrarily withdrawing money from the partnership. No federal law requires partners to make equal or simultaneous withdrawals.

6. Provisions for continuing the business if one partner dies or wants out. Without such a provision, a partner can quit or retire any time the partner wants, sell his share of the partnership to anyone he pleases, or demand to be paid fair value for his or her share of the partnership.

Your biggest problem is determining how much money the departing partner (or estate) should receive and over what period of time. For example, the business may be worth a lot of money because it is established and successful or because it owns a lot of inventory and equipment, but there may be little cash on hand to pay a departing partner. Insurance companies offer "key person" life insurance for partnerships to buy out a deceased or seriously ill partner.

Your buy-out agreement (sometimes called a "buy-sell" or "cross-purchase" agreement) should state how a partner's share of the business is to be valued. Is it based on the value of the business assets; that is, what you actually have invested in the business? Or is it based on what the going business is worth on the open market, what an eager new owner might pay for it? And who will be the lucky person to determine this "worth"?

There are tax consequences to a partner buyout that vary depending on how the agreement is worded. The tax interests of the remaining and outgoing partners are often diametrically opposed. These tax aspects can be substantial; they will probably require professional help.

The agreement might include a non-competing clause so that a departing partner cannot engage in a similar business (for a reasonable period of time and in a limited geographical area).

7. You may want a clause specifying the financial and legal powers of each partner. Such a clause is not binding on outside parties, such as a lender. It will not relieve any partner of partnership obligations entered into by other partners. It only reduces the possibility of misunderstanding among the partners.

8. Can any of the partners have a separate outside business? You would not want a partner to compete with the partnership, possibly siphoning off partnership business.

9. If the partnership dissolves, who will own the right to the business name?

Most of the professional advice I have heard suggests that you hire a knowledgeable lawyer (not all lawyers are familiar with partnership problems) or an experienced accountant to draw up any partnership agreement. I feel that you can avoid the expense, and draft your own agreement if it is a simple one (such as 50-50, equal sharing), if you consider everything in this chapter, and if you know your partners well enough to be confident in your plans.

You and Your Partners

My friend Rory said, "Having a partner is just like having a wife, only more so." Well, Rory is a long-time loner, but his words are basically true. Partnerships are more than business. They are often complex inter-personal relationships. And like marriages, partnerships can bring out the best and the worst in people. By acquiring a partner you are adding a whole new dimension to your business venture, one you should be fully prepared to deal with.

Anyone who has lost a friend after an argument can quickly realize the possible problems and complications of having a business partner. It is not uncommon for partners to have a disagreement, a difference of opinion, or worse. You may feel that your partner is not working as hard as he should (and he may be feeling the same about you!).

When trouble arises between partners, the logical step is to try to work it out: sit down with your partner, get the problems "out front," and get them solved. Much more easily said than done. Like divorces, partnership dissolutions are more common than ever and often just as problematical. The alternatives—dividing up the assets and going out of business, or one partner buying out the other—can be difficult even with a good written agreement, can require lawyers and almost always cause the business to suffer.

Marriage counselors can sometimes save a marriage. But it's a little out of my field, and there is little advice I can give you retrospectively. Knowing that such things happen should warn you to take every precaution prior to going into a partnership to reduce the possibility of problems later on.

The best advice I can offer is to pick your partners *very* carefully. This may seem basic, just common sense; but a poor choice of partners is the root cause of many partnership failures. How well do you know your partners? Are you old

friends? Have you worked together before? What business experience do your partners have? What is his or her "track record?" Look at the way your partners treat their parents, husbands, wives, friends. It may be indicative of how they will treat you.

Partnership Bookkeeping

The basic bookkeeping for a partnership is the same as for a sole proprietorship. But partnerships also keep a separate "partners' capital ledger" which provides a complete record, by partner, of all contributions and withdrawals and of each partner's share of profit or loss.

The partners' capital ledger has two columns for each partner. One column shows *activity* in the partner's account—contributions, withdrawals and the partner's share of profit or loss. The second column is the *balance* of the partner's capital remaining with the partnership.

Contributions and withdrawals should be recorded when they occur. Contributions are shown as positive amounts and increase the partner's balance. Withdrawals are shown as negative, bracketed amounts and decrease the partner's balance. A partner's "guaranteed payment" (wage) is shown as a withdrawal.

Each partner's share of the partnership profit or loss is posted to the partners' capital ledger once a year at year-end. A profit is posted to the Activity column as a positive amount; a loss is shown as a negative amount. Profits and losses increase and decrease a partner's balance accordingly. The Total Balance column is the sum of all the individual partners' Balance columns.

The sample partners' capital ledger below shows activity for 2004 and part of 2005 for a new partnership, Wesley's Farm Fresh Eggs, owned by two partners:

Entry 1: The partnership began on January 1, 2004. Each partner contributed $2,000 to the business. Each partner's balance is $2,000, and the total balance is $4,000.

Entry 2: On March 31, Huck (Partner A) contributed another $800, and Pippi (Partner B) contributed another $400.

Entry 3: The partnership made a $7,000 profit in 2004. At December 31, 2004, the partners' shares of the profit were posted to their individual accounts.

		Huck (Partner A)		Pippi (Partner B)		Total
Wesley's Farm Fresh Eggs						
Partners' Capital Ledger						
Entry		Activity	Balance	Activity	Balance	Balance
1	Contribution 1-1	$2,000.00	$2,000.00	$2,000.00	$2,000.00	$4,000.00
2	Contribution 3-31	$800.00	$2,800.00	$400.00	$2,400.00	$5,200.00
3	Income for Year	$4,000.00	$6,800.00	$3,000.00	$5,400.00	$12,200.00
4	Withdrawal 2-5	($400.00)	$6,400.00		$5,400.00	$11,800.00
5	Withdrawal 5-1		$6,400.00	($350.00)	$5,050.00	$11,450.00

Entry 4: On February 5, 2005, Huck withdrew $400 from the business.

Entry 5: On May 1, 2005, Pippi withdrew $350 from the business.

With each entry, the partners' individual balances and the total balance were adjusted.

A partnership income tax return must sometimes include a balance sheet (explained in the Your Business section) and schedule of partners' capital. For more information, see IRS Publication 541, "Tax Information on Partnerships."

Partnership Post-Mortem

Lara Stonebraker, former partner in Aromatica, a retail coffee store: "It's been my experience that partnerships rarely work, especially if there is an odd number of partners. Because it's always going to be two against one in all decision making. Unless you have such well matched personalities that everybody is always good friends, it creates incredible hassles. That was the most anxiety-ridden period of my life. There were three of us and I happened to be the odd one. I blotted out a lot of that whole experience."

———

Key Dickason, former partner in Xanadu, a computer service: "I was in a partnership once, and my partner and I disagreed, not on the running of the business, but on the way we handled employees. Jack and I disagreed on a philosophical—a better word is ethical—aspect of employee relationships. To Jack, an employee was somebody you used and discarded. To me an employee was somebody you had an obligation and a commitment to. If you have this basic disagreement, no partnership agreement will handle it. Do you put in there, 'You agree to treat employees fairly?' Well, that doesn't mean anything. 'Cause to Jack, Jack was treating them fairly. It eventually led to the dissolution of the partnership.

"The biggest mistake in the world is to start a partnership if there is disagreement in the beginning when you're laying the groundwork for the business. If you enter into basic disagreement on ethics, management, or whatever the objective of the business is, you shouldn't go into business together. Putting your doubts about the situation into a partnership agreement doesn't accomplish anything unless you're prepared to fight, which isn't what it's all about."

———

Jan Lowe, former partner in Midnight Sewing Machine, a retail dress shop: "I went into business with my sister who is a dear person, and who taught me everything I know. I didn't sew a stitch in my life before we bought this dress shop, and she handed me a pattern and scissors and said, 'I'm going to lunch now. If you have any problems, let me know.' So I started off real cold there, which is no way to do it. I'd run into problems when people would want something intricate done or they'd want something altered, and I wouldn't know how to handle it. I wasn't really prepared to do what I did for a living.

"One of our basic problems was non-communication. My partner would borrow money from someone and I didn't know about it, which I thought was a cheap shot. You've got to be in constant communication. If somebody's going to lunch, they've got to tell you. We didn't have anything in writing between us, how things were going to be run. That should be made clear right from the start—exactly what do you want to see happen, how is it going to happen, who's going to make what work, who is best at handling what; and stick to it.

"I think you should be willing to bend when that system does not work. Face it immediately and try something else. To hang onto a system that doesn't work can get you into lots of trouble."

...And a Partnership That Works

"Kipple is a made-up word that means, um, kipple, the dumb stuff that you gather around you that you can't live without." Pat Ellington is a partner in Kipple, a small antique store: "We function pretty well as a four-way partnership. Miriam and I are old friends, friends for fifteen years or more. Her downstairs neighbor is the third partner, and a friend of hers is the fourth. Everybody's really working part time. But this way we can operate a full time business.

"When we first came into this, I was the only one with any kind of business skill. Neither Miriam or Pam ever held an office or business job of any type. Ann has been a housewife all her life.

"We've had personality troubles, but not serious ones, because we squashed them right away. The inter-personal stuff can be worked out if everybody agrees it's going to happen, that there's no blame attached to differences of opinion or feelings. We all agreed when we set out that everybody was going to make mistakes, some of them are going to cost us money, but no blame should be attached to anybody, and we would not throw it up to each other. When Ann joined us, Miriam made a lot of noises, `She did this wrong, she never should have bought that ...' Pam and I would say, `Miriam, you made your mistakes too, back off.' And she slowly but surely got over that. She felt, being the one partner with the most money in at that point, like the business was hers. None of this was conscious. People don't consciously set out to be that way about things, it's sort of inbred. We all have moments of `mine' mentalities: `That's mine. She's threatening it.'

"Miriam is a crackerjack saleswoman. She can sell anybody anything. But she couldn't keep a set of books to save her soul. She can't balance a checkbook. But she can sell. That's a real asset. She doesn't have to keep books if she can do that. Pam's got a good eye when it comes to buying. She's good at that. And Ann, who's much better organized than the other two when it comes to shows and things like that, she's the one who sits down and makes out a list: we're gonna need lights, display material, we need this, we need that. Pam says, `Well, we need so much inventory; where's the rest of it?' These are skills.

"And I'm the bookkeeper. And between the four of us we can really operate."

YOU, INCORPORATED: A Corporation Primer

The corporation is truly a misunderstood animal. People, even business people, have more misconceptions about corporations than about any other form of business. Some small-time operations will benefit by incorporating, but many will not. In order for you to make an intelligent choice between "You" and "You, Incorporated," you will need a basic understanding of what a corporation is and what can and cannot be accomplished by incorporating.

"In Twenty-Five Words or Less"

A corporation is...just another business. The basic day-to-day operations, the management, the bookkeeping, are virtually no different than the operations of an unincorporated business. A corporation can be as tiny as the tiniest unincorporated business; all states allow one person corporations. Just as there are "grey suits and elevators" corporations, there are "blue jeans," home-based and part-time corporations.

A corporation is just another business...but the rules of the game are different. Owners of corporations are the stockholders (also called shareholders). They own shares of stock, pieces of paper. Your corporation may have one or more stockholders (one or more owners) with one or more shares of stock, depending on your needs and your state's laws (discussed later).

A corporation is just another business...but some people are impressed when a business has Inc. next to its name. Some people think they're dealing with a large company instead of, well, just you. At least that's the pitch you hear from businesses that want you to pay them to set you up as a corporation. I really don't know whether a corporation impresses anyone or affects their buying decisions. Do you notice, or care, if some business you buy from is a corporation or not?

Corporate Myth Number One: You're going to lower you taxes by incorporating. Probably not. The fact is, most small businesses will not save tax money by incorporating. Corporate profits (of regular C corporations) are taxed *twice*: once as corporate income and again when distributed to the shareholders (owners) as dividends.

In contrast, the profits from your sole proprietorship or partnership are taxable only to the owners; the business itself pays no federal income tax. So even though corporate tax rates are sometimes lower than individual tax rates, the total income tax, because of the double taxation, is usually higher.

Small corporations do have ways to reduce the combined corporation and shareholder taxes (discussed later), but none will result in taxes lower than those paid by an unincorporated business. (Actually there is *one* situation where incorporating will save you tax money. See "Retained Earnings" below).

Most states impose income taxes on corporations. Some states call their income tax an "excise" tax, not to be confused with federal excise taxes described in the Tax section.

If you don't make mistakes, you aren't really trying.

—*Coleman Hawkins*

Many states impose an additional tax on corporations called a "franchise tax." The franchise tax may be a flat annual fee; or may be a percent of income (like a second income tax); or may be based on the value of stock or assets. In some states the franchise tax is really a minimum income tax: you pay your income tax or the franchise tax, whichever is greater.

Limited Liability

Rules regarding liability are different for corporations. These liability rules, which offer protection to the owners (the stockholders) of corporations from creditors and from some lawsuits, are the most convincing reason for you to consider incorporating your business.

A corporation is recognized by law as a "legal entity," which means that the business is legally separate from its owners. If your corporation does not pay its debts, the creditors usually cannot get their money from your personal, non-business assets. Sole proprietors and partners, by comparison, are personally liable for all business debts and obligations.

The main reason for corporate limited liability is to protect you from creditors—suppliers and others you owe money to in the normal course of business—should the business go broke. A landlord cannot usually enforce a lease if the corporation is bankrupt.

Many people think they should incorporate to protect themselves from lawsuits, but this rarely works. In some cases you will not be personally liable for lawsuits brought against your corporation. But if your company is sued by an angry customer, or someone who was injured or suffered a loss, you as owner or officer of the business will also be named in the lawsuit. Do not be fooled by this common and dangerous misconception about liability protection.

A corporation will not shield you from personal liability that you normally should be responsible for, such as not having car insurance, or acting with gross negligence, or if your company breaks the law. Limited liability will not protect you if your corporation fails to pay any income, payroll or other business taxes.

Professionals such as doctors and lawyers cannot hide behind a corporation to protect themselves from malpractice suits. A corporation, however, will shield you from a malpractice suit brought against one of your partners. This is a major reason that doctors, lawyers, and other professionals set up corporations. Some states have a separate Professional Service Corporation category, with special requirements.

Partnerships often incorporate (or set up Limited Liability Companies—covered in the next chapter) to protect individual partners from possible losses and lawsuits resulting from the actions of other partners.

People who own more than one business sometimes incorporate each business separately so if one business fails, the creditors cannot grab the assets of your other corporations.

Any bank lending money to a small corporation will require the stockholders or officers to co-sign as personal guarantors of the loan.

If you plan to incorporate primarily with the intention of limiting your legal liability, I suggest you find out first, exactly how limited the liability really is for your particular venture. Talk to a good lawyer or accountant.

Small corporations are less likely to be audited by the IRS than unincorporated businesses, though the difference is only about 2%. I would not use this as an excuse to incorporate, but for some people it may well be the icing on the cake.

Change of Ownership

Incorporating a business eliminates much of the legal and tax complications of a change in ownership. New shareholders can be added easily (within certain legal limits, discussed later). Selling a business, passing a family-owned business from generation to generation, giving or selling your employees an ownership interest, and taking on investors in the company are all much easier with a corporation than with an unincorporated business.

Sale of stock or death of a shareholder will not end the business. The same corporation can continue in business with new shareholders. By comparison, a sole proprietorship ceases to exist when the owner sells or gives away the business, takes on a partner, or dies. In some states, a partnership ceases to exist when one partner quits or dies. A sole proprietorship or a partnership can be sold or otherwise acquired by new owners. But the result, legally, is a new business requiring new records, new valuation of assets and liabilities, new business licenses, etc.

Owner-Employees

A corporation is the only form of business that can hire its owners as employees. You are in the unique position of being your own boss and your own employee. Hiring yourself as an owner-employee is one way to reduce corporate income taxes. Every employee's wage, including that of an owner-employee, is a deductible expense of the business. The wage is taxable to the owner-employee as personal income. But unlike regular corporate profits, which are taxable to the corporation and again to the owners, wages paid to owner-employees are not subject to the double taxation. In many small corporations, the owner-employee's salary and year-end bonus eat up all the corporate profits, bringing corporate income taxes to zero. (For tax purposes, year-end bonuses are considered part of regular salaries. As long as salary and bonus combined are not "unreasonable," the IRS allows this tax maneuver).

Many fringe benefits, particularly medical expenses, are 100% tax deductible for the corporation, and are not taxable to the employees at all. This is a much larger tax deduction than that available to sole proprietors, partners in partnerships, owners of Limited Liability Companies (LLC's), and owners of S corporations (who come under different rules than owners of regular C corporations; see below). If your health insurance costs are high, this alone may be an excellent reason to consider incorporation.

Retired people collecting Social Security can lose part of their Social Security income if any outside income, such as earnings from a small business, gets above a certain level. By setting up a corporation, you may be able to pay yourself a low enough salary so it stays under the social security limits. This arrangement cannot be accomplished with a sole proprietorship, a partnership or an LLC because all of the profits of an unincorporated business are considered personal income whether you take a salary or not. This is an area you should discuss with an accountant.

A Warning: If your C corporation is not yet making a profit, I suggest that you do not pay yourself any wages until the corporation is making a taxable profit. Otherwise you'll be paying payroll taxes and personal income taxes on the salary but get no tax breaks for your corporation. A lose-lose situation. Talk to an accountant.

Employee Business Expenses

If you do become an owner-employee of your own corporation, you should be warned about IRS limitations on employee business expenses.

Your corporation can take tax deductions for any allowable business expenses, as long as the corporation itself spends the money. But if you, as an employee, spend the money, your tax deductions are greatly reduced, possibly eliminated, even though you may be the sole owner of the business and even though the expenses may be totally legitimate. It is important that you learn the IRS rules, because it's easy to avoid this trap.

Retained Earnings

The remaining significant difference between incorporated and unincorporated business is the corporation's legal ability to retain up to $250,000 ($150,000 for some businesses) of undistributed profits within the company, and not pay the profits out to the owners. Though the corporation pays income tax on these "retained earnings," as they are called, the owners do not have to pay the "double" or second tax because the profits have not been paid out to them. Retained earnings can be reinvested in the business, distributed to the shareholders at a later date or retained indefinitely by the company.

An unincorporated business can retain the profits in the business, but the owners pay income tax on the profits whether distributed to them or not.

"It's a jungle up here, Martha!"

This is the one situation where incorporating might reduce your taxes. If the corporate tax rate is lower than your personal tax rate (which depends not only on how much profit you earn, but also on marital status, and how many dependents and personal deductions you claim) any retained earnings—profits you choose not to take out of the business this year—will be taxed at the lower corporate rate. If you reinvest those retained earnings in the business in a future year, you're fine. But if you ever withdraw the retained earnings, they become taxable dividends, and you are penalized with the double taxation.

S Corporations

The type of corporation described above is commonly called a "regular" or "C" corporation. (Don't confuse a C corporation with a Schedule C tax return. The two C's are not related. Schedule C is for sole proprietors, not corporations.)

There is another form of corporation different from the C corporation. It is a hybrid between a C corporation and a partnership or sole proprietorship, with some of the advantages of both.

The S corporation (so called because it is covered in Subchapter S of the Internal Revenue Code) has the same basic structure as a C corporation and offers the same limited liability protection to the stockholders. The S corporation, however, pays no federal income tax. Like a partnership, sole proprietorship and Limited Liability Company, the S corporation is what the IRS calls a "pass through entity": profits "pass through" to the owner or owners who pay taxes on the business profit at their regular individual rates.

Unlike an unincorporated business, however, owner-employees of S corporations are treated similarly to owner-employees of regular C corporations. If you work for your S corporation, you must be on the payroll as a regular employee with regular payroll deductions.

Any S corporation profits in excess of your salary are also taxable directly to you, as dividends. Unlike a C corporation, S corporation dividends are taxable to you the year earned, whether you actually receive the money or not. This might be a problem if the business earned a profit but doesn't have the cash to distribute to shareholders to pay their income taxes.

S corporation dividends are taxed, to the owners of the corporation, at the owners' regular income tax rates, not at the lower capital gains rates. Only C corporation dividends benefit from capital gains tax rates. If this seems unfair, keep in mind that a C corporation's profit has already been taxed once, at the corporation's regular tax rate. When that profit is distributed to the corporation's owners, as dividends, it is taxed a second time. By comparison, an S corporation pays no corporate income tax on its profit. S corporation dividends escape double taxation.

Now this is where tax law gets interesting. S corporation dividends, unlike your salary, are not subject to employment taxes. Since you decide how much of a salary you earn, you therefore also get to decide how much of the corporation's annual profit is subject to payroll taxes, and how much escapes payroll taxes as dividends. But look out: if the IRS thinks that your salary is too low and your dividends too high, they may declare that the dividends were a salary in disguise, and hit you for back payroll taxes and penalties. This may require an accountant's help.

As an employee of your own S corporation, you may be eligible for some tax-deductible fringe benefits, but not fully-deductible medical coverage. Owners of S corporations come under the same health insurance rules as partners, sole proprietors and LLC's. Employee-owners of regular C corporations have more generous fringe benefit deductions.

Tax Advantages of an S Corporation

There are three significant tax advantages to an S corporation. The first and most obvious is the elimination of the double taxation. Second, where corporate tax rates are higher than individual rates, as is the case in some tax brackets, S corporations allow you to have the corporate structure without the higher tax rates.

The third advantage is due to some complex tax laws that allow current business losses to be carried back to prior years to offset prior years' taxes, bringing immediate tax refunds. Any business, corporation or otherwise, can avail itself of operating loss carryback laws (explained in more detail in the Tax section). But if a corporation is brand new and sustains a loss, there are no prior years to carry the loss back to. In the case of an S corporation, the loss passes through to the stockholders, and they can carry the loss back to their personal prior years' returns even though

the business did not exist then. Losses that cannot be carried back can be carried forward to offset future years' earnings.

An S corporation can have up to 75 shareholders (stockholders). A husband and wife are counted as one stockholder. Stock ownership is limited to U.S. citizens, resident aliens, estates, certain trusts and some tax-exempt organizations. All shareholders sign and file IRS Form #2553. There are limitations on how profits are to be distributed, how and when the election to become an S corporation is made, and what kind of stock can be issued. An S corporation can own a subsidiary S corporation, a legal maneuver that protects the assets of one of the corporations should the other corporation go bankrupt.

For more information, see IRS Publication #589, "Tax Information on S Corporations."

For state income taxes, most states recognize the S corporation, but a few states do not. Some states impose franchise, income or other corporate taxes on S corporations.

People who like the pass-through tax benefits of an S corporation, but do not meet the requirements, should consider setting up as a Limited Liability Company (covered below).

Close Corporations

Some states have a legal structure called a Close Corporation. Close corporations are limited to 30 (sometimes 50) shareholders. The shareholders, not a board of directors, oversee the operation of the business. Stock sales are restricted. If a shareholder wants to sell his or her stock, the shareholder must first offer the stock to other shareholders. Close corporations are often less costly to set up and have fewer legal restrictions than regular corporations.

Steps to Incorporating a Business

The states, not the federal government, license corporations. The laws vary from state to state, as do the fees. Your state may have filing fees, organization fees, charter fees, license fees, qualification fees, annual report fees—which can run from minimal amounts in some states to thousands of dollars in others.

You will have to prepare articles (or certificate) of incorporation and bylaws. Your state may require you to officially "reserve" your corporate name before you file your articles, and may require you to file separate forms naming the elected officers and to request formal permission to issue stock. Each one of these requirements is likely to have fees.

And unless you are willing and able to study all the corporation laws and file all the necessary forms yourself, add another $200 to $600 for a lawyer's assistance.

Start by contacting the Secretary of State, Office of Corporate Commissioner, or whatever state office registers corporations. Ask for their instructions, forms and fee schedules.

Articles of Incorporation

Generally, the first and most important step in the required incorporation procedures is the preparation of a "certificate" or "articles" of incorporation (sometimes called a "corporate charter" or "articles of association"). In some but not all states, the state itself can give you a printed form for the Articles of Incorporation. All you do is fill in the blanks, much like a deed or a mortgage.

The Articles usually include:

1. The proposed name of the corporation. The state can reject your proposed name if it is too similar to another corporation's name or if it is deceptive so as to mislead the public. Some states prohibit certain words in a corporation's name, typically words that might make the company sound like it is a government agency.

2. The purposes for which the corporation is formed. In some states, the wording of this section can be critical and, if improperly worded, can limit the type of business you can conduct.

3. Names and addresses of incorporators.

4. Location of the principal office of the corporation. Most small corporations officially locate in, and obtain their charter from, the state where the stockholders live.

Much has been written about the benefits of incorporating in a state other than your own, particularly Delaware, where the corporate statutes are lenient and the filing fees minimal. Most states, however, require small in-state corporations, where the majority of stockholders are state residents, to incorporate in that state and abide by state laws and pay in-state incorporation fees and taxes. In most cases, small corporations should incorporate in their home states. Ask your state's Department of Corporations or your accountant about your state's requirements.

5. The names of the future shareholders (called incorporators, subscribers, or promoters) and the number of shares each subscribes to. This is known as a "limited stock offering." Corporate stock is issued either as a "limited offering" or as a "public offering." Most small (closely held) corporations make a limited offering, with each shareholder individually named in the articles of incorporation. After the initial issuance of stock, you need permission from the state to sell new shares or to sell old shares to new stockholders.

A corporation that is "going public"—making a public offering—can sell stock to anyone. States charge much higher fees to charter public corporations. Public corporations must register with the Federal Securities and Exchange Commission (the SEC) and hire CPA's to prepare annual audited financial statements.

When a CPA firm audits your financial statements, they make a thorough examination of your ledgers, examining supporting documents, following the "paper trail," doing their best to prove that your figures are correct. Then they issue an opinion, that your financial statements are accurate and prepared in accordance with "generally accepted accounting principles." This, as you can imagine, is an expensive undertaking. All public corporations are required by law to hire CPA's and publish audited financial statements. Most private corporations (those with limited offerings) are not required to have their statements audited; and, of course, most don't.

6. The type and maximum amount of stock to be issued. Stock is classed as "common" or "preferred." Holders of preferred stock have prior or "preferred" claim on corporate assets over common stockholders. Preferred stockholders are often just investors with no interest in the corporation other than making money on their money.

Stock have either a "par value" (a stated value per share) or "no-par value" (value is not stated). You will probably avoid complications by issuing no-par stock. You specify the number of shares authorized, often an arbitrary figure. Not all authorized shares have to be issued.

As you can tell, there is a lot of legal double-talk here, but the correct wording can make the difference between a complicated and an easy incorporation.

7. Capital required at time of incorporation. This is another important decision and requires a knowledge of corporate "equity," which is comprised of "stated capital" and "paid-in surplus."

"Stated capital" is an amount of money that belongs to the corporation and cannot be paid out to stockholders until the corporation is liquidated. All corporations must have some stated capital. Most states specify the minimum that must be in the corporation's bank account. This is protection for creditors, to prevent stockholders from raiding the company's assets and make it unable to pay its debts. Corporations try to keep stated capital as small as possible.

"Paid-in surplus" is money in excess of stated capital and generally not restricted.

Bylaws

Corporations must have bylaws. Bylaws describe, in much greater detail than the articles, how the corporation is to be run: the rights and responsibilities of shareholders, directors and officers, the fiscal year, when meeting are to be held, how bylaws can be amended, and other issues important to the business.

Acting Like A Corporation

If you are going to incorporate you have to play the corporate game entirely. It is important for even a one-person corporation to play by all the rules and to follow all the formalities.

Your corporation must have at least one stockholder. The stockholders elect directors: you must have at least one director. Directors make policy and oversee the operation. Directors appoint officers: you must have officers (though one person can hold all the positions) who run the business. Officers hire the employees. In a small corporation, one person often wears all four hats: stockholder, director, officer and employee.

Stockholders and directors must hold meetings and keep written minutes of the meetings, or if your state permits, take action by unanimous

written consent. Even if you are the sole owner, corporation law says that you must hold a meeting with yourself (that should be fun) and write down what you decide.

Always identify your business as a corporation, using Incorporated or Inc. or Corp. Make it clear to people you do business with, and anybody loaning money to the business, that you are an officer of a corporation, and not acting as an individual. In correspondence, writing checks, and signing contracts, sign your name "Julia Smith, President, Company Name Incorporated (or Inc., or Corp.)" rather than just Julia Smith. Do not sign "DBA" (doing business as) after your name, as this implies you are acting as an individual.

If you don't act like a corporation— issuing stock, holding meetings, maintaining minimum capitalization, keeping records, filing annual reports, and making sure all documents indicate that this is a corporation—a court might rule that creditors can ignore the limited liability rules and go after your personal assets, like they can if your business is not incorporated. This is called "piercing the corporate veil (or shield)." This is something you do not want to happen.

Joe's Janitorial, Inc.

We had a "credit manager," a "warehouse manager," the whole bit. I'd put people on hold, wait, and pick up again.
    —_John Egard, First Team Sports Co._

A corporations can lose its limited liability protection if it is undercapitalized, if the owners constantly drain the business of cash so it has ongoing problems paying its bills, or pay personal bills from corporate accounts, or commingle personal and corporate assets. If a corporation fails to file state tax returns or pay state taxes owed, your state may be able to suspend or revoke your corporate charter.

Incorporating an Existing Business

A business can incorporate when it first opens its doors or any time afterward. You can start you business as a sole proprietorship or a partnership, both of which cost much less to start and involve a lot less paperwork than a corporation; and incorporate the business later, after you know the business is going to be successful, and you can see a real reason to incorporate.

LIMITED LIABILITY COMPANY (LLC)

The Limited Liability Company is a form of business that combines some of the most desirable features of corporations and partnerships. More and more small businesses are choosing LLCs over corporations and partnerships.

The Limited Liability Company, like a corporation, is a legal entity separate from the owners, who are referred to as "members." For this chapter on LLCs, I use the terms "owner" and "member" interchangeably.

Limited Liability

An LLC has the same limited liability for its members (owners) that a corporation has for its owners—with the same warnings about the limits of "limited liability."

This limited liability is a major reason many partnerships are restructuring as LLCs. Not only are the members' personal assets protected, each member of an LLC is only personally liable for his or her own negligence and not the negligence of other members. In a partnership, all partners are personally and fully liable for the actions of all other partners.

When discussing limited liability, always keep in mind that this is general information. Liability is an ever-shifting area of law. When someone decides to sue, everybody associated with the business is likely to be a target.

Taxation

The Limited Liability Company is taxed like a partnership or sole proprietorship. The company itself pays no income taxes. The profits are taxed to the members at their regular tax rates.

For federal income taxes, an LLC with two or more members is considered a partnership, and files a standard 1065 partnership tax return. A one-person LLC is treated as a sole proprietorship, and files a Schedule C tax return. The members pay income tax on their shares of the profits, whether distributed to them or not, just like partners and sole proprietors.

Like partnerships and sole proprietorships, and unlike corporations, LLC owners are not employees of their business. Members of LLCs are subject to self-employment tax just like partners and sole proprietors, but only if they are active in the business. LLC members who are investors only, not active or minimally active in the business, may be exempt from self-employment taxes; check with your accountant or the IRS.

Members of LLCs come under the same health coverage rules as sole proprietors, partners and owners of S corporations.

And just in case it's not obvious (there are no dumb questions), LLCs *can* hire employees. The LLC members themselves cannot be employees.

LLCs Versus Corporations

LLCs are similar to S corporations, except that owners of S corporations are employees of their business. LLCs offer more generous loss deductions than S corporations, allow more classes of ownership (such as voting and non-voting), have more freedom in deciding how profits and losses are divided, and are not limited to the S corporation's maximum of 75 shareholders nor to the requirement that shareholders be U.S. citizens.

An LLC can expel a member. A corporation cannot expel a stockholder.

Depending on your state's laws, LLCs possibly are not bound by sometimes-troublesome corporate rules such as minimum capitalization. In most states, LLCs do not have to hold director or shareholder meetings, don't have to keep minutes, and don't issue stock certificates.

All of an LLC's profit is subject to self-employment tax (Social Security and Medicare tax). A corporation and the owners of a corporation pay payroll taxes (Social Security and Medicare tax) only on the salaries. Any corporate profit in excess of salaries escapes Social Security and Medicare taxes. (This was explained in the "You, Incorporated" chapter.) For some businesses, there may be a significant difference in what an owner of a corporation pays in payroll taxes compared to an owner (member) of an LLC.

An LLC can change its tax status, and elect to be taxed as a regular corporation, if the members of the LLC see a tax savings to be gained. This option is not available to S corporations.

"If we don't have it, you're out of luck."
—sign on a tiny general store in the middle of nowhere, Branscomb, California

———————

"If it's in stock, we have it."
—sign in farm supply store, Ukiah, California

State Laws

Limited Liability Companies are licensed and regulated by the states, and each state has its own LLC laws.

A few states put a limited life on LLCs, although the LLC can refile with the state and continue its existence. Many states restrict transferability of ownership of LLCs. One of the major reasons people incorporate is to get that ease of ownership transferability.

Some states make an important distinction between LLC owners who are active in the business and those who are investors only, requiring LLCs with inactive investors to register under state securities laws. If your LLC will have investors who are not active in the business, who have no say in how the business is run, you should check your state laws to see what, if any, securities rules apply to your company.

For state income taxes, all but one state tax LLCs as partnerships (Texas taxes LLCs as regular C corporations). Some states have state tax returns especially for LLCs.

Many states exempt LLCs from franchise taxes and organization fees that corporations must pay. But some states have special fees just for LLCs.

Setting Up An LLC

To become an LLC, you register with your state's Secretary of State. An LLC must have Articles of Organization, similar to Articles of Incorporation. Many states require LLCs to have an Operating Agreement, which is a cross between a partnership agreement and corporate by-laws, and is by far the most important document an LLC has. Everything about how the LLC will be managed, who can be a member, how money is to be invested, how money is to be paid out, and just about everything else involving the LLC, are contained in the Operating Agreement. With the Agreement, you get to make your own rules for your LLC. Many of the issues covered previously under "Partnership Agreements" apply equally to LLC Operating Agreements. If you do not have a written Operating Agreement, you are bound by your state's "default" rules, which may not be to your liking.

Members of LLCs, like owners of corporations, should make it clear to everyone you do business with, that you are not acting as an individual but as a representative of a Limited Liability Company. Include "LLC" as part of the business name on all checks, stationery, contracts, business cards, etc. As with a corporation, members of LLCs can lose their liability protection if they fail to follow the rules.

An existing business can convert to an LLC at any time in the future, should you find it suitable to your needs. Converting an existing corporation to an LLC may cause tax problems, but most partnerships and sole proprietorships can convert easily.

LLCs Versus Limited Partnerships

Some limited partnerships are restructuring as LLCs, because LLCs offer limited liability protection to the operating partner, something not available in limited partnerships; and because LLCs usually have fewer state regulations than limited partnerships. Investors prefer LLCs over limited partnerships because they can legally take a more active role managing an LLC. Keep in mind that limited partnerships are closely regulated by the states, Your state may or may not allow a limited partnership to be structured as an LLC. (Don't confuse a limited partnership with a regular general partnership. They are not the same).

Limited Liability Partnerships

Some states do not allow some professional firms, particularly CPAs and lawyers, to set up as LLCs. There is another business form, called a Limited Liability Partnership, or LLP, created for these professionals. LLPs are similar to LLCs. If you can set up as an LLC, there is no reason to consider an LLP.

Do not confuse this Limited Liability Partnership with a limited partnership. They have similar names, but they are not the same thing.

A Few Last Words About Growth...

An unidentified business owner, interviewed in Inc. Magazine: "There's a subtle tendency in our society to belittle the very small business person, to champion growth at the expense of other issues. In my view, there are people for whom growing bigger is a disaster, a promotion to incompetence. So I made a conscious decision to stay small, not because I couldn't get the business, but because it would have changed me in ways I really didn't want to change. Most importantly, if I had grown my business the way the 'experts' say, I would have lost the time to do the little things that make work so enjoyable to me, like taking my wife and children to the mountains for a long weekend."

———————

Terry Dalton, owner, Unicorn Village Mar:ket: "A successful company is not a perpetually larger company with ever increasing sales and ever increasing demands on personal time. A successful business is one that gives you plenty of options. Bigger is not better."

———————

Don Massey, owner, Gulf Coast Publications: "I have no interest in growing larger than a one-person operation. I have complete control over my business and my time. No bureaucracy. No staff reviews. No personnel problems. And I get eight hours of restful sleep every night."

———————

Restauranter Richard Melman, founder, Lettuce Entertain You Enterprises: "I'm comfortable taking one step at a time, getting it right, then moving on. I don't like thinking big. You'll never get hurt by taking a small step, making sure the ground is firm, then taking the next step. I got big by thinking small."

———————

"There is a brick wall out there waiting for everybody who grows too fast. It's invisible until you hit it."
—Arthur Lazere, Northgate Computers

———————

"Take what you can use and let the rest go by."
—Ken Kesey

Section Four
TAXES

"If the adjustments required by Section 481(a) and Regulation 1.481-1 are attributable to a change in method of accounting initiated by the taxpayer, the amount of such adjustments, to the extent such amount does not exceed the net amount which would have been required if the change had been made in the first taxable year, shall be taken into account by the taxpayer in computing taxable income in the manner provided in Section 481(b)(4)(B) and paragraph (b) of this section.

—Internal Revenue Code

Well as through this world I've rambled
I've seen lots of funny men
Some will rob you with a six-gun
And some with a fountain pen.
—"Pretty Boy Floyd" by Woody Guthrie

Deep In the Heart of Taxes

Throughout *Small Time Operator* I've made enough comments—maybe more than enough—about the intrusion of government into all our affairs. And an introduction to taxes is an ideal setting to get into it again. But rather than criticize or defend that Wonderful American Institution known as Income Taxes, I'd just like to give you some information to help you deal with it.

This tax section of *Small Time Operator* will discuss federal income, self-employment and excise taxes; state income and gross receipts taxes; and a few other local taxes.

Because of the nature of the beast—the non-stop modifications and the complexity of the tax laws—this Tax section is handled differently from the rest of the book. The Tax section is like a third grade reader, simple and basic. Rather than presenting a step-by-step "all you need to know" guide to taxes (which would require at least five times the space), the Tax section will provide you with a general education about taxes, including specifics of some of the basic and more important federal laws.

Even if you take your tax problems to an accountant, I think you should familiarize yourself with the information in this tax section. There is more to taxes than just filling out the tax forms every April 15. Many of the tax laws outlined in this section relate directly to every-day management of your business. The federal income tax laws affect your bookkeeping and, through a knowledge of which expenditures are and are not tax deductible, your business profit. What's more, you will be of greater help to your tax accountant, which means your tax accountant can be of greater help to you, if you have at least some familiarity with the federal income tax laws. In fact, the information here may help you think of some tax savings that your accountant may have overlooked.

The Tax Laws As They Apply to You

Many of the federal tax laws are designed solely to keep you from cheating the government out of what they think is rightfully theirs—your money. But a lot of these laws were enacted to save you money, to give you some sort of tax break. The Internal Revenue Service does make an effort, albeit a lame one, to educate people about beneficial tax laws; but basically it's up to you to dig in and find out how to save yourself tax dollars. The problem is that income tax laws tend to overwhelm most people because of their complexity and because of their sheer volume: so many different possibilities, so many "if's, and's and but's."

A lot of special effort has been put into this section of the book to help you understand the tax laws without getting trapped in the octopus tentacles of exceptions. This is accomplished by a four- step procedure:

Step 1: The basic tax rules, those that apply to most small businesses, are explained as simply as possible in plain English; no accounting double-talk and no "if's, and's and but's."

Step 2: Following the basic rules, any special situations, exceptions, or tricky catches in the law are explained. This is designed so you can skim over them rapidly and spot an area that may apply to you.

Step 3: Unusual and complex rules, most of which apply only to a minority of people, are mentioned in order to alert you to their existence but are not explained in detail.

Step 4: Free sources of complete tax information are listed so that you can more thoroughly study the subjects you need to know.

A tax is a compulsory payment for which no specific benefit is received in return.

—*U.S. Treasury*

A Warning

This Tax section does *not* provide complete information on all federal tax laws nor was it ever intended to. It is meant to be a general guideline to help you wade through the maze of rules and regulations that our government in its wisdom has seen fit to enact into law. And remember, tax laws are in a constant state of change. Never assume that any tax law in effect last year is going to be in effect this year. It is your responsibility, and it could be to your benefit financially, to keep abreast of current tax law.

As additional help, you should get a copy of the IRS's *Tax Guide For Small Business* (Publication #334), free from any IRS office, along with a list of their other free small business publications. These are all excellent and reliable references. You can find many of these tax publications on the IRS's web site www.irs.gov. If you use the IRS's tax guides in conjunction with *Small Time Operator* you shouldn't go wrong. (Hopefully.)

The IRS has a toll free help number just for small businesses, 800-829-4933, but a warning about IRS telephone help: Although IRS publications are usually accurate and reliable, the same cannot always be said of tax information the IRS gives out over the phone or in person. The IRS people do, on occasion, give out totally incorrect information. Tax laws are vastly complicated and even the experts make mistakes. Do not rely on verbal information unless you can verify it. Ask the IRS person for a reference in one of their other publications, and look it up.

Keep in mind that these are federal laws, applicable to federal tax returns. For state returns, most state income tax laws are similar or identical to these federal laws; but some states have different laws, different ways to compute depreciation, different deductions allowed or not allowed. Study the instructions that come with your state tax forms. You might find additional state deductions that the IRS does not allow, and save some money on your state taxes. State taxes are covered at the end of this section.

It's an endless sequence of small details.
　　　　　—Business owner Kitson Logue

Accounting Period: Calendar Year vs. Fiscal Year

Every business must keep books and file tax returns based on what the IRS calls a "taxable year", which is either a "calendar year" or a "fiscal year." A calendar year begins on January 1 and ends on December 31. A fiscal year is a twelve month period ending on the last day of any month other than December.

Most small businesses use a calendar year simply because it's easier. All of the federal and state tax procedures are geared to the calendar year: issuance of W-2's, 1099's and dividend and interest statements, and publication of the new tax forms and instructions.

The calendar year is also preferred by the Internal Revenue Service. They have strict and rather complex rules about who can adopt a fiscal year and when the decision must be made. The rules vary depending on how your business is legally structured.

Generally, sole proprietorships must use the same taxable year as the owner, which means the calendar year in most cases. The same rule applies to partnerships, S corporations, Limited Liability Companies (LLCs) and personal service corporations (corporations that primarily sell services performed by the owner-employees). The IRS will allow these businesses to adopt a fiscal year if there is a valid business reason for using a fiscal year. File form #8716, "Election to Have a Tax Year Other Than a Required Tax Year." Regular corporations can choose either a calendar or a fiscal year.

Why choose a fiscal year at all? Some businesses have definite yearly cycles and find that coordinating their taxable year with the business cycle better reflects actual income and expenses. Large retail stores have traditionally chosen a January 31 fiscal year so they can have their January clearance sales, to reduce their stock of merchandise on hand, thereby making the year-end inventory count much easier and less expensive. Corporations sometimes choose a fiscal year coinciding with the month the business first began operation, in order to avoid a short-period tax return and extra taxes the first year.

The tax laws discussed in this tax section apply to both calendar year and fiscal year taxpayers, except where otherwise noted.

Who Must File A Tax Return

Sole proprietors must file a federal income tax return if your *net* earnings from self-employment (your business *net* profit) is $400 or more. Business income minus expenses equals *net* profit.

Your income is taxable to you regardless of the source, even if received from a non-profit corporation or other tax-exempt organization.

Partnerships, corporations and LLCs must file a return no matter what the profit or loss is.

Income tax returns can be filed by mail or over the Internet (www.irs.gov).

Which Tax Return To File

Sole Proprietors: Most sole proprietors will have to fill out a Schedule C, "Profit or Loss From Business." Schedule C is part of your regular 1040 return. The profit or loss on Schedule C is combined with any other taxable income or loss on your 1040. If you have more than one business, file a separate Schedule C for each business.

Some very small service businesses may only need to fill out the much simpler Schedule C-EZ, "Net Profit From Business," which truly is "EZ": one total figure for gross income, one total figure for expenses, and your net profit. That, and a few questions about your vehicle, is it. Schedule C-EZ can only be used by sole proprietors who meet all nine of the following requirements:

1. Business expenses of $2,500 or less.
2. No inventory at any time during the year.
3. Did not have a net loss.
4. Had no employees.
5. Deducted no depreciation, amortization, or first year write-off of depreciable assets.
6. Deducted no expenses for a home office.
7. Used the cash method of accounting.
8. Cannot own more than one sole proprietorship.
9. No prior year passive activity losses (if you don't know what that means, you probably didn't have any).

Partnerships and LLCs: File Form 1065, "U.S. Partnership Return of Income." No taxes are due with this return. Each partner or LLC member gets a copy of Schedule K-1 (1065), "Partner's Share of Income, Credits, Deductions, Etc." Partners and owners of LCCs report their individual share of the business income, whether distributed to them or not, on their 1040 return, using Schedule E, "Supplemental Income and Loss." (LLCs are taxed as partnerships by the IRS, so all federal partnership tax laws apply to LLCs.)

Corporations: Regular C corporations report income and pay taxes on Form 1120 or 1120-A. S corporations file Form 1120-S, but like partnerships, pay no income taxes. Each S corporation shareholder gets a copy of Schedule K-1 (1120-S), "Shareholder's Share of Income, Credits, Deductions, Etc." Shareholders report their individual share of the S corporation income on their 1040 return, using Schedule E, "Supplemental Income and Loss."

More Than One Business

If you have more than one business, you fill out a separate tax return for each business.

If your businesses are all sole proprietorships, you might consider combining them so they are one business, and file one Schedule C tax return. Your income and self-employment taxes will be exactly the same whether you have one or multiple sole proprietorships. There are advantages and disadvantages to setting up multiple businesses, covered in the Your Business section.

If any of your businesses are partnerships, corporations or LLCs, each business must have its own tax return.

People will do silly things to avoid taxes
—J. C. Small, attorney, N.J. Division of Taxation

Filing Dates for Tax Returns

For calendar-year businesses other than corporations, the federal income tax return is due April 15. For corporations, due date is March 15.

Automatic extensions to file returns (but not to pay the taxes):

Sole proprietors, members of LLCs and partners in partnerships (not the partnership itself) can obtain an automatic four-month extension, to August 15, by filing IRS Form #4868, or calling toll free 888-796-1074, and paying the estimated tax due, on or before April 15.

Beyond the automatic four-month extension, the IRS will sometimes allow an additional two-month extension, to October 15, but only for "very good reasons" (those are the IRS's words, and they make the decision). File Form #2688, but only after you first file Form #4868.

Corporations can obtain an automatic six-month extension, to September 15, by filing Form #7004 and paying the estimated tax due, by the March 15 due date.

Partnerships and LLCs can obtain an automatic three-month extension, to July 15, by filing Form #8736 by April 15. Since partnerships and LLCs pay no income taxes, no taxes are due with the extension. Partners and LLC members file their own personal extensions on Form #4868.

All the above extensions (except Form #2688) must be filed by the original due date of the return and must include payment for all taxes due. If you underpay your taxes by more than 10%, the IRS will hit you with a penalty.

Fiscal year taxpayers: For businesses other than corporations, the federal income tax return is due on the fifteenth day of the fourth month following the end of the fiscal year. Corporate returns are due on the fifteenth day of the third month. The same extensions described above are available to fiscal-year businesses.

State tax returns: Many states offer extensions of time to file state returns. Some states go by the federal rules, but some are different. Check your state income tax instruction book.

Just remember, the business belongs to you, not your accountant.   —Columnist Gloria Marullo

TAX CALENDAR for Businesses

The tax calendar lists due dates for federal and state tax reports. Each date shown is the last day on which to perform the required action without penalty. If the due date for filing a return, making a tax payment, etc. falls on a Saturday, Sunday or legal holiday, the date is moved to the next regular work day.

Tax deposits that are due weekly and monthly throughout the year are listed at the end of the calendar.

To help you spot the dates applicable to your business, the first word in each description will tell who the information applies to, such as Employers, Corporations, etc. "Individuals" refers to sole proprietors, partners (not partnerships), corporate stockholders (not the corporations), and LLC members (not the LLCs).

These dates apply to calendar year taxpayers. Businesses using a fiscal year must change some of the dates (see the end of the calendar).

These dates don't usually change from year to year, but they can. Verify them before relying on them.

JANUARY 1-MARCH 16

Corporations that meet certain requirements may elect to be treated as S corporations during current and future years. Use Form 2553. This deadline may be extended to 24 months under certain circumstances.

JANUARY 15

Individuals either pay the balance due on prior year's estimated income tax or file an income tax return (Form 1040) on or before January 31 and pay the full amount of the tax due. See January 31.

Farmers and fishermen may elect to file declaration of estimated income tax (Form 1040-ES) for prior year and pay estimated tax in full, and file income tax return (Form 1040) by April 15. If declaration of estimated tax is not filed, see February 28.

JANUARY 31

Individuals should file an income tax return for prior year and pay the tax due, if the balance on their prior year's estimated tax was not paid by January 15. Use Form 1040. Farmers and fishermen, see February 28.

Employers last day for giving every employee Form W-2 showing income and social security information. Also see February 28.

Employers deposit federal unemployment tax (FUTA) at an authorized bank if the tax is more than

$100. If the amount is $100 or less, you are not required to deposit it, but you add it to the taxes for the next quarter. Then, in the next quarter, if the total undeposited tax is more than $100, deposit it by the last day of the month following the quarter. Use Form 8109.

Employers file Form 941 for income tax withheld and social security and Medicare taxes for the fourth quarter of the prior year and pay any taxes due. If timely deposits were made, see February 10.

Businesses liable for excise taxes file quarterly excise tax return. Use Form 720.

Employers subject to federal unemployment tax file annual return for the prior year. Use Form 940. If timely deposits were made in full payment of the tax, see February 10.

All businesses: most state sales tax returns for the 4th quarter of last year are due.

Corporations that paid $10 or more in dividends or interest, prepare Form 1099 and give one copy to each recipient. See also February 28.

All businesses that paid $600 or more to an individual in commissions, fees or other compensation, prepare Form 1099 and give one copy to each recipient. See also February 28.

All businesses that sold $5,000 or more of goods to independent sales agents, prepare Form 1099 and give one copy to each agent. See also February 28.

All businesses that paid $600 or more in interest prepare form 1099-INT and give one copy to each recipient. See also February 28.

All businesses that paid $10 or more in royalties prepare Form 1099-MISC and give one copy to each recipient. See also February 28.

Operators of fishing boats give each self-employed crew member a statement showing member's share for the year, using Form 1099-MISC. See also February 28.

FEBRUARY 10

Employers who made timely deposits in full payment of all income taxes withheld and social security and Medicare taxes due for the 4th quarter of the prior year file 4th quarter return. Use Form 941.

Employers subject to federal unemployment tax who made timely deposits in full payment of the tax file annual return for the prior year. Use Form 940.

FEBRUARY 28

All businesses that prepared Form 1099 (See Jan. 31) file the 1099's with transmittal Form 1096 with IRS. If filed by computer, due date extended to March 31.

Employers file Form W-3, Transmittal of Income and Tax Statements, with the Social Security Administration if you have issued Form W-2 (See Jan. 31). Copy A of each W-2 accompany Form W-3.

Employers whose employees receive tips report those tips on Form 8027.

Farmers and fishermen who did not file declaration of estimated tax on January 15 should file final income tax return (Form 1040) for prior year.

MARCH 15

Corporations file federal income tax return, Form 1120, or application for extension, Form 7004, and pay to a depositary the balance of tax still due.

S Corporations file federal income tax Form 1120S.

Corporations file state income tax returns for the following states: Ala., Alaska, Ark., Calif., D.C., Ill., Maine, Mass., Md., Minn., Miss., Nebr., N.H., N. Mex., N.Y., N.C., Okla., R.I., S.C., Vt., W. Va., Wis.

MARCH 31

All businesses: Electronic filing of Form 1099.

Corporations file state income tax returns for the following states: Conn., Del., Fla., Ohio, Tenn.

APRIL 15

Individuals file a federal income tax return for the prior calendar year. The tax due must be paid in full with this return. File Schedule C or C-EZ (Schedule F for farmers), and Schedule SE. If you desire an automatic 4-month extension, file Form 4868 accompanied by payment of your estimated unpaid income tax liability.

Individuals file a declaration of estimated income tax (including self-employment tax) for the current year and pay at least 25 percent of such tax. Use Form 1040-ES.

Partnerships and LLCs file a return for the prior calendar year. Use Form 1065 (no tax due).

Corporations deposit first installment of this year's estimated income tax.

Individuals file a state income tax return for all states collecting income tax except Del., Hawaii, Va., La., and Iowa.

Corporations file state income tax returns for the following states: Ariz., Colo., Ga., Idaho, Ind., Kans., Ky., Mo., N.J., N.D., Ore., Pa., Utah, Va., La.

APRIL 20

Individuals in Hawaii file state income tax return.

Corporations in Hawaii file state income tax returns.

APRIL 30

Individuals living in Del., Va. or Iowa file a state income tax return.

Corporations in Mich. and Iowa file state income tax returns.

All businesses: most states sales tax returns for the first quarter are due.

Employers file Form 941 for income tax withheld, Social Security and Medicare taxes for the 1st quarter, and pay taxes due. If timely deposits were made, see May 10.

Employers deposit federal unemployment tax (FUTA) at an authorized bank if the tax is more than $100. If the amount is $100 or less, you are not required to deposit it, but you must add it to the taxes for the next quarter. Then, in the next quarter, if the total undeposited tax is more than $100, deposit it by the last day of the month following the quarter. Use Form 8109.

Businesses liable for excise taxes file quarterly excise tax return. Use Form 720.

MAY 10

Employers who made timely deposits in full payment of income tax, Social Security and Medicare taxes for the 1st quarter, file 1st quarter return. Use Form 941.

MAY 15

Individuals in La file state income tax returns.

Corporations in Mont. file state income tax returns.

JUNE 15

Individuals pay 2nd installment of estimated income tax.

Corporations deposit second installment of estimated income tax.

JULY 31

Employers file Form 941 for income tax withheld and Social Security and Medicare taxes for the 2nd quarter and pay any taxes due. If timely deposits were made, see August 10.

Businesses liable for excise taxes file quarterly excise tax return. Use Form 720.

Employers deposit federal unemployment tax (FUTA) at an authorized bank if the tax is more than $100. If the amount is $100 or less, you are not required to deposit it, but you must add it to the taxes for the next quarter. Then, in the next quarter, if the total undeposited tax is more than $100, deposit it by the last day of the month following the quarter. Use Form 8109.

All businesses: most state sales tax returns for the 2nd quarter are due.

Employers with an employee benefit, pension, profit sharing, or stock bonus plan, file Form 5500 for the previous calendar year.

AUGUST 10

Employers who made timely deposits in full payment of all income tax withheld and Social Security and Medicare taxes due for the 2nd quarter, file 2nd quarter return. Use Form 941.

AUGUST 15

Individuals who received an automatic 4-month extension for filing last year's federal income tax return must now file the return. Form 1040.

AUGUST 31

Heavy-duty truck owners and operators pay the federal use tax on highway motor vehicles used on the public highways. Use Form 2290.

SEPTEMBER 15

Individuals pay 3rd installment of estimated income tax. Use Form 1040-ES.

Corporations deposit 3rd installment of estimated income tax.

Corporations that received an automatic 6-month extension for filing last year's federal income tax return must now file the return, on Form 1120, 1120-A or 1120-S.

OCTOBER 31

Employers file Form 941 for income tax withheld and social security and Medicare taxes for the 3rd quarter and pay any taxes due. If timely deposits were made, see November 10.

All businesses: most state sales tax returns for the 3rd quarter are due.

Businesses liable for excise taxes file quarterly excise tax return. Use Form 720.

Employers deposit federal unemployment tax (FUTA) at an authorized bank if the tax is more than $100. If the amount is $100 or less, you are not required to deposit it, but you must add it to the taxes for the next quarter. Then, in the next quarter, if the total undeposited tax is more than $100, deposit it by the last day of the month following the quarter. Use Form 8109.

NOVEMBER

Employers should request a new Form W-4 from each employee whose withholding exemptions will be different next year.

NOVEMBER 10

Employers who made timely deposits in full payment of income tax withheld and social security and Medicare taxes due for the 3rd quarter, file 3rd quarter return. Use Form 941.

DECEMBER 15

Corporations deposit the 4th installment of estimated income tax.

WEEKLY AND MONTHLY ALL YEAR

Corporations that meet certain requirements may elect, any time during the year, to be treated as S corporations in future years. Use Form 2553. To be treated as an S corporation this year, see Jan. 1.

Employers: tax deposits of social security and Medicare (NOT self-employment) and withheld income taxes required monthly (by the 15th of the following month) whenever amount due is $500 or more; required 8 times a month whenever amounts due are $3000 or more.

Businesses liable for excise taxes are required to make monthly deposits on the last day of the month when more than $100 in excise taxes is collected. For more information, see IRS publication #510.

FISCAL YEAR TAXPAYERS

Individuals: federal tax return 1040 is due the 15th day of the 4th month after the end of your tax year.

Partnerships and LLCs: federal tax return 1065 is due the 15th day of the 4th month after the end of your tax year.

Corporations: federal income tax return 1120 or 1120-S is due the 15th day of the 3rd month after the end of your tax year.

All fiscal year businesses: many states follow the same schedule as the federal government for filing state income tax returns, but some states have different dates. Consult your own state.

Individuals: federal estimated tax payments are due on the 15th day of the 4th, 6th, and 9th months of your tax year, and on the 15th day of the first month after your tax year.

Corporations: federal estimated tax payments are due on the 15th day of the 4th, 6th, 9th and 12th months of your tax year.

Corporations electing to be S Corporations file Form 2553 by the 15th day of the 3rd month of the tax year.

Employers maintaining an employee benefit, pension, profit sharing, or stock bonus plan, file Form 5500 by the last day of the 7th month following the end of the taxable year.

BUSINESS EXPENSES

All legitimate business expenses, except those specifically disallowed by law (covered later), are deductible in computing your taxable income, as long as they meet the IRS's three basic rules:

One: The expenses must be "ordinary." "Ordinary" expenses are ones that are common or accepted in your type of business. They do not have to be recurring or habitual.

Two: The expenses must be "necessary." A "necessary expense," according to the IRS, is one "that is appropriate and helpful in developing and maintaining your trade or business." The word "necessary" in this context of IRS tax law, does not have the same definition we usually associate with "necessary," as in "required," "indispensable," "must be done." It is not necessary that you buy nice stationery. It is not necessary that you air condition your office. These are not mandatory requirements of your business, but they pass the "necessary" test.

Three: The expenses must be "reasonable," or, to quote the IRS, "not be lavish or extravagant under the circumstances."

Defining what is or is not "lavish or extravagant under the circumstances" depends on, well, depends on the circumstances. The bigger the business and the more income the business earns, the more likely you can deduct large amounts of money and call the expenses "not lavish or extravagant under the circumstances."

Full time, ongoing businesses can usually get away with a bit more lavishness than part time and new businesses.

Expenditures that are partly personal (non-business) and partly business can be prorated and the business portion expensed or depreciated. Sometimes your home or your automobile fall in this category. Business expenses that you pay on your personal credit card are fully deductible.

Any asset that you originally purchased for non-business purposes or before going into business, that you are now using for business or using partly for business, can be depreciated as of the date you began using the asset in your business. See the "Depreciation" chapter.

Try to get receipts for everything, and keep them. Receipts are your best documentation should questions come up or if you are audited.

Partners in partnerships, and owners of corporations and LLCs: Try not to pay business expenses out of your personal funds. Business deductions are sometimes disallowed when claimed by owners or employees, instead of by the companies themselves. If you do pay any business expenses out of your own pocket, have the business reimburse you, so the business itself can claim the deductions.

Multiple businesses: If you have more than one business, shared expenses (such as the same office, telephone, computer, etc.) should be split between the businesses. 50%-50% (if you have two businesses) is common, but you can use any reasonable percentage that reflects how much each businesses uses.

Prepaid Expenses

Most prepaid expenses are deductible the year paid, as long as they do not extend beyond twelve months. So, for example, if you pay an insurance bill in December that is good until the following December, you can deduct the entire bill when you pay it, even though only one month of it applies to the current year. Prepaid expenses that extend beyond twelve months must be prorated; only the current year's portion can be deducted.

This twelve-month rule is new. The IRS has previously stated that prepaid rent, prepaid property taxes, and prepaid interest are not deductible until the year to which they apply. The IRS has not yet changed its written rules, so check with your accountant before deducting prepaid expenses.

Start-Up Expenses

Business expenses incurred before you start your business (called start-up expenses, though they are really pre-start-up expenses) come under two different tax rules.

General preliminary costs incurred before you actually pick a specific business, such as investigating different business possibilities, are usually not deductible at all. The IRS considers these "personal expenses," no tax write-off ever.

Once you've decided on a particular business, the start-up expenses (not including the general preliminary costs mentioned above) are deductible, but not 100% the year you incur them. You have the option to capitalize them, which means no deduction at all until you quit or sell your business; or to write them off ("amortize" them) over a 60-month period, or longer if you prefer, starting the first month the business is open.

To figure your deduction, divide your total start-up costs by the number of months in the write-off period (60 or more). The result is the amount you can deduct each month. Use Form 4562, the part labeled "Amortization," to show your calculations. You must file this form your first year in business. Otherwise, you lose the op-

tion and will be required to capitalize the start-up expenses.

Start-up expenses are a real sore spot for new businesses, because the expenses include any and all business expenditures incurred before you are open for business. They include organizational expenses, such as hiring a lawyer to draft up legal documents; and even conventional pre-opening expenses such as rent, telephone, advertising, stationery, etc.

The IRS has often wrangled with taxpayers over which costs are and aren't "start-up," and at what point a new venture is actually "in business." The IRS has stated that a business hasn't actually started until it produces income. Tax Courts have disagreed and have ruled that once a business is set up and "open for business," it is officially started even if it has not made a sale yet. This is an area to discuss with an accountant. I suggest you put off as many expenses as possible until after the business is operating.

One way around some of the start-up expense hassles is to start your business at home if that's feasible, just as small an operation as possible to meet IRS requirements. Once you have generated a little income, *then* spend your money on finding a new location, on stationery, furniture and equipment, and on accounting and legal advice. Since you are now officially in business, the expenses are deductible as regular business expenses, no longer subject to the start-up rules.

If you do incur start-up expenses but never actually start a business, the expenses may, in some situations, be deductible as a capital loss. You will probably need an accountant's help.

If You Already Are In Business: If you are expanding a business, adding a new outlet, adding a new division, etc., it is not considered a start-up. The expenses are deductible. If you are starting a second business, if possible try to structure it as an expansion of your current business to avoid these start-up rules.

100 Typical Business Expenses

Below is a listing of over 100 typical business expenses that can be deducted on your income tax return. If you would like a much more extensive list of deductions, my book *422 Tax Deductions For Businesses and Self Employed Individuals* (Bell Springs Publishing, 800-515-8050)

SCHEDULE C
(Form 1040)

Department of the Treasury
Internal Revenue Service (0)

Profit or Loss From Business
(Sole Proprietorship)

► Partnerships, joint ventures, etc., must file Form 1065 or 1065-B.
► Attach to Form 1040 or 1041. ► See Instructions for Schedule C (Form 1040).

OMB No. 1545-0074

Attachment
Sequence No. **09**

Name of proprietor	Social security number (SSN)
Samuel Thesham	123 45 6789

A Principal business or profession, including product or service (see page C-2 of the instructions)
pinball machine sales and repair
B Enter code from pages C-7, 8, & 9 ► 4 5 3 9 9 0

C Business name. If no separate business name, leave blank.
Bell Springs Pinball
D Employer ID number (EIN), if any

E Business address (including suite or room no.) ► P.O. Box 1240, Willits CA 95490
City, town or post office, state, and ZIP code

F Accounting method: (1) ☒ Cash (2) ☐ Accrual (3) ☐ Other (specify) ► ....
G Did you "materially participate" in the operation of this business during 2003? If "No," see page C-3 for limit on losses   ☒ Yes ☐ No
H If you started or acquired this business during 2003, check here .... ► ☐

Part I Income

1 Gross receipts or sales. Caution. If this income was reported to you on Form W-2 and the "Statutory employee" box on that form was checked, see page C-3 and check here ► ☐	1	$32,364
2 Returns and allowances	2	0
3 Subtract line 2 from line 1	3	$32,364
4 Cost of goods sold (from line 42 on page 2)	4	2,008
5 Gross profit. Subtract line 4 from line 3	5	$30,356
6 Other income, including Federal and state gasoline or fuel tax credit or refund (see page C-3)	6	0
7 Gross income. Add lines 5 and 6	7	$30,356

Part II Expenses. Enter expenses for business use of your home only on line 30.

8 Advertising	8	150	19 Pension and profit-sharing plans	19	
9 Car and truck expenses (see page C-3)	9	480	20 Rent or lease (see page C-5):		
			a Vehicles, machinery, and equipment	20a	
10 Commissions and fees	10		b Other business property	20b	4,850
11 Contract labor (see page C-4)	11		21 Repairs and maintenance	21	218
12 Depletion	12		22 Supplies (not included in Part III)	22	1,218
13 Depreciation and section 179 expense deduction (not included in Part III) (see page C-4)	13	136	23 Taxes and licenses	23	1,267
			24 Travel, meals, and entertainment:		
14 Employee benefit programs (other than on line 19)	14		a Travel	24a	
15 Insurance (other than health)	15	650	b Meals and entertainment		
16 Interest:			c Enter nondeductible amount included on line 24b (see page C-5)		
a Mortgage (paid to banks, etc.)	16a		d Subtract line 24c from line 24b	24d	
b Other	16b	637	25 Utilities	25	221
17 Legal and professional services	17		26 Wages (less employment credits)	26	
18 Office expense	18	78	27 Other expenses (from line 48 on page 2)	27	70

28 Total expenses before expenses for business use of home. Add lines 8 through 27 in columns ►	28	9,757
29 Tentative profit (loss). Subtract line 28 from line 7	29	20,599
30 Expenses for business use of your home. Attach Form 8829	30	
31 Net profit or (loss). Subtract line 30 from line 29.	31	$20,599

- If a profit, enter on Form 1040, line 12, and also on Schedule SE, line 2 (statutory employees, see page C-6). Estates and trusts, enter on Form 1041, line 3.
- If a loss, you must go to line 32.

32 If you have a loss, check the box that describes your investment in this activity (see page C-6).
- If you checked 32a, enter the loss on Form 1040, line 12, and also on Schedule SE, line 2 (statutory employees, see page C-6). Estates and trusts, enter on Form 1041, line 3.
- If you checked 32b, you must attach Form 6198.

32a ☐ All investment is at risk.
32b ☐ Some investment is not at risk.

For Paperwork Reduction Act Notice, see Form 1040 instructions.   Cat. No. 11334P   Schedule C (Form 1040)

Schedule C (Form 1040)   Page **2**

Part III Cost of Goods Sold (see page C-7)

33 Method(s) used to value closing inventory: a ☒ Cost b ☐ Lower of cost or market c ☐ Other (attach explanation)

34 Was there any change in determining quantities, costs, or valuations between opening and closing inventory? If "Yes," attach explanation   ☐ Yes ☒ No

35 Inventory at beginning of year. If different from last year's closing inventory, attach explanation	35	$100
36 Purchases less cost of items withdrawn for personal use	36	1,958
37 Cost of labor. Do not include any amounts paid to yourself	37	
38 Materials and supplies	38	
39 Other costs	39	
40 Add lines 35 through 39	40	$2,058
41 Inventory at end of year	41	50
42 Cost of goods sold. Subtract line 41 from line 40. Enter the result here and on page 1, line 4	42	$2,008

Part IV Information on Your Vehicle. Complete this part ONLY if you are claiming car or truck expenses on line 10 and are not required to file Form 4562 for this business. See the instructions for line 13 on page C-4 to find out if you must file.

43 When did you place your vehicle in service for business purposes? (month, day, year) ► ... / ... / ...

44 Of the total number of miles you drove your vehicle during 1998, enter the number of miles you used your vehicle for:

a Business .... b Commuting .... c Other ....

45 Do you (or your spouse) have another vehicle available for personal use? .... ☐ Yes ☐ No
46 Was your vehicle available for use during off-duty hours? .... ☐ Yes ☐ No
47a Do you have evidence to support your deduction? .... ☐ Yes ☐ No
b If "Yes," is the evidence written? .... ☐ Yes ☐ No

Part V Other Expenses. List below business expenses not included on lines 8-26 or line 30.

Pinball repair manuals	$70
48 Total other expenses. Enter here and on page 1, line 27	48	$70

♻ Printed on recycled paper

---

lists and explains many more than I can fit into this book. Think of it this way: you get a raise every time you find a legitimate tax deduction! It's worth the hunting.

The expenses marked with an asterisk (*) are explained on the following pages. The number following each expense refers to the column number in the expenditure ledger, so you can tell at a glance in which column to post the expense. "Y/E" after an item means that the expense is recorded on the year-end summary only.

Any business expense that meets the IRS's basic rules (ordinary, necessary, and reasonable), if not specifically disallowed, should be taken whether it is on this list or not. Those expenses specifically disallowed are listed later in this section.

This listing is also a guide to filling out your income tax return. The Schedule C tax form, "Profit or Loss From Business," lists only 20 or so categories of expense. These are broad, general categories. There are many legitimate, deductible expenses not listed on the tax form.

To help you figure out your tax form, I've grouped the 100-plus expenses by tax return category.

But don't feel this is cemented in stone. It is not critical which expenses go on which lines on the tax form. The IRS is not going to be upset if an expense that belongs on one line winds up on another. Even I'm not sure whether some expenses should be called "office expenses" or "supplies." If you have an expense you don't know where to put on the tax return, just pick a reasonable category and put it there.

It is a good idea to make a worksheet showing which expenses you combined for the tax return, and keep it with your copy of your return (no need to send it to the IRS). This will make things a lot easier should you ever face an audit, or if you need to check your figures later, or if you are just looking back a year later trying to figure out how to fill out the next year's tax return.

The bold categories below are from a recent Schedule C, though there's no telling if the IRS will suddenly decide to redesign the tax form, *again*, and change these.

Advertising
Advertising (5)
Business gifts (5)*

Car and truck expenses
Vehicle expenses (9 or Y/E)*
If you rent or lease a vehicle, the expense goes under "Rent or lease," not here.

Commissions and fees
Commissions (3)
Consultant fees (3)

Contract labor
Independent and outside contractors (3)
Subcontractors (3)

Depreciation
Amortization of intangibles (Y/E)*
Equipment, machinery, tools (see Depreciation)
Office furniture (see Depreciation)
Software (Y/E)*

Insurance
Bonding fees (10)
Insurance (10)*

All deductible business insurance except health (unless incorporated as a C corporation), and vehicle (if taking the Standard Mileage Allowance or if included in "Car Expenses" above).

Interest
Interest on business debt (10)*

Legal and professional services
Accounting fees (3)
Auditing fees (3)
Bookkeeping services (3)
Burglar alarm service (10)
Cleaning services (3)
Collection agency fees (10)
Credit bureau fees (10)
Dues, business and professional associations (10)
Dues, union (10)
Employment agency fees (10)
Fees to organizations (10)
Internet and web host services (10)
Janitorial services (3)
Lawyers (3)
Legal expenses (10)
Merchant's associations (10)

Night watch service (10)
Professional organizations (10)
Security service (10)
Tax preparation (business portion only)(3)

Office expense
Bank service charges (2)
Books (2)
Business cards (2)
Coffee service (2)
Credit card fees (2)
Ledgers (2)
Office and computer supplies (2)
Postage (2)
Publications (2)
Safe deposit box (2)
Software (useful life one year or less)(2)*
Stationery (2)
This book (2)

Rent or lease
Rent (6)
Rent or lease of a vehicle goes in this category, not under "Car and Truck Expenses".

Repairs and maintenance
Minor repairs (10)*

Supplies
This category refers to industrial supplies. Office supplies should be included with "Office Expense." This "Supplies" category does not include manufacturing supplies or supplies that are part of inventory. Such supplies are part of the Cost of Goods Sold calculations.
Clothing, special (10)*
Shipping supplies (10) (but see Inventory)
Tools (small, useful life one year or less)(10)
Uniforms (10)

Taxes and licenses
Business license (8)
Employer's taxes (8)
Floor tax (8)*
Income taxes (state only)(8)*
Inventory tax (8)
Gross receipts tax (8)*
License fees (8)*
Passport fees (8)
Permit fees (8)
Property taxes (8)*
Sales tax (collected from customers)(8)*

Travel, meals and entertainment
Conventions (see Travel Away From Home)(10)*
Entertainment (10)*
Trade shows (see Travel Away From Home)(10)*
Travel away from home (10)*

Utilities
Electricity, heating, water (7)
Garbage (7)
Telephone (7, or its own column if you want to keep separate track of telephone bills).

Wages
Payroll (4)
Withheld payroll taxes (4)
Employee benefits
Employee pension and profit-sharing plans

Other expenses
Some casualty losses (burglary, vandalism, fire, storm, etc.) may be deductible here. See Casualty Losses (10 or elsewhere)*
Charitable contributions (corps. only)(10)*
Education expenses (10)*
Moving expenses (10)*
Research & experimentation (in some cases)(10)
Bad Debts (Y/E)*

Cost of goods sold
Cost of goods sold (1)*
Freight (see discussion)*
Inventory (1)*
Shipping (see discussion under Freight)(1 or 2)*

DEDUCTING BUSINESS EXPENSES

Below are explanations of some of the most common, and some of the most asked about, business expenses.

INVENTORY
and Something Very Important
Called Cost-Of-Goods-Sold

Inventory is merchandise—goods, products—held for sale in the normal course of business. Inventory also includes materials that will go into the making of a finished product, and work in process (partly finished goods you are making). Repair parts are considered inventory.

Inventory does not include tools, equipment, furniture, office supplies or anything purchased for reasons other than resale.

(If you have no inventory, if you do not sell goods or parts, you can skip this entire chapter).

Not all of your inventory purchases can be deducted as current year expenses. *Only the cost of those goods actually sold is deductible.* This is an important distinction; you should understand it completely. The cost of inventory *un*sold at year-end is an asset owned by you and will not be a deductible expense until sold (or until it becomes worthless; covered later in the chapter).

If you sell or manufacture goods, cost-of-goods-sold is your most important and usually your largest item of expense. The federal income tax form has two main categories of expense: (1) cost-of-goods-sold, and (2) all other. You will be required to show on your tax return how you calculated your cost-of-goods-sold.

Let's first use a simple example of cost-of-goods-sold. My friends John and Karen Resykle buy antiques and old clothes at garage sales and then resell the merchandise at a profit at flea markets. Last year, John and Karen purchased a total of $8,200 worth of merchandise (cost to them). At year-end, they still had $300 worth of merchandise on hand and unsold (again, at their cost, *not* the selling price). John and Karen's deductible cost-of-goods-sold is $7,900 ($8,200 purchased, less $300 unsold).

The above example assumes that there was no inventory on hand at the beginning of the year. Let's now say there was $400 on hand (their cost) at January 1. John and Karen's cost-of-goods-sold is now $8,300:

Inventory on hand at January 1	$ 400
Add: Inventory purch. during the year	8,200
Total inventory available for sale	$8,600
Subtract: Inventory on hand at Dec. 31	(300)
Cost-of-goods-sold	$8,300

Inventory On Hand At Start of Business

If you are starting a new business and already have inventory that you purchased before going into business, you can add the cost of that inventory (or the market value if less than cost) to the current year's purchases—even though you did not buy it this year—and include it in your cost-of-goods-sold calculations. Record this inventory in your expenditure ledger in Column #1 as "Inventory on hand at start of business."

Taking Inventory

As you can see, at the end of the year you need to make a list of inventory on hand. This is called "taking inventory" or "taking a physical inventory." (Business folk use the word "inventory" to refer both to the goods and to the procedure of counting the goods.) Do not value the inventory at sale price. The inventory should be valued at your cost. Cost includes sales tax if your paid sales tax and any shipping and handling charges.

Manufacturers and Crafts Businesses

For manufacturers and crafts businesses, computing the cost of your inventory will be a difficult task, for two reasons.

First, you calculate the cost not only of your raw materials but of your finished and partially finished goods as well. This will require a lot of educated guesswork—it always does. Value your inventory at its cost to you. That cost includes materials and paid labor. It does not include your own labor (unless you are an employee of your own corporation).

The second complication in computing cost-of-goods-sold is a nasty law called Uniform Capitalization Rules. The rules apply to all manufacturers and other businesses that, to quote the IRS, "construct, build, install, manufacture, develop, improve, create, raise, or grow property." Crafts businesses come under this rule. The term "manufacture" applies to making crafts.

Under Uniform Capitalization Rules, the cost of a manufacturer's inventory must include the cost of overhead attributable to the manufacturing operation. Such manufacturing overhead becomes part of the cost of the manufactured product, just like the cost of the materials, and cannot be deducted until the product is sold.

"Overhead" in this context is very broad and refers to almost everything related to manufacturing: repairs, maintenance, utilities, rent, indirect labor and production supervisory wages, indirect materials, tools and equipment, warehousing costs, administrative costs, insurance, taxes, employee benefits, you name it.

You only have to deal with the Uniform Capitalization Rules if you have goods that you have manufactured (finished or partly finished) on hand and unsold at the end of the year. If all your manufactured goods are sold, then all the overhead is also "sold" and can be fully deducted this year. The Uniform Capitalization Rules do not apply to inventory that has not yet been worked on (unused parts and raw materials). This untouched inventory is valued at its cost without adding these overhead costs.

I'll try a "simple" example. Let's say that the space in your shop is divided, half for manufacturing and half for sales. Your expenses for the year included $5,000 for rent and utilities (half of which is for manufacturing, half for sales), and $10,000 for inventory. At the beginning of the year, there was no inventory. At year-end, there was $1,000 (cost) on hand. Your cost-of-goods-sold is computed as follows:

Inventory on hand January 1	$0
Inventory purchased during year	10,000
One-half rent and utilities (manufacturing portion)	2,500
Cost of goods available for sale	$12,500
Subtract: inventory on hand Dec. 31	(1,000)
$1,000 is 10% of the inventory purchased during the year; therefore, 10% of the manufacturing portion of the overhead is also still "on hand". So you subtract 10% of the manufacturing half of rent and utilities	(250)
Cost-of-goods-sold	$11,250

This $1,250 inventory ($1,000 goods and $250 overhead) "on hand" at year-end will become the inventory on hand January 1 of the next year, to be written off next year when it is sold. This example assumes no other overhead expenses related to the inventory, no paid salaries in the manufacturing, no inventory stored in the sales area. These costs would have to be included in computing cost-of-goods-sold.

In the above example, the entire $1,000 inventory on hand at year-end is finished goods. Had it instead been untouched parts or materials, the entire $2,500 in manufacturing overhead could have been deducted instead of only $2,250.

If the $1,000 inventory included both manufactured goods and untouched inventory, well, as you probably already figured, the computations get all the more complicated (but relax, we won't go through them).

Artists, authors, composers, photographers and designers who sell original works are exempt from the Uniform Capitalization rules. The exemption applies only to original (one-of-a-kind) work. The exemption does not apply to reproductions, copies, published works, "limited editions," or other production pieces.

Inventory Loss of Value

In computing cost-of-goods-sold, inventory on hand at year-end is usually valued at its cost to you and not at its sales price, which normally is higher than its cost. If for any reason your year-end inventory is worth less than what you paid, the inventory should be valued at this lesser amount.

"Worth" refers to its retail value, what you can sell it for. Clothes no longer in fashion, obsolete goods, damaged or destroyed goods, broken lots and remnants, "excess inventory" (more than you can sell), goods unsalable for any reason—all such items should be reduced to their market (sales) value. If year-end inventory is totally worthless, it should be valued at zero. This inventory valuation method is known as "lower of cost or market."

You may have figured out by now that reducing the value of your inventory—"writing it off" as a loss—increases your expenses, thereby decreasing your profits and your taxes. Let's look again at our first example, John and Karen Resykle, the flea market entrepreneurs. Their purchases during the year were $8,200; cost of inventory on hand at year-end was $300. Originally, their cost-of-goods-sold was $7,900 ($8,200 less the $300 on hand). Karen finds, however, that she made some bad purchases, and the inventory on hand at year-end for which she paid $300 cannot be sold for more than $200. Year-end inventory is therefore reduced to $200, that being the lower of cost or market. The cost-of-goods-sold, instead of being $7,900, is now $8,000 ($8,200 purchased, less $200). The additional $100 cost-of-goods-sold increases deductible expenses by $100. Since John and Karen's income is unchanged, the additional expense reduces their profits by $100 and, therefore, reduces their taxes also.

If you do value your inventory at less than its cost, the IRS expects you to offer the devalued inventory for sale at the lower-than-market price, either before year-end or within thirty days after the year end. You don't have to actually sell the inventory if you cannot find a buyer, but you do need to offer it for sale.

Inventory Lost, Stolen or Given Away

The cost of stolen or missing inventory and the cost of samples given away are deductible as part of cost-of-goods-sold. This inventory is not on hand at year end, so it is not included in your year-end inventory count. Therefore, it automatically becomes part of your cost-of-goods-sold (even though it really wasn't sold—the term cost-of-goods-sold really should be "cost of goods sold, lost, stolen, given away, damaged, unsalable, etc."). No additional write-off is allowed.

Inventory Valuation—LIFO and FIFO

Businesses may value inventory using the first-in, first-out method (FIFO), which is calculated as though the oldest inventory is sold first and the newest inventory is on the shelves; or the last-in, first-out method (LIFO), which is calculated as though the newly purchased inventory is sold before the older inventory. The actual inventory on hand doesn't have to actually correspond to the method you choose. You can sell your inventory first-in, first-out yet account for it using the LIFO method, and vice-versa.

Most businesses use the FIFO method. It is easier to calculate and the IRS rules are straightforward. LIFO calculations can get confusing. I suggest you ask your accountant if you should consider the LIFO Method.

Consignment

Consigned inventory is merchandise a business or an individual places with another business for the other business to try to sell. A dress maker may consign inventory to a dress shop. The person consigning the goods (the dress maker) has not made a sale and does not get paid until the business that has taken the goods in on consignment (the dress shop) sells the goods.

For tax and inventory purposes, the consignor (in our example, the dress maker) has not sold the dress. There is no income to report. The dress should be included in the dress maker's year-end inventory. The consignee (the dress shop) has not purchased the dress until it re-sells the dress to its customer. The dress shop does not include the dress in its year-end inventory.

Consignors should be warned that these consignment laws are income tax laws only. They may not hold up in bankruptcy court. If the dress shop files for bankruptcy before it sells the dress, the court can seize and sell consigned inventory to pay off the creditors of the dress shop, even though the shop doesn't legally own the goods. The dress maker will have to stand in line with all the other creditors hoping to get paid.

The dress maker may be able to protect herself by filing a UCC #1 Form (UCC stands for Uniform Commercial Code) with the county or state where the dress shop is located. This is a legal notice that the goods belong to the dress maker and not to the dress shop. It will usually hold up in bankruptcy court, enabling the consignor to get the unsold merchandise back.

If the dress was sold by the dress shop, but the shop filed for bankruptcy before paying the dress maker, the courts hold that this was a sale, that the dress maker is just another creditor who probably will never see her money. The UCC #1 filing will not help in this situation.

BUSINESS ASSETS

Business assets—equipment, machinery, furniture, vehicles, buildings, etc.—can be depreciated (written off over several years), or if the assets meet certain requirements, can be written off the year of purchase. The assets are called capital, or fixed, or depreciable assets.

This chapter covers first-year write off of assets. The next chapter covers depreciation.

Most business assets except buildings can be written off (with limitations) the year of purchase: machinery, equipment, tools, furniture, fixtures, display cases, computers, faxes, copiers, software, some leasehold improvements (parts of the interior of buildings), and some vehicles. The IRS calls these assets "Section 1245 Property."

The first year write off is optional. If you prefer, you can depreciate the assets instead of writing them off (more on this below).

There are two separate first-year write-offs allowed. The first write-off is called the Section 179 Deduction (also called the Expensing Allowance, or Expensing Election). The second write-off, which can be taken in addition to the Section 179 Deduction, is the 50% First-Year Special Depreciation Allowance.

Section 179 Deduction

The total Section 179 write-off, all assets combined, cannot exceed $102,000 in any one year (2004 maximum; the maximum changes from year to year). Both new and used assets qualify as long as they were purchased for the business and not before going into business.

This write-off rule does *not* apply to intangible assets such as patents, copyrights, trademarks, goodwill, etc.; to inventory, parts, or office supplies; or to buildings (two exceptions: some livestock and horticultural structures and some storage buildings can be written off).

Here are the requirements:

1. If you have more than one unincorporated business, the $102,000 is the maximum for all combined businesses.

2. Married couples are allowed a maximum write-off of $102,000 between them.

3. If you purchase more than $410,000 in depreciable assets in any one year, the $102,000 maximum is reduced, dollar for dollar, by the amount in excess of $410,000.

4. The write-off cannot exceed your total taxable income. For sole proprietors, total taxable income is all income, both business and non-business, reported on your tax return (husband and wife combined if filing jointly). Any write-off disallowed because of this income limitation can be carried forward to the next year, and future years if necessary, until the assets are fully written off. But you must elect the write-off the year the assets are acquired in order to get the carry-forward. Use Form 4562.

5. If an asset is used partly for business and partly for personal, non-business use, the business portion can be written off, but only if the asset is used more than 50% for business the first year. If the asset is used 50% or less for business the first year, you are not eligible for this Section 179 deduction.

6. Automobiles, even if used 100% for business, have a maximum Sec. 179 deduction. See

"Limitations on Automobiles" below. Trucks and heavy SUVs are not subject to this limitation.

7. Assets converted to business use, owned before going into business, are not eligible.

8. Assets bought one year but paid for in the next year, and assets bought in installments with payments over more than one year, can be written off under Section 179 the year you acquire and use the assets, even if you are on the cash basis.

9. If you sell assets you've previously written off, or convert them to non-business use, you may have to "recapture" the amount you wrote off (add it back into income) the year of sale or conversion, depending on how many years you own the asset. See "Selling An Asset" in the "Depreciation" chapter below.

50% Depreciation Allowance

If you purchase more assets than the maximum allowed under Section 179 above ($102,000 for 2004), you can deduct an additional 50% of the remaining cost of the assets the first year. This is known as the Special Depreciation Allowance, and it is quite special if your business buys expensive machinery and equipment.

For example, lets say that this year you bought business assets costing a total of $150,000. Under Section 179, you can write-off $102,000. That leaves $48,000 to depreciate ($150,000 less $102,000).

Under the 50% Allowance, you can also write-off 50% of the that remaining $48,000 (another $24,000) the first year. So, the total first-year write off allowed is $126,000 ($102,000 plus $24,000). The balance of the $150,000 purchase, $24,000, must be depreciated (explained below).

Assets eligible for the 50% Depreciation Allowance must meet the same requirements as Section 179 with two important exceptions:

(1) Only new assets are eligible. Assets purchased second-hand are eligible for the Section 179 Deduction but not for the additional 50% Depreciation Allowance.

(2) Assets purchased before going into business are eligible for this 50% deduction but not for the Section 179 deduction.

This 50% Allowance is scheduled to expire December 31, 2004, unless extended by Congress.

Both of the first-year write-offs (the Sec. 179 Deduction and the 50% Depreciation Allowance) are optional. If you prefer, you can depreciate some or all of these assets over a period of years rather than write them off the year of purchase.

Why would anyone choose complex, multi-year depreciation over this simple, write-it-off-now deduction? Many businesses make little or no profit the first year or two and may not have any use for the additional tax savings the write-off offers. It might be better to depreciate the assets, deducting the bulk of the expense in future years when you can use it to save taxes. You might want to calculate your profit and taxes under both methods to find the bigger tax savings.

You can write off some assets and depreciate others. It is not all-one-way or all-the-other.

You fill out IRS Form 4562, Depreciation and Amortization. For more information, see IRS Publication 946, "How to Depreciate Property."

Any assets ineligible for the Sec. 179 write-off or for the 50% deduction, or in excess of the maximums, must be depreciated. See below.

DEPRECIATION

Depreciation is a tax term and means that the tax deduction for an asset you purchase is spread out over several years. Each year, a portion of the cost is deducted. The assets are variously called fixed, capital, or depreciable assets. The same rules apply to both new and used assets.

The assets described above under Business Assets—equipment, furniture, vehicles, etc.—are depreciable assets. Buildings are depreciable assets. Major improvements and major repairs that increase the value or that extend the life of an asset are considered depreciable assets.

All office supplies and all inventory, regardless of cost, are not depreciable assets and may not be depreciated. Inexpensive tools and equipment should not be depreciated, but should be deducted as an expense the year purchased.

Some special rules:

Buildings: If your business is located in a building that you own, you can depreciate the portion of the building being used for business (including your home if you meet the home office requirements). If you rent, the rent is a direct expense; there is no need to compute building depreciation.

Leasehold Improvements: Components of a building that are not structural, such as portable air conditioning, some fixtures, support for heavy machinery, partitions, awnings, etc. are known as "leasehold improvements" (even though they are not leased). Leasehold improvements can be depreciated over a much shorter time than buildings, and may be eligible for the First Year Write Off. When you purchase a building, separate out the cost of the leasehold improvements in order to get faster write-offs.

Land: While a building can be depreciated, the land the building sits on cannot. Land is considered a permanent asset that cannot be expensed until sold. If the cost of land and building are not separately stated, most accountants figure 80% of the cost was the building, 20% the land, but you can use any reasonable allocation. The cost of parking lots and cost of landscaping can be deducted or depreciated, so these should be separated out from the cost of the land.

Antiques: According to the IRS, valuable antiques and art treasures cannot be written off until sold. Only property that has a "determinable useful life" can be depreciated. The Tax Court, however, has ruled that antiques that wear out and lose value from use may be depreciated. You'll need an accountant's help here.

Vehicles: Your vehicle can be depreciated if you do not take the Standard Mileage Allowance. But there are limitations, discussed below.

Films and Recordings: Motion picture films, video tapes, and sound recordings—originals, not duplicates for sale or rent—come under a different set of IRS rules not covered in this chapter.

Rental and licensing businesses: Businesses that rent out equipment can depreciate or write-off the equipment. Movie-rental stores can write off movies when purchased (if they won't last more than a year) or depreciate them. Photographers, illustrators, software developers and others who license their work can usually write off their expenses rather than depreciate them.

Intangibles: Intangible assets (also called intellectual property) such as trademarks, copyrights, patents, goodwill, etc., are depreciable property. The term for writing off intangibles is called "amortization" instead of depreciation. The assets are "amortized" instead of "depreciated." The two terms mean the same thing. (A trademark licensed from another business can be written off; it does not have to be amortized).

Warning: The Rules Change All The Time

IRS depreciation rules change almost every year. With every change, I swear, the rules get lengthier and more complex.

Whatever rule was in effect when you purchased an asset (or when you first used it in business if you purchased it before going into business) is the rule you use for that asset for as long as you own the asset. So if you have been in business and buying depreciable assets for several years, you may be calculating depreciation using several different sets of rules!

The depreciation rules explained below are only for newly-acquired assets, under IRS laws in effect when this edition of *Small Time Operator* was published. These are federal rules only. For state income taxes, some states use the same depreciation rules and some, God bless 'em, require entirely different calculations.

How Much Can Be Depreciated?

You are allowed to depreciate the cost of your depreciable asset. "Cost" is defined as the purchase price and includes sales tax, freight and any installation charges. If you bought your equipment inexpensively, your cost is what you paid, not what the equipment is "worth." When equipment is purchased in installments (on time) the cost is the total purchase price as if you had paid cash for it.

Finance or interest charges can usually be written off as a regular business expense the year paid, completely separate from the cost of the asset. (One exception: for buildings or equipment that you construct yourself or have built for you, if they take more than two years to build or if they are depreciated over 20 years or more, the finance or interest charges are added to the cost of the asset and treated as part of the asset.)

Depreciable assets used in your business that were purchased before going into business can be depreciated regardless of when acquired. These assets are valued at their cost or at their market value at the time the assets are first used in your business, whichever is less. If some old machinery, or an old computer, which cost you $2,000 eight years ago, was only worth $500 (market value) when first used in your business, you may only depreciate $500.

Write Off Period

There are several categories of assets, each with a different write off period (also called a recovery period), how many years the assets are to be depreciated. The categories most used by small businesses and farmers are:

3 Year Property: on-road tractor units, hogs, race horses over two years old, all horses over 12 years old, web site design, some software (see "Software" below).

5 Year Property: cars, trucks, trailers, aircraft, and buses; most equipment used for research and experimentation; computers, copiers, fax machines, and similar office equipment; carpeting; movable partitions; semi-conductor manufacturing equipment; solar, wind and some other alternative energy property; appliances and furniture in residential rental property; some electronic equipment; cattle, sheep, goats.

7 Year Property: machinery, equipment, furniture, fixtures; small signs; railroad track; horses other than those listed as 3-year Property.

10 Year Property: boats, barges and tugs (except pleasure craft, which are not deductible, period); single-purpose agricultural and horticultural structures; fruit and nut trees and vines.

15 Year Property: large outdoor signs. Gas stations, including their mini-marts (with some exceptions). Some intangible property such as goodwill, trademarks, trade names, franchises, customer lists, and covenants not to compete. Patents and copyrights are 15 year property only if acquired as part of a business you purchase.

20 Year Property: some farm buildings.

27½ Year Property: residential rental buildings, including built-in elevators.

39 Year Property: all buildings other than residential rental property, farm buildings, and some gas stations.

Other: Patents and copyrights are depreciated over the life granted by the government (except see 15 year property above).

Methods of Computing Depreciation

Business assets are depreciated under a system called MACRS, which stands for Modified Accelerated Cost Recovery System. "Cost recovery" is the government's term for depreciation. "Modified" refers to the fact that it is a modified version of an out-of-date depreciation method. "Accelerated" means faster write-offs than other methods (which is no longer true: some MACRS calculations are "accelerated," some aren't. IRS changed the rules but left the description).

Under MACRS, there are four methods of depreciation. All four methods result in the same tax write-off eventually, but each method involves different amounts that can be written off in any given year.

General Depreciation System (GDS) #1. The most commonly used depreciation system, GDS #1 (also called the "200% declining balance" system) offers the fastest write-offs: larger write-offs in the first few years, smaller write-offs in later years. Most business assets other than buildings, intangibles, farm assets, and certain "listed property" can be depreciated under this method (see below for the exceptions). The Depreciation Table will help you compute GDS depreciation quickly and easily.

At your option, assets eligible for this method can be depreciated under the other three methods described below. If you already have reduced your taxes down to nothing and don't need any more deductions this year, the other methods will bring larger deductions in future years.

General Depreciation System (GDS) #2. Also known as the 150% Declining Balance Method. Required for most farm buildings and equipment, and some land improvements. The method is similar to GDS #1 but with smaller write-offs in the early years.

Straight Line. This method must be used for intangibles, most buildings (other than farm buildings), vineyards, and fruit and nut trees.

The straight-line method distributes depreciation equally over the write-off period. Each year, the same amount is depreciated (except the first year, when only part of a year's depreciation is allowed; more on this later).

Don't worry about your mistakes. Everybody makes them. Everybody. And that nonsense about learning from them: don't worry, you won't. From most of them, you won't learn a thing except "Ouch that hurts."

—Columnist Jeffrey Dobkin

DEPRECIATION TABLE

Year	3 Yr. Assets			5 Yr. Assets			7 Yr. Assets		
	GDS #1	GDS #2	St. Line	GDS #1	GDS #2	St. Line	GDS #1	GDS #2	St. Line
1	33%	25%	17%	20%	15%	10%	14%	11%	7%
2	45	38	33	32	26	20	25	19	15
3	15	25	33	19	18	20	17	15	15
4	7	12	17	12	17	20	13	13	14
5				11	16	20	9	12	14
6				6	8	10	9	12	14
7							9	12	14
8							4	6	7

Alternative Depreciation System (ADS). This method is required for certain assets if used 50% or less for business (called "listed property"): vehicles (unless you take the Standard Mileage Allowance, in which case you take no depreciation at all); boats; airplanes; cell phones; computers (*if* you use the computer away from your business premises); and entertainment and recreation property. ADS is required for assets used primarily outside the U.S., and assets imported from certain trade-restricted countries.

Under ADS, the write-off periods are different than those shown above, and the depreciation runs over a longer period of years. If you are required or want to use ADS, IRS Publication #534, "Depreciation," lists the different write-off periods.

Depreciation Table

This table will help you compute depreciation using GDS #1, GDS #2, and straight-line, and to compare the three methods. The fourth method, ADS, can't be included in a simple table because there are too many asset categories.

"Year" refers to the calendar year, not to the first twelve months you own the asset. Percentage is the percentage of cost you can write off that year.

This table is only for assets qualifying for the half-year convention (see "First Year Depreciation" below). Do not use for assets requiring "mid- quarter" calculations.

First Year Depreciation

At your option, you can first take the Section 179 Deduction and the 50% Special Depreciation Allowance, explained above under "First Year Write-off." The balance of the cost of the assets is depreciated.

You are not allowed a full year's depreciation the year you acquire an asset. For assets other than buildings, you are allowed only a half year's depreciation the first year. "Year" refers to the calendar year, not to the first twelve months you own an asset.

If you compute your own depreciation, just divide the first year's depreciation in half. At the end of the write-off period, you add the remaining half year's depreciation. If you use the Depreciation Table, the half year is figured into it.

In effect, this "half-year convention" adds an extra year to the write-off period. A 7-year asset, for example, will be depreciated over an eight year period: a half year the first year, a full year the second through the seventh years, and a half year the eighth year.

There is an important exception to the half-year rule. If more than 40% of your depreciable assets (other than real estate) are purchased in the last three months of the year, you do not use the half-year calculation. You group the assets according to which quarter of the year they were purchased and then make four separate computations.

(The half-year rule and the quarter-year rule are for calculating depreciation, not for the First

Year Write-Off explained under "Business Assets" above. You are entitled to the full First Year Write Off regardless of when during the year you purchased the asset.

Buildings: First year depreciation on buildings is calculated building by building using what's called a "mid month convention." Whatever month a building is acquired for business (or first used for business), you are allowed a half month's depreciation that month, and then full depreciation for the remaining months of the year. So if you purchased a building in April, you are allowed 8½ months depreciation the first year. Then at the end of the depreciation period, you get an additional 3½ month's depreciation.

Part Business, Part Personal

Depreciation may be deducted only for the business portion of a depreciable asset. If your tools are used 50% for work and 50% for pleasure, compute depreciation on 50% of the cost.

Special limitations apply to certain "listed property" used 50% or less for business, as mentioned under the ADS method above. Try to keep business use above 50%, and keep detailed records—dates, hours, miles, etc.—to prove it.

Software

Software that you purchase can be depreciated over three years, or less if the software has a shorter life (such as a tax program, which is only good for one year). Or at your option, the software can be written off the year of purchase (explained above under "Business Assets").

Software that was packaged with your computer when you bought it is considered part of the cost of the computer. It can be depreciated or written off according to the computer depreciation rules explained above.

If you develop software programs, you can, at your option, write off the development costs as current expenses. You also have the option to depreciate software development costs over five years, using the straight line method.

Doing taxes is not an effective use of a business owner's time.
　　　　　　—Business executive Jane Wesman

Limitations on Automobiles

Regardless of the percent used for business or the depreciation method used, automobile depreciation (and the first-year write-off) is limited to a maximum of $10,710 the first year, $4,900 the second year, $2,950 the third year, and $,1775 each succeeding year. (2003 amounts. Dollar limits change from year to year.) Due to this limitation, expensive cars cannot be fully depreciated in the five years normally allowed. Depreciation is spread out over a longer period.

This limitation is for automobiles only. Trucks, vans, large SUVs and other vehicles with a gross weight over 6,000 pounds are not subject to this limitation.

Selling An Asset

When you sell an asset that has been written off, or fully or partly depreciated, there may be a taxable profit on the sale. This is known as "recapture" and is somewhat complex, depending on how many years you've had the asset, how much depreciation or write-off you've taken, and what method of depreciation you've used.

The basic concept: The cost of the asset is reduced by the first-year write off or the total depreciation *allowed*, to come up with what's called "adjusted cost" (or "cost basis"). If the selling price is higher than the adjusted cost, you have a taxable profit. If the selling price is lower, you have a tax-deductible loss.

It is important to understand that if you did take the first-year write off, your cost basis is zero (assuming you were able to write off the entire asset). If you did not take a first-year write off, you must reduce the cost basis by the depreciation *allowed*, whether you take depreciation or not. If you don't take the allowable depreciation each year, you are cheating yourself.

For example, let's say you bought a piece of equipment a few years ago for $4,000, and you already deducted $3,000 of depreciation. Your adjusted cost is $1,000 ($4,000 original cost less $3,000 depreciation). Let's say you sell the asset for $2,500. You will have a $1,500 taxable profit:

Original cost	$4,000
Accumulated depreciation	(3,000)
Adjusted cost	$1,000
Sale price	(2,500)
Profit	$1,500

1	2	3	4	5	6	7	8	9	10	11	12	13	14	15	16	17	18
DATE	DESCRIPTION	METH.	WRITE OFF PERIOD	NEW OR USED	%	COST	BAL. TO BE DEPR.	DEPR. Year ___	BAL. TO BE DEPR.	DEPR. Year ___	BAL. TO BE DEPR.	DEPR. Year ___	BAL. TO BE DEPR.	DEPR. Year ___	BAL. TO BE DEPR.	DEPR. Year ___	BAL. TO BE DEPR.

Now, let's change the example and say you sold the same asset for $600. You will have a $400 deductible loss:

Original cost	$4,000
Accumulated depreciation	(3,000)
Adjusted cost	$1,000
Sale price	(600)
Loss	$ 400

Record the sale of a depreciable asset in your income ledger the month of sale, but below the regular sales figures for the month. Although the sale may be subject to income tax, it is not a regular business sale and should be shown separately. You should also record the sale on your equipment ledger. No depreciation is allowed for any asset sold the same year it was purchased.

Discarding or Junking an Asset

If an asset is fully depreciated or fully written off when it becomes worthless/useless/unsalable junk, that's as far as the taxes and bookkeeping go—there is no profit and no loss. But if the asset is only partly depreciated, you can write off the balance of the cost (the undepreciated part of the cost) the year the asset becomes worthless.

For example, a piece of equipment cost $3,000 a year ago, and so far you've deducted $800 in depreciation. The thing burns up. This year you can write off $2,200, the undepreciated balance ($3,000 cost less $800 depreciation). This example assumes, besides no selling price, no insurance. If the asset is insured, any insurance payment is treated the same as income from the sale of an asset (see "Selling an Asset" above).

When you junk an asset, no entry should be made to your income ledger, but you should note it on your equipment ledger.

IRS Reporting

IRS Form #4562, "Depreciation and Amortization" can be used to figure depreciation.

The Depreciation Worksheet

The combination Equipment Ledger and Depreciation Worksheet will help you keep track of your depreciable assets and the depreciation on them, and will help you prepare Form #4562. Some people simply photocopy the Worksheet and attach it to their tax form.

Use a separate line on the worksheet for each asset. Fill out the columns when you purchase an asset and you'll never have to hunt up the information a second time. Even if you hire an accountant to prepare your taxes, you will save the accountant time, and save yourself money, if you fill out Columns 1, 2, 5, 6 and 7 (the basic information). Enter the information as follows:

Column 1, Date. Date purchased or date first used in business.

Column 2, Description. Be specific enough to distinguish this particular asset from all others.

Column 3, Method. The depreciation method you've selected. If you are writing off the asset instead of taking depreciation, put "W/O" (for first-year write off) in this column.

Column 4, Write Off Period. How many years the asset is being depreciated. If you are writing off the asset instead of depreciating it, leave this column blank.

Column 5, New or Used.

Column 6, Percent Used for Business.

Column 7, Cost. See the discussion of cost in this chapter.

Column 8, Balance to be Depreciated. Column 6 x Column 7 = Column 8. This column is the cost adjusted for the percentage used for business. The amount you arrive at here is commonly called the "cost basis." This is the amount that is actually depreciated or written off the first year.

The five sets of paired columns, 9 & 10, 11 & 12, 13 & 14, 15 & 16, and 17 & 18, provide five years of depreciation scheduling for each asset. The first column in a pair is the depreciation for the year, and the following column is the remaining undepreciated balance. Column 9 less Column 10 equals Column 11, and so on.

This ledger may not be adequate for businesses purchasing, repairing and maintaining heavy or expensive equipment. Manufacturing equipment, construction equipment and the like will require separate records for each item. The basic ideas and the depreciation laws are the same.

A Last Word on Depreciation

If you are totally dismayed by this chapter, you are not alone. Depreciation is vastly complex, a real struggle to compute correctly. Few business owners are willing and able to make these calculations, and they usually turn to tax accountants for help. Most accountants have computer programs that can automatically compute depreciation under all of the different methods, select the correct method for you, and compare methods to find the biggest tax savings.

VEHICLE EXPENSES

Most expenses of operating a vehicle for business are deductible except regular commuting expenses between your home and your usual place of business, which are not deductible.

There are two ways of figuring vehicle expenses. As in so many other situations, one is difficult and one is easy:

Method One: You can keep itemized records of all your vehicle expenses. These include gasoline, oil, lubrication, maintenance, repairs, insurance, parking and tolls, garage rents, license and registration fees, interest on the purchase, even auto club dues. The purchase price of the vehicle and the cost of major repairs such as an engine overhaul may have to be depreciated over several years. See the Depreciation chapter.

Vehicle expenses are prorated between per-

sonal use (not deductible; commuting to and from the office is considered personal use), and business use (deductible). The most common method of proration is based on the miles driven. For example, if you drove 10,000 miles last year of which 2,500 miles was for business, 25% of all your vehicle expenses are deductible, and 25% of the cost of your vehicle can be depreciated.

Keeping itemized records of all your vehicle expenses is tedious work. The IRS realizes this also. In one of their rare helpful moods they have come up with...

Method Two: An optional Standard Mileage Allowance (Standard Mileage Rate). Instead of recording each fill up and every oil change, you may take a standard flat rate for every business mile driven (not including the commute). The 2004 rate is 37½¢ per mile. The Standard Mileage Allowance is in lieu of depreciation and all vehicle expenses except parking, tolls, interest, and state and local taxes, which are deductible in addition to the mileage allowance (sales tax on the vehicle is not deductible).

The Fine Print

You may not use the Standard Mileage Allowance if you use the vehicle for hire such as a taxi, or if your business operates more than four vehicles at a time. You may not use the Standard Mileage Allowance if you take the First Year Write Off on your vehicle (covered under "Business Assets"). Business vehicles that do not qualify for the Standard Mileage Allowance may still use Method One, itemizing expenses.

Using the standard mileage rate reduces the cost basis of your vehicle (for figuring profit or loss when the vehicle is sold). You reduce the basis by 16¢ for each business mile driven.

The method you choose the first year you use your vehicle for business determines what methods you can use in future years (for that vehicle). If you use Method One (itemizing) the first year, you must stay with that method as long as you use that vehicle. If you use the Standard Mileage Allowance the first year, you can switch back and forth if you want, itemizing some years and using the mileage allowance other years. If you do switch from the mileage allowance to itemizing, you must use straight line depreciation.

If you choose Method One, depreciation is

limited if the vehicle costs over a certain amount or if the vehicle is used 50% or less for business. See the "Depreciation" chapter.

Leasing a Vehicle

The business portion of a vehicle lease is deductible, with exceptions. You can deduct the actual expenses or use the standard mileage rate.

If you lease an automobile for 30 days or more, your lease payment is not fully deductible. The lease payment must be reduced by something called an "Inclusion Amount." The Inclusion Amount varies depending on the cost of the car and the date of purchase, and is a rather confusing calculation because the Inclusion Amount is actually added to your income rather than reducing the deduction. An Inclusion Amount table is in IRS Publication 463, "Travel, Entertainment, Gift and Car Expenses."

If you take the Standard Mileage Allowance, you don't have to worry about the Inclusion Amount. You get the full 37½¢ per mile.

The Inclusion Amount applies only to automobiles, not to trucks, vans, large SUVs, any vehicles with a weight of 6,000 pounds or more. And again, the Inclusion Amount is only for car rentals that run 30 days or more. The typical day or week-long car rental is fully deductible.

A lease-purchase is considered a purchase, and not a lease, for tax purposes.

Sole proprietors report vehicle expenses on form #4562 if you are required to fill out that form for depreciation or first-year write-off of any assets; or on the back of Schedule C, if form #4562 isn't otherwise required.

For more information on vehicle expenses, see IRS Publication #463.

REPAIRS

Repairs on business property, buildings, and equipment are fully deductible as a current expense.

Major repairs that involve structural changes, remodeling, or that adapt an asset to a new or different use, must usually be treated as a permanent (capital) investment and handled in the same manner as the purchase of a depreciable asset. See the "Depreciation" chapter.

The IRS often challenges businesses that deduct expensive repairs, particularly on buildings, arguing that the repairs are really capital improvements and must be depreciated. You may want to discuss this with your accountant.

BAD DEBTS

A business bad debt (money owed to you that is uncollectible) is fully deductible, but only if it was posted to your income ledger when you made the sale. Businesses using the cash method of accounting cannot take a bad debt expense for unpaid and uncollectible accounts, because the income was never recorded in the first place. (Cash-method businesses record income when the cash is received, not when the sale is made).

Bounced checks, however, are deductible bad debts, because they were posted to the income ledgers.

If you take credit cards, charge card charge-backs (if a customer refuses to pay his bill) are deductible as bad debts, because the money was received and posted to your income ledgers. (If this does not make sense to you, read the chapter Cash Accounting Vs. Accrual in the Bookkeeping section.)

The chapters "Return Checks" and "Uncollectible Accounts" in the Bookkeeping section, explain how to set up a bad debts folder.

Businesses sometimes set aside money in a bad debt reserve fund, sort of like self-insurance. Such reserves are not really business expenses and are not tax deductible.

LOSSES: Casualty / Theft

Business losses from fire, storm or other casualty, or from theft, shoplifting or vandalism are fully deductible to the extent they are not covered by insurance.

Inventory that is stolen or destroyed is not deducted as a casualty loss. The inventory loss is part of your cost-of-goods-sold (discussed in this section) and cannot be deducted a second time.

Depreciable property that is stolen or destroyed can be deducted as a casualty loss, but only to the extent of the undepreciated balance. For example, let's say a tool was stolen. You paid $200 for it two years ago and have already taken $40 depreciation on it. You may show a theft loss of only $160 ($200 less the $40). If you wrote the entire $200 off the first year, you have no deductible loss.

The IRS says that business losses are not deductible if covered by insurance even if no claim is filed with the insurance company.

Theft losses are deductible the year discovered, not the year the theft occurred.

Operating Losses: If your business lost money this year, you may be able to use the loss to offset other income, reducing taxes. See the chapter "Operating Losses."

DONATIONS / Charitable Contributions

Sole proprietors, partnerships, LLCs, and S corporations cannot deduct charitable contributions. Only C corporations are allowed a business deduction for charitable contributions.

However, if instead of making a non-deductible donation, your business purchases an advertisement in a charitable organization's directory or event program, the cost of the ad (if "reasonable") would be fully deductible.

Political donations are not deductible, period.

C Corporations: There are special rules about who can receive a donation and how much the corporation can write-off. Donated inventory can be written off at up to twice its cost.

Lots of things can happen if you don't keep the right records, and none of them are good.
                                    —*CPA Dan Smogor*

INTEREST EXPENSE

Interest paid on business debts (including interest on credit-card purchases) is deductible, with a few important exceptions:

Interest on loans to construct real estate (if you are building a new building) must be capitalized; that is, added to the cost of the property.

Interest on back taxes is not deductible, except for corporations. (If Microsoft or WalMart gets audited and hit with back taxes, the interest charges are fully deductible. But if you get audited and owe back taxes, well, sorry about that.)

If you borrow money to purchase an existing business, the laws can get complicated. If the business is a sole proprietorship, partnership or S corporation, part of the interest may be deductible as a current business expense, but part may have to be capitalized. Generally, the interest on the part of the loan that applies to actual business assets (equipment, inventory, etc) is deductible. The interest that applies to intangibles (goodwill, trademarks, etc.) must be capitalized. If you are purchasing a regular C corporation (not an S corporation), you are actually buying stock, and the interest comes under a different set of rules (investment income and expense) and is not deductible as a regular business expense. You will probably need professional help.

Prepaid interest is deductible if it does not extend beyond 12 months. But read the "Prepaid Expenses" chapter before taking this deduction.

Corporations: If you are an employee of your own corporation, and you get a personal loan to purchase business assets, the interest is not deductible as a business expense. If the corporation itself borrows the money, the interest is deductible. How you structure corporate finances has a major effect on how much you pay in taxes.

ENTERTAINMENT

Only 50% of entertainment expenses are deductible on your tax return.

In some cases there is a fine line as to what is entertainment (subject to the 50% limit) and what is not entertainment and therefore fully deductible. For example, sometimes "promotion" is also called "entertainment." But promotion expenses are 100% deductible, and entertainment is limited to 50%. You get to define your own expenses. The right choice of words will get you the right deduction.

Entertainment is a Red Flag to the IRS. Large entertainment expenses are likely to invite an audit. So don't classify an expense as entertainment unless it truly is.

A company or holiday party where all employees are invited (as well as customers and prospective customers) is 100% deductible.

Entertainment facilities and pleasure craft are not deductible, period.

For more information, see IRS Publ. #463, "Travel, Entertainment and Gift Expenses."

Entertainment businesses: If you are in the business of entertaining, the cost of entertainment sold to your customers is fully deductible.

BUSINESS GIFTS

Tax deductions for business gifts are limited to $25 per recipient in any one year.

Samples of your merchandise, given to prospective buyers or to people who might review or publicize your products, are not considered gifts and are not subject to these gift limitations. You write off the cost of the free samples as part of cost-of-goods-sold. See the chapter on Inventory.

Gifts to employees come under stricter rules. Gifts of nominal value, such as a turkey, a bottle of wine, a framed photo of the boss, are deductible and not taxable to the employee. But any gift of significant value, and any cash gift or cash equivalent such as a gift certificate, even for a small amount, is considered taxable wages to the employee, reported on the W-2, subject to all payroll taxes. The same rules apply to awards given to employees (exception: up to $1,600 for an Employee Achievement or Employee Safety Award can be tax free; special rules apply).

MEALS

Regular meals at work are generally not deductible.

Some meals, however, are deductible. The famous business lunch, wining and dining a current or prospective customer, is 50% deductible but only if business is specifically discussed at the meal and if the cost is not "lavish or extravagant." You must have a receipt and write on it who you took out and why. Tips are considered part of the meal and are also 50% deductible.

Meals while traveling away from home on business are 50% deductible. See the "Travel" chapter. Truck drivers who qualify under special Department of Transportation rules are allowed a 70% deduction.

The following are fully deductible: Food samples made available to the general public. Cost of the annual company picnic. Thanksgiving turkeys you give your employees. Meals provided to employees on the business premises for the employer's convenience.

Taking employees out to lunch is deductible but taxable to the employees. That's right: treat a hard working employee to lunch, and the poor guy has to pay income and payroll taxes on it!

Businesses selling meals (restaurants, caterers, etc.): The cost of meals sold to your customers as part of your regular business are 100% deductible. Meals that you provide as part of a business meeting or seminar are fully deductible.

Child Care Businesses can deduct the full cost of meals provided or can take a special Standard Meal Allowance.

TRAVEL

Local business travel, when not going somewhere overnight, is limited to transportation expenses only. Regular commuting expenses, home to work and back, are not deductible. Side trips to customers or to suppliers are deductible.

You are allowed deductions for food and lodging and miscellaneous expenses only if you are away from home overnight. "Home" is defined as your place of business, not where you live.

For years, the IRS has been in and out of tax court with people, arguing the definition of "home." Self-employed itinerant workers, traveling contractors, and salespeople are continually challenged by the IRS on travel deductions, the IRS claiming that the road is home, so no deductions allowed. If your business is of this nature and if travel expenses are substantial, I'd advise consulting a good tax accountant.

If you are working away from home for over one year, the IRS automatically considers the road to be home, and disallows travel expenses.

Business Trips

A business trip within the United States that is 100% business is 100% deductible. That includes round trip travel, lodging, transportation, and incidental expenses such as phone, laundry, etc.

Three exceptions: Meals and entertainment are only 50% deductible. Deductions for travel on luxury boats or cruise ships have some limitations (check with the IRS).

What about a trip that is part business and part vacation? You may be able to write some of it off, and you may be able to write all of it off, if you carefully follow the rules.

If the reason for your trip is primarily personal (more than half the days are for vacation), none of the traveling expenses to and from your destination are deductible. Only expenses directly related to your business can be deducted.

If your trip is primarily for business (more than half the days are for business) and it is within the United States, the cost of the round-trip travel is fully deductible even if some of the trip is for pleasure. So you *can* tack a short vacation onto a business trip, and the only costs that aren't deductible are the non-business expenses, such as the extra days' lodging and meals and entertainment.

And if you have a business trip that overlaps a weekend, requiring you to be there Friday and the following Monday, lucky you: you can write off the weekend as well, as a business expense, even though all you did was sit on the beach and dance in the clubs (as long as it is less expensive to stay the weekend than to go home Friday and come back Monday morning).

If you take your husband or wife, the spouse's expenses are not deductible unless he or she is an employee or partner and has a legitimate business reason for accompanying you.

Fill what's empty, empty what's full, and scratch where it itches.
—Alice Roosevelt Longworth

Travel Outside the U.S.

A business trip outside the United States may be 100% deductible, with the same exceptions of meals, entertainment and luxury water travel. But if you attend overseas conventions, seminars or meetings, a deduction is allowed only if, in the IRS's opinion, there is a valid business reason for holding the meeting overseas. Some countries are exempt from this restriction; check with the IRS.

If you travel outside the U.S., more stringent rules apply. If the trip is no more than one week *or* the time spent for pleasure is less than 25 percent, the same basic rules apply as a trip within the U.S. But if the trip is more than a week, or if the vacation days are 25% or more of the trip, you allocate travel expenses between the business and the personal portion of your trip.

When counting business versus vacation days, a "business day" does not require you to do business all day. Any day you put in at least four hours of work is considered a business day. Any day your presence is required, for any amount of time, is also considered a business day. And travel days count as business days.

The IRS Does Not Like Business Trips

As you can tell from the generous way the law is written, it's a bit too easy to write off a business trip that is really a disguised vacation. The IRS knows this all too well, and they are forever suspicious of business travel expenses, particularly sole proprietorships where the owner is accountable to no one else: you feel like taking a business trip (and you can afford it), you take it. The IRS wants to be sure it's not a vacation in disguise. You want to be sure you can prove, if audited, that the trip wasn't a vacation. A log of daily activities and business contacts is not required by law, but it may help convince a skeptical IRS auditor that your trip to the Bahamas or to New Orleans really was for business.

One tax client of mine who owned a retail coffee shop took an expensive trip to Scandinavia and wrote it off as a business deduction. When she was audited, which didn't surprise either of us, she was able to show the IRS auditor photos she took of coffee shops she visited throughout her travels. She showed the auditor Scandinavian coffee mugs that she is now importing. She got through the audit successfully.

Keeping Track of Expenses

For meals, you can keep a record of actual expenses or, at your option, you can use a standard "per diem" rate set by the IRS—so much per day. If you use the per diem meal allowance, only 50% of the allowance is deductible, because only 50% of meal expenses are deductible. The standard rate varies from city to city. For lodging, corporations can use a per diem rate if they choose, but unincorporated businesses must use actual expenses. For current rates, see IRS Publication #1542, "Per Diem Rates."

For more information: IRS Publication #463, "Travel, Entertainment, and Gift Expenses."

DUES

Dues for business groups, professional organizations, merchant and trade associations, chambers of commerce, etc. are deductible. Dues to community service organizations, such as Rotary, Lions, etc., are also deductible.

Dues and membership fees in clubs run for pleasure, recreation or other social purposes are not deductible.

FREIGHT

"Freight" refers to all shipping and delivery charges. Freight-in on inventory you purchase is included as part of the cost of the inventory. Freight-in on expensive assets (machinery, furniture, etc.) should be added to the cost of the asset. Freight-out on goods you sell are fully deductible expenses.

EDUCATION EXPENSES

Here is an opportunity to get some additional education and charge the cost to your business, *if* you are careful in selecting your courses.

The cost of education is deductible only if the education maintains or improves a skill required in your business. Education expenses are *not* allowed if the education is required to meet minimum educational requirements of your present business or if the education will qualify you for a new trade or business.

Here's that book you ordered, "Income Taxes Made Easy."

A self-employed welder who takes a course in a new welding method can charge the expense to the business. A self-employed dance teacher who takes dance lessons can deduct the cost of the lessons. On the other hand, a leather craftsperson who takes a woodworking course cannot deduct the expenses. The education must be directly related to the business you already operate. Taking a course in pottery *before* opening your pottery shop is not deductible.

Any self employed person can take a course in bookkeeping, or taxes, or computers, and deduct the cost.

Education expenses include tuition, fees, books, and travel expenses while away from home overnight (with limitations).

Employers: Employers can deduct up to $5,250 per employee for employer-paid educational expenses for the employees. The education does not have to be employment related.

INSURANCE

Most business-related insurance premiums are deductible.

Vehicle insurance is deductible if you don't take the Standard Mileage Allowance. See the chapter "Vehicles."

Workers compensation insurance is deductible for your employees. Workers comp on yourself may or may not be deductible; see the "Insurance" chapter in the Getting Started section.

Life insurance premiums are not deductible.

Premiums for business interruption insurance may or may not be deductible, depending on what the insurance covers. See the Insurance chapter in the "Getting Started" section.

Prepaid insurance, as long as it does not extend beyond twelve months, is deductible when paid. See the chapter "Prepaid Expenses."

HEALTH (MEDICAL) INSURANCE

Sole proprietors, partners in partnerships, members of LLCs, and owners of S corporations can deduct the full cost of health insurance for themselves, spouses, and dependents.

The health insurance deduction, however, is not considered a business expense, does not reduce your business profit, and is not included on the business tax return. The deduction is taken on your 1040 return. The deduction, however, may not exceed the net profit from your business.

The deduction does not apply when computing self-employment tax. You pay self-employment tax on your net profit before taking the health insurance deduction.

The deduction is not allowed if you are eligible for employer-paid health insurance through your own employer (if you have another job) or through your spouse's employer.

Long term care insurance is eligible for this deduction, with certain dollar limitations. Disability insurance that pays you for lost earnings if you are disabled, is not considered health insurance and is not deductible.

In addition to health insurance, you can make tax-deductible contributions to a Health Savings Account (HSA). You can withdraw money from the account, tax free, to pay medical bills. Ask your bank or insurance company for details.

Health Insurance for Employees

Health insurance you pay for your employees, their spouses and dependents is 100% deductible for you and not taxable to the employees.

Instead of, or in addition to, health insurance for your employees, you can pay your employees' actual medical, dental and eye care bills, and get a 100% deduction. (Self-employed individuals cannot get a deduction for paying their own medical bills; they only have the deduction for medical insurance).

You are not required by law to provide health insurance for your employees. But providing employee health insurance, if you can afford it, will be a key selling point to attract and keep good workers. Health insurance is a major reason employees come, and stay. I often hear the story of some business that finds a good employee, trains and nurtures the employee, comes to depend on the employee, just to lose the person to another company that offers health benefits.

Corporations: In a regular C corporation (not an S corporation), you and your family come are eligible for tax-free employee health benefits, and your corporation is allowed a full deduction for the cost, but only if all of your employees are covered, not just yourself.

You file a 1099-MISC form with the IRS if you paid any physician or insurance company $600 or more during the year.

NON-DEDUCTIBLE EXPENSES

Certain expenses are specifically disallowed by law and cannot be deducted, no way, no how:

1. Business expenses not meeting the "ordinary and necessary" or the "reasonable" test.

2. Federal income tax and tax penalties. State income tax is deductible on your federal return.

3. Fines or penalties for violation of the law. Even though you were parked on business, you cannot deduct that parking ticket. Other business fines or penalties, if they don't involve breaking the law, are deductible.

4. Payments to yourself. The only way you may pay yourself a wage and deduct it as an expense is to incorporate.

5. Loan repayments. The loan was not income when received and is not expense when paid. Interest on the loan is usually deductible.

6. Regular clothing. Uniforms, clothes with your company logo or advertisement, and clothes used exclusively for work and unsuitable for street wear are deductible.

7. Regular meals at work, but see the "Meals" chapter for exceptions.

8. Regular commuting expenses between your home and usual place of business.

9. Cost of land, until you sell it. Only the structure on the land may be depreciated.

10. Certain start-up expenses as explained in the "Start Up Expenses" chapter.

11. Some club dues. See the "Dues" chapter.

12. Purchase or lease of entertainment facilities or pleasure craft.

13. Charitable donations (except for corporations) and political donations.

SELF-EMPLOYMENT TAX (SECA)

Self-employment tax, also known as SECA (Self Employment Contributions Act), is combined Social Security/Medicare tax for self-employed individuals. Self-employment tax is based on your taxable profit from the business.

Sole proprietors, partners in partnerships, and active owners of LLCs are subject to self-employment tax. (LLC members who are investors only, not active or minimally active in the business, may be exempt from self-employment taxes; check with your accountant or the IRS).

Corporations: The tax is not imposed on corporations; if you own a small corporation, you are an employee of your business and pay regular Social Security and Medicare instead of self-employment tax. Director's fees not included as part of a regular salary are subject to the self-employment tax.

Only "business income" is subject to self-employment tax. (The difference between business and non-business income is explained in the Bookkeeping Section under "Defining Income").

Income from a brief one-shot job that is neither continuous nor regular is usually exempt from self-employment tax.

Self-employment tax is apart from and in addition to federal income tax. You may owe no income tax but still be liable for self-employment tax. Retirement deductions, deductions for health insurance, and the regular personal deductions and exemptions, which reduce income tax, cannot be used to reduce self-employment tax.

Self-employment tax often comes as quite a shock to new businesses. People, particularly in part-time and sideline businesses, are not making enough profit to worry about income taxes, but they never realize they may have a substantial self- employment tax bill.

Special note: If you business profits are $400 or less, you do not have to pay any self-employment tax and can skip this entire chapter. If you net $401, you pay self-employment tax on the entire $401, not just the dollar over the $400 minimum (go back and round off those pennies).

If you made $400 or less but want to pay self-employment tax, to increase your Social Security account, the IRS provides an optional method so you can pay into Social Security and Medicare. It is explained on the SE tax form.

Figuring The Tax

For 2004, the self-employment tax rate is 15.3% (combining 12.4% Social Security tax and 2.9% Medicare tax) on profits up to $87,900. On profits above $87,900, the tax rate is 2.9% (no ceiling). Your actual tax will be lower than these rates indicate, because of two deductions:

The first deduction reduces the self-employment tax itself. You figure the tax not on your full profit, but on a reduced amount. You reduce your profit by 7.65%, and figure the tax on the reduced profit. You accomplish this by multiplying your profit by .9235.

For example, if your taxable profit was $30,000, multiply the $30,000 by .9235, which comes to $27,705. The self-employment tax will be 15.3% of $27,705, or $4,239 (pennies rounded). If your business made more than $87,900, the formula is different; see below.

The second deduction is an income tax deduction, taken on your 1040 tax form. After you figure your self-employment tax, reduce your business profit by half the self-employment tax before figuring your income tax.

Using the same example (a $30,000 profit, and self-employment tax of $4,239): Half the $4,239 is $2,120 (rounded). So you reduce your $30,000 profit by $2,120, to get $27,880, and figure your income taxes on the $27,880.

Understand that the two deductions are completely separate calculations, using different figures. In the example, a business with a $30,000

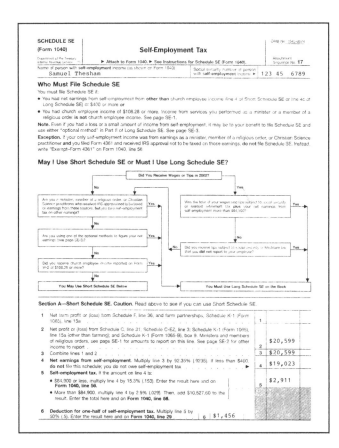

profit, self-employment tax is figured on $27,705 (the first deduction), and income tax is figured on $27,880 (the second deduction). Some idiot in Washington actually dreamed this up.

Self-employment tax is computed on your 1040 federal income tax return, using Form 1040-SE. If you have more than one unincorporated business, combine all profits and losses to figure self-employment tax. You file only one #1040-SE.

Businesses with profits above $87,900: You compute self-employment tax and the two deductions differently, because your profit is taxed at two different rates: 15.3% on the first $87,900, and 2.9% on all profits above $87,900. You follow the same procedures, but using two tax rates.

Husband and wife businesses: If a husband and wife operate a business together, who pays self-employment tax depends on how the business is set up. If the business is a partnership or an LLC, both spouses pay self-employment tax. Each spouse files his and her own Form 1040-SE. If the business is a sole proprietorship, only one spouse owns the business, and only one spouse pays self-employment tax. See "Husband and Wife Partnerships" in the Your Business section.

Outside Employment (You Also Hold a Job): Self-employed people who are also holding jobs where Social Security and Medicare is withheld from their pay should combine the two incomes to arrive at the self-employment tax maximum. You will be in one of these situations:

1. If the combined incomes, outside job and business profit, are under $87,900, nothing changes. You figure self-employment tax (and the two deductions) exactly as described above, but only on your business profit. Your outside wages are subject to regular employee payroll taxes.

2. If the combined incomes, outside job and business profit, are over $87,900, you pay a reduced self-employment tax. How you figure the tax depends on several factors:

(a) If your outside job pays more than $87,900, all of your business profits are subject to the lower 2.9%, less the two deductions.

(b) If your outside job pays less than $87,900 (but combined earnings, job and business, are over $87,900), you first subtract the outside job wages from $87,900. The result is how much of your business profit is subject to the 15.3% self-employment tax. For example, let's say you have a job paying $30,000. $87,900 minus the $30,000 comes to $57,900. So the first $57,900 of business profit is subject to the 15.3% tax (less the deductions). Any business profit above $57,900 is subject to the 2.9% tax (less the deductions).

Although the above calculations sound confusing, you will find them much easier to do than to explain. And be warned: the maximum amounts change every year. Verify them with the IRS.

Remember that if your business profit is $400 or less, you owe no self-employment tax, period.

For more information, see IRS Publication #553, "Information on Self-Employment Tax."

RETIREMENT DEDUCTIONS

You may invest a portion of your business profit in a retirement plan and pay no income taxes on the money invested or the earnings until you retire and withdraw the funds.

There are several tax-deferred retirement plans available to business owners and their employees. Some plans are like bank accounts, paying fixed interest; some plans are investment arrangements, with possible risks. Some plans have set-up and administration fees, some plans charge no fees at all.

	Maximum Contrib. for Yourself	Minimum Contrib.	50-or-over Catch-up Contrib.	Include Employees?	Deadline
IRA	$3,000 (add'l $3,000 for spouse)	none	$500 (add'l $500 for spouse)	no	set up & contribute by tax return filing date (no extensions)
SEP (SEP-IRA)	18.59% or $41,000	none	none	yes	set up & contribute by tax return filing date (including any extensions)
SIMPLE	$18,000	none if no employees	$1,500	yes	set up by October 1. Contr. by tax return due date (extended)
QUALIFIED 401k, Keogh	$41,000	varies	$3,000	yes	set up by last day of year, contribute by tax return filing date (including extensions)

Each plan has different contributions, different deadlines for making contributions, and, most important to employers, different requirements for including employees in the plans. Some plans require you to include some or all of your employees, some don't.

You can choose one plan, or you may be able to set up multiple plans. Contributions you, as employer, make for your employees are tax deductible, assuming you meet IRS requirements.

Please note: The maximum contributions listed below only apply to you, as the owner of your business. Contribution percentages and maximums for your employees are sometimes different. And the amounts change almost every year. Get advice from your accountant or your plan provider before setting up a plan.

Individual Retirement Account (IRA)

The simplest plan is the IRA. Any business owner, any self-employed individual, any owner-employee of a corporation, any wage earner can set up an IRA. An IRA is like a bank account. There are no fees or IRS forms to file.

You as an employer have no obligation to cover any employees.

Maximum annual contribution is $3,000 ($6,000 if you have a non-working spouse) or your taxable earnings, whichever is less. If you are 50 years old or older, the maximum annual

contribution increases by $500 ($1,000 if your spouse is also 50 or over). Maximum is reduced if you or your spouse has an outside job that includes a retirement plan.

You can set up or contribute to an IRA anytime up to the due date of your tax return, not including extensions (April 15 of the next year). Once the IRA is set up, you can change the contribution, or make no contribution at all, each year; although there are maximum tax-deductible contributions, there are no minimums.

There is a different kind of IRA, called the Roth IRA (named after the senator who created it) where contributions are not tax deductible, but withdrawals from the Roth IRA, including the interest earned, are tax free, just the reverse of the regular IRA.

Simplified Employee Pension Plan (SEP)

A SEP (also called a SEP-IRA) is for self-employed individuals and for your employees. SEPs are easy to set up and maintain. Like an IRA, a SEP is similar to a bank account. There are no administration fees or IRS forms to file.

With a SEP, however, if you have employees, you will have to make contributions for employees who meet certain requirements. You, the employer, pay the full cost of the SEP plan for your employees.

The maximum contribution for yourself is 18.59% of your earnings, up to a maximum contribution of $41,000. (The law says that the maximum contribution is 20%, but due to the confusing way the IRS calculates self-employment earnings, it actually works out to 18.59%.)

You can set up or contribute to a SEP right up to the due date of your tax return: April 15 of the next year, or later if you file an extension. Like IRAs, SEPs have no minimum contribution requirements; you can change the contribution, or make no contribution at all, each year.

You can have both a SEP and an IRA.

SIMPLE Plan

SIMPLE stands for "Savings Incentive Match Plan for Employees." Unfortunately, the rules are not all that simple.

If you have no employees, you can set up a SIMPLE just for yourself and contribute up to $18,000 a year. (The title of the plan says it is for "employees" but self-employed individuals can participate. For retirement plans, the IRS definition of "employee" often includes self-employed people.)

The maximum contribution you can make depends on your income and how the plan is set up. If you are age 50 or older, you can contribute an additional $1,500 a year. There is no minimum annual contribution if you have no employees.

If you have employees, you, the employer, contribute to the plan on behalf of employees who meet the plan's requirements. Your employees can also contribute their own money, if they choose to, but they are not required to do so. Whether employees contribute on not, you the employer contribute for them. How much the employer must contribute for employees depends on how the plan is set up.

A SIMPLE can be set up as an IRA, with an individual plan for each employee; or as a company wide 401(k) plan. A SIMPLE has to be set up by October 1 of the current year. You have until the tax return due date to make contributions.

Qualified Plans (401k and Keogh)

The term "Qualified Plans" actually refers to several different IRS-approved retirement plans, better known as 401(k) plans and Keogh (or HR10) plans. These plans also are known as defined benefit plans, defined contribution plans, money purchase plans, and profit sharing plans.

Qualified plans are more complicated than other retirement plans, more paperwork, more forms to file, often more expensive to administer.

Under a Qualified Plan, you can contribute up to $41,000 per year for yourself, plus an additional $3,000 per year if you are 50 years old or older. Computing the actual maximum contribution is a bit complicated, as it includes two separately computed contributions: an employer's and an employee's share. A self-employed individual is considered both employer and employee.

Under a Qualified Plan, if you have employees, you, the employer, contribute to the plan on behalf of employees who meet the plan's requirements. Employees can also make contributions for themselves. Some Qualified plans have annual minimum contributions, some don't.

You must set up a Qualified plan by year-end. You have until the due date of your tax return, including extensions, to make contributions.

More Details: All Plans

Withdrawals: Under all of the plans, you cannot withdraw money without penalty until age 59½. Some plans can be tapped penalty-free for medical bills, health insurance, buying a first home, or for college tuition.

Calculating Income: For self-employed individuals, the income figure you use to calculate retirement contributions is not the full profit from your business. You reduce the profit by one-half your self-employment tax. You also have to include your non-business income and losses in determining total income.

Start-Up Tax Credit: You are allowed an annual tax credit of 50% of the cost of setting up and maintaining a retirement plan (administrative cost, not the cost of contributions to the plan) for the first three years—but only if you have at least one "non-highly compensated employee." If you are the only person in your retirement plan, you cannot take the credit. Maximum annual credit is $500.

Self-employment tax: Retirement plan contributions for yourself are not deductible for computing self-employment tax. You base self-employment tax on your business profit before the retirement contributions made for yourself.

State taxes: Not all states allow retirement deductions in calculating state income tax. You may still owe state income tax on your full profit.

Employers: If you want to set up a retirement plan just for yourself, without having to pay for your employees, many insurance companies offer non-qualifying plans. But under the non-qualifying plans (so called because they do not qualify for an income tax deduction) you pay regular income taxes on your entire business profit.

Corporations: A corporation cannot have an IRA or Keogh plan. SEPs, SIMPLEs, and 401(k) plans are available to all businesses.

More Information

Banks and insurance companies offer all the above plans. The interest or return on investment will vary with different plans and contribution amounts. See IRS Publication 590, "Individual Retirement Accounts," and Publication 560, "Retirement Plans for Small Business."

ESTIMATED TAX PAYMENTS

If your federal tax for the current year, income and self-employment combined, is estimated to be $1,000 or more ($500 for corporations), you are required to pay the tax in quarterly installments. The IRS wants your tax money just like the taxes withheld from employees' paychecks.

The four quarterly installments are due April 15, June 15, September 15, and the following January 15. You do not have to pay the fourth estimate if you file your tax return by January 31 and pay the balance due.

How do you estimate your taxes? You can base your estimate on your prior year's taxes, even if you were not in business then. Whatever your total tax came to last year, divide it by four and send the IRS four equal installments. If your total federal tax last year, income and self employment tax combined, was less than $1,000, you are not required to make any estimated tax payments. If your income was over $150,000, or $75,000 for married couples filing separately, the estimate is 110% of last year's tax.

If you base your estimates on the prior year's taxes, you must have been a U.S. citizen or resident for the entire previous year.

You have the option to estimate your taxes based on your current year's income. Four times a year, you figure your taxable income for that quarter and send in the correct tax. As you can imagine, this is not an easy task. Under this method you may be hit with an interest penalty if you underestimate by more than 10 percent.

When you compute your actual tax at year-end, any overpayment of estimated taxes will, at your option, either be refunded or applied to the following year's estimates.

If you pay low estimated tax or none at all, and if you are having a profitable year, be prepared when April 15 rolls around. You may have to come up with a lot of cash to pay this year's taxes *and* to pay next year's first quarterly estimate; both are due the same day. You may want to make voluntary estimated payments or set some money aside to cushion the blow.

If you have more than one business, you file

134

one Schedule ES combining the taxes on all the businesses.

Estimated taxes are filed on Form 1040-ES. The form can be filed by mail or electronically.

If you are holding a job where taxes are withheld by your employer, instead of filing a Schedule ES, you can have your withholding increased to cover the additional income and self employment taxes. The IRS doesn't care whether it gets your money through withholding or through estimated payments.

Farmers, fishermen and fisherwomen who derive at least 2/3 of their total income from farming or fishing, only have to make one estimated tax payment for the year, due January 15 of the new year. You do not have to pay the estimate if you file your tax return by March 1 and pay the balance due.

BARTER

"In the beginning, there was no money."

But there always was the tax man, and barter does not escape his grasp. Barter transactions are taxable just like all other business transactions.

When you exchange or trade your business goods or services for someone else's goods or services, it is called barter. The "fair market value" of the goods or services you receive must be included in your regular business income and treated just like any other business income.

If the goods or services you receive are to be used in your business, you get a business write-off on your taxes, just as though you paid cash.

For example, let's say you are a cabinetmaker, and you build some custom cabinets for the person who owns the local office supply store. In exchange for the cabinets, you get $1,000 worth of "free" office supplies (or maybe some equipment or a computer). You have taxable income of $1,000. If you use the supplies or equipment 100% for your business, you also have a $1,000 expense you can write off. If any of what you receive in trade is for personal, non-business use, the personal portion is not deductible. The owner of the office supply store also has $1,000 to report as business income. If she uses the cabinets in the store, she has a $1,000 business expense. If she uses the cabinets in her kitchen at home, she does not have a deductible expense.

If the exchange is valued at $600 or more, and if it includes services (not goods), the business receiving the service must report it to the IRS on Form 1099-MISC. This is the same law that applies to independent contractors (see "Hiring Help" in the Growing Up section).

If you are bartering for services, be careful that the person providing the service is not an employee in disguise, one who should be on the books with payroll deductions, worker's compensation insurance and the rest. An employee who gets paid in goods or services, instead of cash, is still an employee. The "fair market value" of the goods or services the employee receives is considered wages, 100% taxable.

If you join a barter club (exchange, network), the rules are basically the same. But you recognize the income at the time you receive the "barter credits" even if you haven't yet "spent" them.

Barter organizations are required to report all transactions to the IRS.

Barter transactions should be posted to your ledgers the same way you post cash transactions.

In most IRS audits of businesses, one of the first questions often is, "Do you engage in trade or barter?" A yes answer is a red flag to expand the scope of the audit.

OPERATING LOSSES

If your business suffers a loss this year you will owe no income tax on the business, which I'm sure you know. You may not know that this loss will also offset other income, such as a salary from an outside job or your spouse's wages, to reduce this year's income tax.

You can also use this year's loss to offset income, and reduce taxes, from other years. You are allowed to carry back what the IRS calls a Net Operating Loss (NOL) to apply against prior income and receive a refund of prior years' taxes, even if you were not in business then. For most businesses, the loss can be carried back 2 years. And if your taxable income for the 2 prior years is not sufficient to absorb the entire loss, you may carry the balance forward as many as 20 years. (Farmers and ranchers have a 5 year carryback).

At your option, you can forego the two-year carry-back period and apply your NOL entirely to the 20 future years. If the two preceding years generated little or no income tax, you probably will do better to forego the carry-back, and apply the entire NOL to future years.

Net Operating Loss is not simply the business loss shown on your tax return. It is a complicated combination of business and non-business income and deductions. NOL calculations are complex, and there's no way to simplify the procedure. Step-by-step instructions are in the IRS's Publ. 536, "Net Operating Losses." Don't be put off by their complexity; the NOL deduction may save you a bundle in income taxes.

Examining Your Loss

Saving on income taxes because your business lost money is a consolation prize of sorts, but you are losing money. If you don't know why, it's time to stop and figure out why. You need to determine whether you can turn the business around or whether you should pack it in, and try something else. "Businesses always lose money the first year" is not a good answer, and isn't true. If you are puzzled, get help. Hire an accountant for an hour's worth of advice. It will be worth every penny.

YEAR-END TAX STRATEGIES

Put a little Post-It note on the front cover of this book to remind yourself to read this chapter somewhere around the first of December. Within reasonable limits, if you act before January 1, you can juggle your income and expenses to decrease or increase your taxable profit, and your taxes, for the year just ending.

Here are several year-end strategies:

1. If you are on the cash basis (see "Cash Accounting Vs. Accrual" in the Bookkeeping section), you can reduce this year's taxable income, and this year's taxes, by waiting until the new year to bill your customers, or by encouraging your customers to pay their bills after the new year. Cash-basis businesses do not report income until they receive it. Even though you earned the money in December, if you get paid in January the income is considered January's income, and the taxes on it are delayed a full year.

On the other hand, if your tax bill is already

about zero for the current year, you may want to try to get paid by December 31, so *next* year's income (and taxes) will be lower.

This year-to-year shuffling of income does not apply to businesses using accrual accounting.

2. Cash-basis businesses can accelerate—or delay—making payments on bills you owe. Pay the bills by December 31 and get a deduction this year; or pay the bills after January 1, and get the deduction next year.

Checks written and mailed or delivered by December 31 can be deducted the year written, even if cashed in the new year.

Bills paid electronically are deducted the year your account is debited. If a bill is paid electronically in December but not processed by your bank until January, the expense cannot be deducted until the next year.

You can charge purchases to a bank credit card (VISA, MasterCard, Discover or American Express) by December 31 and get a full deduction for the current year, even though the bill is not paid until next year. By some mysterious quirk of legal logic, the IRS considers a charge to a credit card as paid in the year you make the charge, not in the year you pay the bill. This applies even to cash basis businesses. This rule does NOT apply to charges made to store or gasoline company credit cards. Those charges are deducted when you pay the bill. (Go figure...)

3. Assets purchased for your business can be written off the year of purchase, within limits (see the chapter "Business Assets"). A new computer, business equipment, office furniture, even a vehicle can be purchased right up to December 31 and get the full deduction. If you are short on cash, you can finance your purchase, pay for it next year, and get the full deduction this year (even if you are on the cash basis).

Or, at your option, you can choose to depreciate the equipment, deducting only a part of the cost in the current year, and deducting the rest of the cost in future years.

Or, if you don't need any more deductions this year, postpone your purchases until January.

4. Stock up on—and pay for—business and computer supplies, stationery and other consumables, and write off the entire expense in the current year. (You cannot do this with inventory;

inventory cannot be written off until sold; see the chapter "Inventory").

5. Pay your January monthly bills in December and take a deduction in the current year. But see the chapter "Prepaid Expenses."

6. If you are planning to sign up for a service that lasts up to a year—a new insurance policy, cell phone contract, Internet connection, maintenance contract, etc.—if you start the contract and pay for the contract in December, you can write off the entire amount in December. See the chapter "Prepaid Expenses."

7. December 31 is the deadline for setting up a new Keogh or 401(k) plan (a Qualified Plan), although you do not have to make contributions to the plans until the next year.

8. Hire your kids for the holidays. If you need extra help in December, the kids are on school vacation, put them to work in the business. Generally, a child under the age of 18 can earn up to $4,750 a year tax free; and you, the parent-employer, get a full tax deduction. The rules are explained in the chapter "Family Employees" in the Growing Up section.

9. Give your hard-working employees a year end bonus. The bonus is taxable to your employees as wages, and you (and your employees) pay payroll taxes, but you get an income tax deduction—and you generate a whole lot of goodwill from the people you rely on.

10. C corporations can pay year-end bonuses and dividends in December, or January of the new year, depending on the tax needs of the stockholders. You should discuss this with your tax accountant. (Does not apply to S corporations).

After December 31, there are still things you can do to reduce taxes for the year just ended:

1. For accrual businesses only: Take a good look at your accounts receivable, what your customers or clients owe you. If any are uncollectible, you can write them off and take a bad debts loss for the year just ended, but ONLY if you recorded the income in your income ledger. If you don't record income until you receive it (cash method) you cannot take a bad debts write-off. See the chapter "Bad Debts."

2. If you are depreciating equipment, furniture, machinery or other business assets, if any of these assets are no longer functioning, are worthless, obsolete, broken, missing (!), etc. you can write off the entire balance (the undepreciated cost) on your taxes for the year just ended. See the "Depreciation" chapter.

3. Evaluate your inventory. Damaged, obsolete, unsalable inventory can be written off on your tax return, as part of cost-of-goods-sold. Inventory that is salable, but worth less than what you paid for it, can be reduced in value for figuring your taxes. See the "Inventory" chapter.

4. You can open and contribute to an IRA or a SEP (or both) up until your tax return filing date: April 15 for the IRA, extended date for the SEP. You pay no income tax on the contributions until you withdraw the money. You do, however, still have to pay self-employment tax on the money contributed to a retirement plan.

TAX CREDITS

Tax credits are special tax incentives created by Congress to stimulate the economy or to encourage businesses to act in socially or environmentally responsible ways. Unlike regular business deductions that reduce your profit, tax credits directly reduce your income taxes dollar for dollar. They can be a real gold mine.

Tax credits come and go, available one year and not the next. If you fail to take a tax credit you are entitled to, the IRS will not tell you.

Last year, there were tax credits for purchasing electric vehicles, producing alcohol fuels, conducting new research, providing low-income housing, making your business accessible to disabled people, producing electricity from renewable resources, hiring employees who meet certain eligibility requirements, rehabilitating historic structures.

Tax credits do not reduce your business income (or your self-employment tax). The credits appear on your 1040 form, not on Schedule C. Some credits appear on partnership or corporation returns. IRS Publication #334, "Tax Guide for Small Business," lists the tax credits currently available.

TAX SOFTWARE

Tax-preparation software can organize your ledgers so they match tax-return categories, suggest tax options, ask questions, and prepare your entire tax return.

But business taxes can be quite complicated, as you know. It would take a clever and sophisticated program—and one without bugs—to know just the right questions to ask. The software would have to be fully up to date for the latest changes to tax law, which come constantly. And like any other computer program, you need to learn how to use the software. This may be a lot of work considering you will be using it only once.

I have talked to several tax accountants about tax programs, and every one thinks you'd be making a mistake to trust your business tax return to a computer program, one that may or may not include all the peculiarities of small business tax law.

Now, I admit that accountants would loose a lucrative chunk of their income if people started using computers instead of them, but their warnings are valid. A face to face discussion with a tax accountant is much more likely to turn up tax savings than typing answers to formula questions on your computer. An accountant can spot possible problems you might avoid, by rewording an answer to a question, or re-labeling an expense, or maybe by not claiming some deduction that might be a red flag to the IRS.

An accountant can show you how you might do things differently next year, to reduce future tax bills. An accountant can answer your questions, without you having to filter them through some "search" programming.

Of course, I am an accountant...

People get very nervous when talking to the IRS and don't know when to be quiet. When a simple yes or no will do, they go into a whole explanation of all kinds of things that the agent doesn't need to hear.

—Accountant Howard Rosenbloom

The INTERNAL REVENUE SERVICE and You

Small Time Operator is not a manual for beating the IRS at their own game nor is it intended to be another "101 Ways to Reduce Your Taxes." Still, a general knowledge of the Internal Revenue Service and its inner workings may benefit you in your dealings with the agency and may even add to your peace of mind.

Most people, including most small businesses, file their tax returns and never get audited. The IRS audits 3-5% of all sole proprietors, 2% of all small corporations. IRS agents have to earn their keep, and they are not going to be nickel-and-diming every little business that files a return. In almost all instances, returns selected for audit are those obviously out of line with the IRS's idea of the "norm."

The IRS does conduct "random" audits—and they are a nightmare if you are selected—but the audits are truly random, and there is no predicting who will be among the chosen few.

All tax returns, big and small, are automatically checked on IRS computers for mathematical errors: addition, multiplication, tax computation. If there is an arithmetical error, you will be notified of the error and any change in your taxes due to it. This is not an audit; and if you make an error, it does not increase your chances of being audited.

Many income tax returns are checked against other documents sent to the IRS, particularly W-2s, 1099 forms, and other Information Returns. If your tax return does not include income that was reported to the IRS on a W-2 or 1099 form, you may get an inquiry, or even a tax bill, from the IRS.

Federal income tax returns are entered into the IRS computers and automatically compared to what is known as the "Discriminate Input Function Formula," a computer program of the average American's financial profile. If your return falls within the "DIF" formula, you will be deemed An Honest Taxpayer. Your return will be filed away in the deep recesses of computer storage and will probably never be seen again.

If the computer does kick out your return, flags it for a possible audit, it will be sent back to an IRS district office. An agent in the district office will review the return and decide whether or not to initiate an audit. Not every tax return rejected by the computer is audited; usually, only those returns the agent feels are potential money makers for the IRS are selected.

When examining a small business, the IRS will probably be looking for some of the following:

1. A reasonable profit, comparing total expenses to total sales. If your sales are $10,000 and your expenses $9,990, you may arouse suspicion that all is not right.

2. Consistency from one year to the next. Large fluctuations or unusual changes from year to year might invite an audit.

3. Unusual or unreasonable expenses. Large expenses not usually found in your type of business will be suspect. Large deductions for entertainment or travel away from home invite audits.

If you are taking a deduction for a large, unusual expense or for an expense that may be suspect, such as travel, you might include a statement with your tax return explaining the deduction and include written documentation to prove the validity of the expense. This is not required or even suggested by the IRS, but it might help you avoid an audit if an IRS agent winds up looking at your return. You may want to ask your accountant about this.

4. Estimated numbers. The IRS is suspicious of round numbers.

5. Whether you've been audited before. If you have been audited in the past and wound up owing more tax, your chances of being audited again are increased. On the other hand, if prior audits did not result in more tax, you probably will not get audited again even if the computer does "kick out" your return.

6. What kind of business you own. The IRS has a "Market Segment Specialization Program" (MSSP) where they select a specific industry, and audit a large number of restaurants, or maybe lawyers, or insurance agents, often a type of business where "problems" have typically shown up in prior audits.

This program especially targets businesses that conduct transactions in cash, such as laundromats, cab drivers, vending machine operators. The IRS believes that cash businesses have a higher degree of "noncompliance" (i.e. cheating) than other businesses. What you write in the "occupation" box and the business code number on your tax return may affect your chance of being audited.

7. The IRS has an agreement with most states to exchange tax information. If your state tax return was audited, the state may notify the IRS about the results of the audit. The IRS may notify your state about results of IRS audits. The IRS may examine state sales tax reports, comparing sales reported on sales tax returns with sales reported on income tax returns.

Home Businesses: A lot of people think that home-based businesses (those claiming a home-office deduction) are more likely to be audited. In my experience, this is not true. A home business is no more likely to be audited than any other small business—unless the home-office deduction is large compared to the size and income of the business. Any unreasonable or out-of-line deduction could trigger an audit.

Business Loss and "Hobby Losses"

A loss on your tax return is by no means a sure cause for audit. It is not uncommon for new businesses to show a loss the first year, with high start-up costs and early, slow business.

A warning, however, to people who manage to show a loss year after year: if you do not show a profit for at least three out of five consecutive years, the IRS, if it audits you, might rule that your business is not really a business, but a hobby. The IRS treats any income from a hobby as taxable income, but losses are not deductible. By contrast, a business loss is deductible. (If you breed, train, race or show horses, the IRS hobby loss test is 2 out of 7 years instead of 3 out of 5).

The Hobby Loss Rule is not a firm rule. A business can deduct losses for several years in a row without ever being challenged by the IRS. In the event of an audit, the IRS will allow the on-going losses if they are convinced that you are operating a real business and trying, though unsuccessfully, to make a profit. The key issue is *intent*. What are you really doing? Trying to earn some money or just having fun? It will help if your business looks like a business (licenses, ledgers, bank account, business cards, etc.) and if you're devoting time to it in a businesslike manner.

If your business is showing losses in the first year or two, you can keep the IRS from invoking the hobby-loss rule until the full five year period is up, by filing Form 5213, "Election to Postpone Determination" within three years of the due date of your first business tax return (April 15 of the fourth year in business). Filing this form is **not** required. In fact, many accountants think it may be a red flag to increase your chance of an audit. I suggest that you ask your accountant about filing this form.

Notice of An Audit

Your first notice of an audit will be a letter from the IRS informing you of the audit and the year or years to be examined. You may be asked to come in person to a meeting with an agent or merely to send in written information. The IRS may want to see a bill or proof of payment to support a specific expense, or they may want to see your entire set of ledgers. You may be asked to supply copies of your prior years' tax returns. The auditor may want to visit your business. If your business has a web site, the auditor may visit your web site looking for information.

When audited, you may be required to prove the accuracy of your ledgers, supplying bank statements, invoices, cancelled checks, or whatever else the IRS requests. Federal law requires you to keep adequate records to support your numbers, and the IRS has the legal right to examine those records.

If you are audited, it may be a costly decision to face the IRS without an accountant there to help. IRS agents are trained to ask leading questions in order to get information from you that may increase your tax bill or lead to an expanded audit. A good accountant knows what to expect and can help answer questions, honestly and legally, but in a way that may avoid unnecessary trouble. The accountant can possibly help narrow the scope of the audit, and arrange to meet the auditor at the IRS office or the accountant's office, instead of your own business location.

The accountant, being a professional and used to dealing with IRS agents, can defuse any personal animosity. Business owners often get angry at IRS agents. And IRS agents, being human beings, are sometimes harder on owners who are unable to control themselves. A little politeness can go a long way in helping an audit along.

Federal income tax laws and their legal interpretations fill entire bookshelves. Small business law by itself is full of special rules, exceptions to those rules, and Tax Court rulings overthrowing or restricting those rules. IRS agents are tax

"You're saying that as a professional writer, your expenses totaled $22,000 more than your income? What kind of way is that to make a living?"

experts, but they do occasionally make mistakes. Honest mistakes, I'm sure. But if you don't know the law, you don't know if the IRS agent is right or wrong when he says that you cannot deduct some expense you thought you could. A good tax accountant, one experienced in small business, knows those rules inside and out. I have saved some of my tax clients lots of money by being at the audit, tax books in hand, showing an IRS agent that his ruling is incorrect.

If the audit goes against you, and you still feel you are in the right, the IRS provides all taxpayers an elaborate system of appeals, starting with informal meetings with agents and going right up to the Supreme Court.

Penalties

Generally, no penalties are assessed where there is an honest mistake on a tax return. You will owe only the back taxes and interest, as long as you pay up when the IRS says pay up.

There are a large variety of IRS penalties, some mild and some severe, for various offenses: Failure to file. Failure to pay (the more you owe, the bigger the penalty). Negligence. "Intentional disregard of rules and regulations without intent to defraud." "Willful attempt to evade or defeat taxes" (that means fraud). Where fraud is involved, the IRS can impose both civil and criminal penalties. Civil penalties (fines) can be imposed in the normal course of an audit. Criminal penalties (large fines and/or jail) may only be imposed after full due-process of law, a trial, etc.

If you cannot afford to pay the taxes when your tax return is due, file the return on time anyway. The penalties will probably be less. Quite often, the IRS will waive penalties where failure to file a return or failure to pay the tax is due to "reasonable cause."

Except for special situations, the general statute of limitations—the length of time the IRS has to audit a return and assess back taxes—is three years from the time the return is filed. If you omit more than 25% of your gross income, the statute of limitations is increased to six years. If your return is "false or fraudulent" or if no return is filed, there is no time limit. Most IRS audits, however, are initiated within 18 months of filing the return. If you haven't heard from them by then, you probably won't.

This chapter is full of vague terms: reasonable cause; without intent to defraud; intentional disregard of rules and regulations; willful attempt to evade; "unusual" this and "unreasonable" that. Many people make their living arguing over these and other godawful terms. As with so many other legal situations, the words often wind up meaning whatever the agent or the judge wants them to mean. This is not an area for amateurs. If you are caught up in an audit involving these issues, your philosophy and your finances will have to dictate your reactions. Good luck.

Failure to File a Tax Return

I would like to cover an area about which I have received a surprisingly large number of questions over the years: what if someone has been in business a few years and never filed a tax return? It's rarely a case of intentional dishonesty. A typical example is a craftsperson who starts out with a hobby. At Christmas, he sells a few hundred dollars worth of merchandise, and he never thinks of his craft as a business. But now, two or three years have passed, and he realizes that $5,000 or $10,000 a year is going through his bank account, and he's never filed a tax return. Now what?

Contrary to what many people think, the Internal Revenue Service is not all-powerful nor all-seeing. Their computers are not set up for Big Brother snooping—not yet, anyway. The IRS will not know you have earned money unless you or someone else reports it to them. For most Americans, this information comes to the IRS on a Form W-2, report of income of employees, or on a report of bank account interest.

A self-employed person is most likely to be known to the IRS via something called a Form 1099-MISC, report of income paid an individual other than an employee. If you sell your services to another business (not goods, just services) and that business paid you $600 or more during one year, they are required to file a Form 1099, notifying the IRS that you have received this money. If you are an independent sales agent and you purchase $5,000 or more in goods for resale (from one company in one year) that company will report the purchase to the IRS on a 1099 form. In both of the above situations, the business that files the 1099 must send you a copy of the form.

If you receive a Form 1099, the IRS has your name. If the amounts paid exceed the minimum requirements for filing, you are likely to get a letter of inquiry or possibly even a tax bill.

Forms you yourself file might alert the IRS to your existence, such as employment reports, sales tax reports, even state tax returns.

If no one reports you, and if you file no reports or other documents, the IRS will probably not know of your existence. Probably. But you are breaking the law, and there is no statute of limitations on how many years later they can come after you.

The law says, and I recommend, that you file returns for all those prior years, pay the back taxes and interest. Some people will just go on their merry way and never file and never be found; we've all heard of someone with that kind of experience. Other delinquent folk may decide that this is the year to file their first return, and let the prior years lie, hopefully, unnoticed.

AMENDING OLD TAX RETURNS

There may be gold in old income tax returns. Two facts few people know: (1) Most income tax returns, especially small business returns, have errors no one, not even the IRS, discovered; and (2) You may amend prior years' tax returns and get refunds of overpaid taxes.

The IRS catches glaring and obvious errors on tax returns: mistakes in addition or tax computation, missing forms, entries on the wrong line, improper procedures. Beyond the obvious, unless you get audited—and less than 5% of small business tax returns are audited—your return will be accepted as is, errors and all.

How do you know if there is an error or omission on your tax return? If you prepared the return yourself, there's probably an error. The tax laws are so complex, even the experts don't know it all. Unless you studied the tax laws thoroughly, you probably missed something.

If you took your taxes to one of those tax chains or storefront tax operations, your return was probably prepared by someone with little experience and brief training. These people do not take the time to look into your business finances in search of tax savings. If the tax preparer took your numbers and asked few or no questions, chances are good your return is not all it could be.

The most common omissions and errors I've found on business tax returns are: not taking tax credits you are entitled to; failing to accrue expenses at year-end (see the chapter "Accrual Accounting"); overlooking legitimate business expenses that didn't get into your ledgers or your business checkbook, such as out-of-pocket cash payments, business expenses paid out of your personal checking account, automobile expenses, home office expenses, purchases that are partly personal and partly business, bank service charges, equipment and furniture used in your business but purchased prior to starting your business; incorrectly computing depreciation; miscalculating cost-of-goods-sold.

If you find or suspect an error or omission, ask your accountant about it. If you prepared your own return or if it was prepared by someone of questionable competence, locate an experienced accountant (see the chapter "Professional Help" in the Your Business section), and ask the accountant to look over your return. Most accountants will give it at least a glance. Some will catch and correct an error. Others will want to re-do the entire return: they're less likely to make a mistake if they are not working from someone else's mistake.

Tax returns are amended on form 1040-X for sole proprietorships, 1120-X for regular corporations, 1120-S (marked "Amended") for S corporations, and 1065 (marked "Amended") for partnerships and LLCs. Refunds are fairly prompt.

Amended tax returns must be filed within three years from the date you filed your original return or within two years from the time you paid your tax, whichever is later. A return filed early is considered filed on the due date. So for 2004 tax returns filed and paid on time (April 15, 2005) or ahead of time, you have until April 15, 2008, to amend the return.

If your federal return was in error, your state return was probably also in error. States have similar procedures for amending returns. Some states require you to amend the state return if you amend your federal return.

An amended return is more likely to get the once over from an IRS or state tax auditor. My experience, however, is that amended returns are not more likely to be audited than original returns. Still, if the refund is only a small amount, maybe you should just skip it. Why chance involving the IRS in your business if you're only getting a few bucks?

FEDERAL INFORMATION RETURNS

Certain business transactions must be reported to the IRS on special "information returns." These reports are not tax returns, and no taxes are paid with them. In most cases, you also give a copy of the information return to all parties involved in the transactions.

Many, but not all, states require similar information returns to be filed with the state.

Below are the federal Information Returns currently required.

Outside services. Businesses paying $600 or more a year in fees, commissions or prizes to non-employees or independent contractors, file Form 1099-MISC.

Independent sales agents. If you make direct sales of $5,000 or more of consumer products to outside sales agents in any one year, you file Form 1099-MISC.

Tips. Restaurants with more than 10 employees earning tips, file Form #8027.

Interest payments. If you pay $600 or more in interest in any calendar year on a business debt, report the payment on Form #1099-INT.

Real estate transactions. The person responsible for closing real estate transactions (usually the title company but sometimes the broker) files Form #1099-S with the IRS.

Royalty payments. If you pay $10 or more in royalties to one person in a calendar year, report the payment to the IRS on Form #1099-MISC.

Dividend payments. Corporations paying $10 or more in dividends report each payment to the IRS on Form #1099-DIV.

Owners or operators of fishing boats report all payments to crew members on proceeds from sale of catch, on Form #1099-MISC.

Interest received. If your business receives $600 or more of mortgage interest from an individual in a calendar year, report the income to the IRS on Form #1098.

Lenders. If you lend money in connection with your business, and in full or partial satisfaction of the debt, you acquire an interest in property secured for the debt, file form 1099-A.

Stock brokers. Report sales of stocks, bonds commodities, etc. on Form 1099-B.

Rent. Businesses paying $600 or more a year in rent (for business premises, machinery or equipment, etc.) file Form 1099- MISC.

Lawyers. Any payment to a lawyer must be reported on Form 1099-MISC.

Medical coverage. Businesses paying $600 or more for health insurance, or paying $600 or more directly to a physician for an employee's medical expenses, file Form 1099-MISC.

Fish resellers. File 1099 if you buy more than $600 of fish from fishing boats.

Large cash transactions. Businesses that receive $10,000 or more in cash (currency), money orders, travellers or cashier's checks (but not personal or business checks) in a single transaction or in two or more related transactions, report it to the IRS on Form #8300.

Suspicious Activity. Businesses that issue or redeem money orders or travellers checks of $2,000 or more that seem to be "suspicious" (whatever that means) must report the transaction to the IRS within thirty days on a "Suspicious Activity Report Form." Welcome to the United States of America, Home of the Brave, Land of the Free.

FEDERAL EXCISE TAX

Most small businesses are not liable for federal excise taxes.

Excise taxes are imposed on manufacturers of trucks, truck trailers, truck parts, tires, inner tubes, fishing equipment, outboard motors, bows, arrows, firearms, ammunition, coal, gasoline and gasohol, lubricating oils, and cars that do not meet fuel economy standards; on businesses operating aircraft; on businesses using fuel in inland waterways; on retailers of heavy trucks and trailers; on retailers of diesel, gasoline substitutes, noncommercial aviation and marine fuels; and on retail sales of new automobiles over $32,000. The excise tax is payable quarterly on Form 720, Quarterly Federal Excise Tax Return.

Excise taxes are also imposed on brewers; on wholesale and retail beer, wine and liquor dealers; on manufacturers of stills; on tobacco; and on importers and dealers in firearms. These excise taxes are paid on Form #11.

A highway motor vehicle Federal Use Tax is imposed on owners of large highway trucks, truck trailers and buses. Form 2290 is filed annually. For more information, see IRS publication #349, "Federal Highway Use Tax."

Businesses that are required to file excise tax returns must have an Employer Identification Number (EIN) even if you are not an employer. Use Form SS-4 to request a number.

Some states call their corporate income tax an excise tax, not to be confused these excise taxes.

For more information on excise taxes, see IRS Publication #510, "Excise Taxes."

STATE INCOME TAXES

As of last year, every state had some form of income tax on resident unincorporated businesses except Alaska, Florida, Nevada, New Hampshire, South Dakota, Tennessee, Texas, Wyoming and Washington, though New Hampshire has a "business profits tax" (see below).

Most states compute state tax as a percentage of your federal income tax, or based on a percentage of the income shown on your federal return. Five states have income tax rules just different enough from the federal rules to require separate calculations. The Royal-Pain-In-The-Butt Award goes to Alabama, Arkansas, Mississippi, New Jersey, and Pennsylvania.

State income taxes, like federal income taxes, are based on your net income (net profit). Total (gross) income less deductible expenses gives you net income.

Generally, states allow businesses to deduct the same expenses as the IRS allows with a few important exceptions: you may deduct state income tax on your federal return but not on your state return (in most states; you should check your state's laws on this); you may not deduct federal income taxes on your federal tax return, but several states allow a deduction for federal income taxes; depreciation rules and charitable contribution rules are sometimes different; some states do not make allowances for Net Operating Loss carry-back and carry-forward or have different years allowed for NOL carry-back and carry-forward; self-employment tax is a federal tax only, although some states allow a deduction for it; not all states allow the same nontaxable retirement contributions the IRS allows. Many states offer tax credits, reducing state income taxes. Some of these credits are similar to federal credits, some are completely different.

Most state income tax returns for calendar-year taxpayers are due April 15. Five states have later due dates: Delaware—April 30; Hawaii—April 20; Iowa—April 30; Louisiana—May 15; Virginia—May 1. Many states have extended due dates to file returns, three to six months, if the taxes are paid by the original due dates.

Corporations: The above due dates are for unincorporated businesses. Corporate due dates vary considerably from state to state. Many states require corporations to file income tax returns a month earlier (often March 15).

STATE GROSS RECEIPTS TAXES

A gross receipts tax is a tax on total business receipts—sales, income—before any deductions

for expenses. The tax is in addition to any income or sales tax.

Some states call their sales tax a gross receipts tax, but the tax referred to here is not a sales tax. Sales tax is collected from your customers. Gross receipts taxes are paid out of your own pocket.

As of last year, the following states had a gross receipts (or other unusual) tax:

Alabama has a Business Privilege Tax, varying from 25¢ to $1.75 per $1,000 of business net worth, with a minimum tax of $100.

Alaska has a gross receipts tax on the fishing industry.

Delaware has a gross receipts tax called a Merchants and Manufacturers Tax. The amount is $75, plus .1% to .72% of receipts in excess of $50,000 a month.

Michigan has a special state Single Business Tax, 1.8% of net profits (*not* gross receipts), but only after a $45,000 deductible. This tax is in addition to the sales and income tax.

Minnesota has a Fur Clothing Tax, 6.5% of gross retail sales.

Nebraska has a $175 Litter Tax on all manufacturers and wholesaler; and on carry-out food and beverage retailers that gross $100,000 a year or more.

New Hampshire has a Business Profits Tax, 8.5% of the profits on your federal tax return if your business grossed more than $50,000. New Hampshire also has a Business Enterprise Tax of 0.75% of the business' tax base, but only for businesses grossing $150,000 or more or having a tax base (value) of $75,000 or more.

New Mexico has a gross receipts tax and per-vehicle surcharge on vehicle leasing businesses.

South Carolina has a $50 Retail License Fee ($20 for artists and craftspeople).

South Dakota has a 2% Excise Tax on some building contractors.

Washington has a Business and Occupations gross receipts tax varying from .47% to 1.5% depending on type of business. Washington also has an Enhanced Fish Tax, a gross receipts tax on the fishing industry.

West Virginia has a Business Franchise Tax, the greater of $50 or 0.7% of the business' capital. West Virginia also has a gross receipts tax on soft drinks.

OTHER STATES TAXES

The list of state taxes on businesses is virtually endless. Many (but not all) states tax:

Manufacturers, wholesalers and retailers of alcoholic beverages, fuels, tobacco, motor vehicles, boats and airplanes.

Mining, logging, forest land, and real estate dealings.

Admissions on theaters, amusement parks, clubs, music halls, etc.

Freight, delivery, transportation and tour bus companies.

Chain stores, for businesses with more than one location.

Hotel rooms and restaurant meals.

Grain handlers and processors.

Financial and investment businesses.

Some states have state business licenses and annual fees (sometimes called a "business privilege tax").

You should make an effort to find out about your state's tax laws on small businesses. Call state offices, ask other business owners, ask your accountant. You don't want to be caught by surprise or hit with some whopping penalty for failure to file a tax return you didn't know about.

LOCAL TAXES

Counties almost always impose property taxes (also called ad valorem taxes) on real estate. Some counties impose a property tax on business assets such as equipment, furniture and tools. This is called a "personal property" (ad valorem) tax, and it can be quite high if your assets are assessed at a high value. Examine this tax bill. Make sure retired or sold assets are not included, and that older assets are not overvalued.

Some counties impose an inventory tax (sometimes called a "floor" tax), a property tax on business inventory on hand at a given date, or based on an average inventory over the last twelve months.

Some large cities impose income taxes, gross receipts taxes, and/or sales taxes on businesses. These taxes are in addition to any similar state tax. A few cities impose a flat "Business Tax" or "Business Registration Fee," which is in addition

to the regular business license. Your business may have to pay special sewage or disposal fees.

You should contact your county or city offices to inquire about business taxes, on general and specific types of businesses. Don't be caught by surprise, and find out too late about a tax you didn't know about and can't afford.

With the exception of some income taxes, business taxes are tax deductible.

He says we're free.

It is our Patriotic Duty to keep as much money out of the hands of our government as we can.
    —*Philosopher Walter Camp*

The best thing Congress can do is go home for a couple of years.

    —*Will Rogers*

145

Section Five
HOME BUSINESS

Once a month I venture into rush-hour traffic
to remind myself of what I'm missing.
—Jeannette Scollard, SCS Manufacturing

HOME, Inc:
Starting a Home-Based Businesses

I'd guess that on every city block and on every rural road in the United States, someone is operating a business out of a home.

Some of the largest and best-known businesses in the United States were started in someone's home. Bill Hewlett and David Packard started their legendary company in Mr. Hewlett's garage. Walt Disney created Mickey and Donald and the Walt Disney Company at his kitchen table. William Harley and the Davidson brothers, Arthur and Walter, started their motorcycle business in a shed in the Davidson's backyard. Steve Jobs started Apple Computer in his home, Bill Gates started Microsoft in his, Michael Dell Started Dell Computers in his. Mrs. Fields started her cookie business at home. Lillian Vernon started her mail order business at home. Jeff Bezos founded Amazon.com in his apartment in Seattle.

The number of home-based businesses in the U.S., especially since the growth of the Internet, has increased tremendously in recent years. Today, according to the U.S. Small Business Administration, 56% of all businesses in the United States are home-based. The U.S. Department of the Census and the U.S. Bureau of Labor Statistics report that there are over ten million full-time home based businesses in the United States, and an additional nine million part-time and sideline home businesses. And despite the huge growth of Hewlett Packard, Harley Davidson, and many other famous former home businesses, 80% of all businesses that start in the home stay there.

The Low-Cost, Low-Stress
Business Training Ground

People who start businesses are often portrayed as "risk takers." But the smart new business owner is really just the opposite, what I call a "risk minimizer." A home-based business is the easiest and least risky way to test your untested business ideas and build your business at your own speed.

You can start with a minimum investment, in your spare time. You can keep your job, you don't have to refinance your home, you don't have to gamble your savings. Find out if the business will work, find out if you are cut out to run a business. Some people think they have the world's greatest idea, and maybe they do, but maybe they don't. Some people think they'll love being their own boss and find out they hate it.

When you start at home, your mistakes are less costly than if you were going at it full-time with lots of overhead, bills to pay, can't afford any mistakes, a real pressure cooker. Every new business person makes mistakes. And some of those mistakes are going to cost you money. You charged too little. You paid too much. You said the wrong thing to the wrong person, and lost a customer. You forgot an important detail when agreeing to a job, and lost your shirt.

If you start part-time, as cheaply as possible, out of your home, your disasters will always be small ones: A $200 mistake and a $20,000 mistake could be the same mistake. Your business can afford to make low-budget mistakes. The start-slow-and-learn-as-you-go home business eliminates most of the pressure. You can learn from your mistakes. You'll be able to learn your trade and learn business in general in a more relaxed, low-pressure environment.

Defining a Home Business

The term "home business" (or "home-based business") applies to anyone working for himself or herself, whose main business location is in the home or in a separate structure on the home property. The term "home business," and the laws specifically addressing home businesses, apply not just to businesses that buy and sell goods, but to home based inventors, contractors, professionals, freelancers, designers, consultants, Internet entrepreneurs, anyone who is self-employed.

It's riskless. You can test it. If it tests no-go, you don't go.
—Doris Christopher, Owner, The Pampered Chef

Everything in this book applies to home businesses as well as businesses operated from a separate business location. But home businesses subject to government rules and restrictions, and income tax laws, that apply only to home-based businesses. Home businesses, just because they are in your home, have their own unique problems and rewards.

Kind Of Business

Some businesses are naturally suited to being operated out of a home, and others, of course, are not. Ideal home businesses are those where the location of the business is not a significant factor in the success of the business; businesses that require little physical space; and businesses that do not intrude on neighbors and the character of the neighborhood. So, retail stores, manufacturing operations, restaurants, auto repair shops, and businesses where a lot of customers come to the business premises are usually not suitable for operating out of the home. Also, most jurisdictions prohibit the use of a home kitchen for preparing foods for public sale or consumption.

Ideal home businesses include:
1. Mail-order businesses.
2. Internet businesses.
3. Publishing.
4. Professionals, consultants, freelancers, designers, writers, computer programmers, bookkeepers, and other office services.
5. Any service business where you go to your customers instead of having them come to you, such as cleaning, repairs, sales agent.
6. Crafts, as long as the workshop isn't too noisy or smelly, and assuming you deliver your goods to your customers as opposed to having a retail shop or showroom at home.
7. Inventors (don't blow up the workshop).

The Good, The Bad, and the Family

When a business is in the home, constantly staring at you 24/7, people business owners tend to put in many more hours than they would if they had to get in the car and drive to the office. After dinner, early in the morning, the middle of the night. It's life for a lot of home business owners.

More than in any other endeavor, a home business demands that you find a balance, that you make time for your family and for yourself. Successful home business owners set regular business hours, and stick to them—most of the time, anyway. At 5 pm, they turn off the phone, turn on the answering machine, lock the door to the office, and "go home."

But the opposite is also true. For some people, the special advantage of a home business is that they can work when the inspiration hits. The middle of dinner or the middle of the night is not off limits. The family, if they have a family, understands it, or tolerates it, or maybe hates it, but the bottom line is that it is your business. It will only be successful if you run it the way you want.

Perception is Reality

Home business was once thought to be the poor stepchild of the business world, a second-rate way to make a living. Part time hobbyists, stay-at-home parents, laid-off executives. Why aren't you good enough to have an office downtown? Times and perceptions, fortunately, have changed. Many professionals and tradespeople work from their homes. Most Internet entrepreneurs work from their homes.

The old stereotype is fading. But it is not completely gone. Everything you do to help create an image of professionalism will help. Design professional looking stationery, business cards, brochures. Don't skimp. Create the image you want to convey.

If your customers and clients will be coming to your home, you have a lot of work to do to make the business look professional, to separate it from the living part of your home, to make the entire home and surroundings look clean and prosperous. Wash the windows. Mow the lawn. Sweep the stairs. If you have animals, keep in mind that many people don't like animals. Many people are allergic to animal hair. The little things add up. People do judge you by the clothes you wear. They judge your business the same way. Remember, you are your business. And now your home is also your business.

Privacy is extremely important to many people. They do not want to discuss their business or their finances with your family sitting nearby. If it is possible to have a separate entrance, neither you nor your clients need to deal with your living area.

Safety First

Make sure your home business is safe for visitors. Business customers and clients will not be forgiving of a spill that makes them slip and fall, or an obstacle that makes them trip. Even if you don't get sued, you'll lose a customer for sure.

Keep walkways well lit. Check for icy paths, slippery steps, obstacles underfoot, loose rugs. If there is an unexpected step up or step down, post a warning. If there are sliding glass doors, put some decal or decoration on the glass so someone doesn't walk right into it. Tie up the dog.

The Well-Hidden Home Business

Many home businesses might benefit by, if not out-and-out hiding the fact that the business is in the home, at least downplaying the fact. You also may not want strangers, salesmen and the like coming to your home, bothering your family or the neighbors.

If you do not want people dropping by your home unannounced, don't include your street address. Use a Post Office box or a private mail box (PMB) at a mail box store. Make sure the telephone directory does not list your home address.

Post Office Boxes / PMBs

Some businesses use a post office box or a "personal mail box" (PMB) at a commercial mail box store, instead of their street address to hide their location. Unfortunately, this often backfires because a lot of people, particularly those who don't know you, are suspicious of businesses with PO box and PMB addresses. Is this a real business, or some scam or fly-by-night operation? It's too easy for you to close the box and disappear.

A lot of suppliers ship by UPS (United Parcel Service) or some similar service. Unless the UPS driver knows who you are and where you are located, you might not get your delivery.

Some magazines and newspapers will not accept advertising with PO and PMB box addresses. A few states require businesses to put a street address on all advertising, order forms,

etc. (a law few people know about and that is rarely enforced).

Some businesses, particularly home mail-order businesses, find that they often get a P.O. box. Mail left in a rural delivery box, or on your porch, can get stolen or blown away. And there are still many places in rural America where there is no house-to-house mail delivery available.

Businesses that have a P.O. box often list their street address as well as the box number on stationery, mailing labels, ads, brochures, listings, etc. You might want to discuss this with the local postmaster. The post office is more cooperative than you might think, particularly in rural areas and small post offices; there may be a simple solution to your problem.

William A. Tannenbaum, The Internet Group, New York City: "Home business owners should be open about the nature of their operations and not project any embarrassment or lack on confidence about being based at home. That should be a completely neutral factor provided the entrepreneur handles it correctly. Don't be apologetic. Don't be defensive. These days, a person's office is wherever his computer is, and there are very few limits to what can be done at home. But the essential message you must convey to clients, to suppliers, to bankers, to investors, is that you are every bit as serious, sophisticated, and growth minded as you would be in any other location."

Deliveries

United Parcel Service (UPS) and similar delivery services will make deliveries to your door. You don't have to be signed up with the company to get deliveries. If you regularly ship out via UPS or some other company, and you want them to come to your home for pick-ups, you can sign up with the company. They will come to your business five days a week to see if you have anything to go out. They bill you a flat-rate weekly charge plus the charges for packages you ship. If you only ship once in awhile, you can instead arrange for a pick up only when you request it.

Trucks (common carrier shippers) will deliver freight to home businesses. If you are expecting a large or heavy shipment, you should discuss the delivery with the trucking company ahead of time. Some trucks can make street-level deliveries; their doors are low to the ground or they have hydraulic lift gates. Many trucks, however, have high doors requiring unloading at freight docks or with fork lifts. Some truck drivers will help unload freight, and some will expect you to do the unloading. Some trucks will deliver only to the curb or as close as they can drive to your door, and they expect you to haul the stuff inside. Freight companies charge extra, sometimes quite a bit extra, for inside delivery. If the freight charge is coming C.O.D., find out ahead of time if you will need cash or if the trucker will take a check.

Zoning

Home businesses are often subject to restrictive zoning laws. Zoning laws vary considerably from one location to another. Some communities outlaw home businesses entirely (though I still stand by the first sentence in the introduction to this chapter!). Some communities restrict the type of business that can be operated out of a home, the size of home businesses, the number of employees, number of visitors, the amount of inventory on hand, number of vehicles, parking, signage, even the hours of operation. Some communities allow home businesses in the residence but not in a freestanding garage or shop on the property. Some communities, hallelujah, have no restrictions whatsoever.

For specific zoning regulations, contact city hall if you are in city limits, or county offices if you are outside city limits. Don't tell them who you are; just ask if there are zoning restrictions on home businesses. And don't rely on verbal information. Get a copy of the written law, and read it. If certain types of home business are allowed, find out what types of businesses are and are not allowed. Try to define your business to meet the zoning requirements. Sometimes all you have to do is get the terminology right.

Before you get totally bogged down in zoning prohibitions, you should consider the reasons for zoning laws. People do not want a lot of noise, odors, trash, traffic, parking problems and strangers near their homes. They want quiet and peaceful residential neighborhoods. So they banish businesses, which often bring noise, traffic

and strangers, to other areas of the community.

If you plan to start a home business where you will be operating noisy machinery in the garage, where you'll be storing stuff outside, where people will be coming to your home, or where the sign in the window and the business appearance of your home detracts from the neighborhood image, you can expect complaints from your neighbors and problems with zoning authorities.

But if you have some small office business or some quiet (and odorless) crafts business, and if few if any customers come to your door, you are not likely to disturb your neighbors, and you are not likely to get in trouble with the zoning authorities, even if you are technically breaking the law. Zoning officials don't go snooping around looking for violations; they almost always act only when they receive a complaint.

The first and foremost zoning law, in my opinion, is: Be Considerate Of Your Neighbors. Put yourself in their situation. How would you feel if a neighbor started a business like the one you plan to start? If it seems appropriate to you, talk to your neighbors and tell them of your plans. Find out, before you start your business, if there will be opposition or bad feelings.

Find ways to minimize the impact of your business on the neighborhood. If you will be having several people come for a conference, consider renting a small back room in a local restaurant instead. If you receive or ship a lot of packages, consider using a mailbox store for pick up and drop off of packages. Have a parking space in front of your home or on your driveway for visitors. Keep signs small and tasteful; a small plaque next to the door may be all you need. Consider renting storage space for your inventory.

What happens if you are operating a home business and are suddenly visited by an official of the zoning board, advising you that you are breaking the law? Ask if a complaint has been filed, and if so, why? Are you causing a genuine nuisance? Will the zoning people allow you to alter your practices to eliminate the nuisance? Can you file a petition or request a waiver, variance or special use permit that will allow you to continue in business?

A public hearing is part of the variance application in most cities. If any neighbors show up to oppose the variance at that hearing, your chances are pretty much shot. So it is a good idea to get on friendly terms with your neighbors, and let them know just what you are doing before you apply for a variance. Your neighbors might help by writing letters or signing a petition in support of your business.

If worst comes to worst, and you are forced to shut down, can you have 30 or 60 or 90 days to relocate? I am not suggesting that you may have to move in order to run your business without zoning hassles, but you wouldn't be the first person who did. This is more true of someone who operated a retail shop or an intrusive workshop as opposed to a quiet office or service business.

The small town of Yellow Springs, Ohio enacted a zoning ordinance restricting home businesses, limiting the number of employees and the number of client visits per day, forbidding outdoor storage, and adding other regulations the local newspaper described as, "at best useless, at worst potentially harmful to the community." The editor added, "I wrote that hesitantly, because the people who created the law are smart people who intended to create nothing at all like this mess we have. But when you get into the details of defining just what is a home business that does not disturb a residential area, it becomes almost impossible to draw a fair line that will be applicable to all cases. The best defense of the law is that it won't be enforced. But of course it will be; not equally against all home businesses but against some in some neighborhoods, when a neighbor demands it. Home businesses can exist, or not exist, according to their neighbors' preference, mood, personality or whim."

Landlords, Condominiums, Co-ops and Homeowners Associations

A bigger problem than zoning regulations are residence contracts. If you rent your home, live in a condo or co-op, or live in some type of restricted housing development, be sure the lease, ownership agreement or real estate covenant does not prohibit a home business. Co-ops in particular often have strictly-enforced restrictions on home businesses.

No one will likely be spying on you. If you are quiet, not troubling your neighbors, chances are you could operate a business undetected and unharrassed just about anywhere. Most rules are

ignored, aren't they? As one famous former politician said, "Don't ask, don't tell."

Setting Up Your Office

Just because corporate America defines an office as a claustrophobic cubicle doesn't mean you have to set up your own office as such. The luxury of a home office is that you can spread out wherever you want. And, often, the problem of a home office is that you can spread out wherever you want.

When home and home office overlap, chaos starts creeping in. It is too easy to mingle personal and businesses expenses, equipment, cash, paperwork, and everything else. The result is inaccurate business records, inaccurate tax returns and wasted time sorting out what's business and what's personal. Keep your business and your personal life as separate as possible.

Linda Blair Design, Scarsdale, N.Y.

If at all possible, have a separate room, or at least a separate area, desk, files and shelves, dedicated to business and nothing else. The simple act of physical separation will make your office more organized, your business more manageable, your life more sane. Most studies have shown that people who mix residential space with work space tend to become disenchanted with working at home. If the kids need a computer to do their homework, buy a second one and put it someplace else.

153

The more office equipment you have, the more electricity you'll be using. If you find you are overloading your home circuits, tripping circuit breakers, you may need to get an electrician to help rewire the house. Or you may not need any rewiring. You may only need to reconfigure where equipment is plugged in. Different electrical outlets in the same room may be on different circuits, enabling you to break up the current draw. If you know where the circuit breakers are for your house, you can shut off one breaker at a time, and see which wall outlets are wired to which circuit breakers. You could run your computer off of one circuit, the electric heater off another, avoiding current overload.

The Business Telephone

Many home businesses, particularly when getting started, do not get a business listing. But if you want your customers to take you seriously, a dedicated business telephone line, answered as though it was a business and not the kitchen phone, is the first major step. Picking up the phone and saying "Hello" doesn't exactly sound professional. The customer is confused. "Is this, uh, is this a real business?"

With a separate business phone, you can decide not to answer the business phone in off hours. People will call a business in the middle of the night, and East Coast people will call at 8am their time when it's 5am and you're still asleep in California.

With a separate business phone, the kids can answer the phone without having to pretend they work for some business.

New suppliers who are unfamiliar with your company will sometimes call directory assistance, just to find out if you are listed, before they sell something to you on credit. The telephone listing is some assurance to people that you are most likely legitimate.

Many self employed individuals who use their own name as their business name, use their residential listing for their telephone. This may save you money, but it does not always work to your benefit. Telephone directories are separated between business and residential. A business listing will put you in the business section, which is where your clients expect to find you.

A business listing usually includes a free Yellow Pages listing a one-line listing; an ad costs

extra). Your business is also listed with the directory assistance operator. If your business is not listed, lots of people won't be able to find you. When you have a business listing, you can also include your name in the residential pages for a few extra dollars a month.

When you do list with the telephone company as a business phone, you can also list your personal name in the white pages and with directory assistance under the same number if you want.

You are not required to list an address for a business phone or for a personal phone. So if you don't want people to know where you are located, if you don't want strangers driving up to your home uninvited, you can request that your address be left off your listing.

Telephone Company Rules

Telephone company rules for home-business phones vary from company to company and from state to state. The rules are set either by the company or by the state Public Utilities Commission. Most telephone companies require you to have a business listing if you use your home phone for business. Business listings are usually more expensive than personal listings, sometimes substantially more expensive. Installation charges, monthly rates, extra services, and sometimes local outgoing calls cost more.

If you are required to have a business listing and do not have one, and if the telephone company finds out (which, truthfully, is not likely), they will probably demand that you switch to a business listing, effective today. Your new business rates will start the day they switch you. You won't be billed additional charges for previous months. You can keep the same phone number.

Telephone Etiquette 1

If the business has a name, answer using the business name. If you are working as a self-employed professional, answer with your name. "Good morning, this is Hugo Hackenbush."

If a baby's crying in the background when you're talking to a New York client, you have to drop your rate in half.
—Neil Rabinowitz, home-based photographer

Customers don't expect business phones to go unanswered, and they don't expect business phones to be constantly busy. If you will not be available to the phone during regular business hours, hire an answering service, or voice mail, or at least get an answering machine. Answering machines are less expensive than voice mail. But answering machines cannot take a message if your line is busy. Voice mail can. Most people think voice mail sounds more professional, more business-like, than answering machines. Forget call waiting. I can't think of a faster way to lose clients than to put them through the call waiting routine.

If you want to encourage people to leave a message, keep your own message brief. People do not want to sit through a musical interlude, a recorded chat and a plug for your product. You may enjoy being the star of your own telephone recording, but to many people answering machines and voice mail are irritating to start with. Long messages just increase the irritation and make it more likely a customer will simply hang up. Don't make your customers push buttons, and, for goodness sake, don't tell them that your call is important to us...

If you drive around a lot, particularly if you provide urgent services such as a plumber or a locksmith, a cell phone will be a valuable investment. When someone's water pipe bursts, they need a plumber *now*. If you are not at the phone, they'll call someone else. For a small monthly fee, your regular telephone company will list your cell phone number in the phone book.

Gene Logsden, In Business Magazine: "I want a device to circumvent recorded phone messages. I do not see why I have to pay for a long distance call that is answered by a recording that informs me the person I am calling is not in. If no one answered the phone I would be smart enough to figure that out for free. I do not want the person I am calling to spend his money calling me, only to learn that I am not in either, even though I thought I would be. This kind of recorded non-communication has been known to go on for days. How many millions of dollars do we spend a year to find out we are not in?"

Yellow Pages

Once you have a business listing, it won't be long before a salesperson from the telephone company will call and try to sell you Yellow Pages advertising. A business phone usually includes a one-line listing in the Yellow Pages at no extra cost. Longer listings, bold listings and display ads cost more, sometimes a lot more.

A display ad in the Yellow Pages can be quite valuable if you are selling to the local public, particularly if you are trying to reach local people who don't know you. When people look in the Yellow Pages, they are usually attracted first to the display ads. The smallest business can look big-time with a good Yellow Pages ad.

There is a real skill to designing effective Yellow Pages advertising. The phone company will be of some help, but you may want to get a professional designer to help (maybe you can find someone who will trade design help for your product or service). Study other ads in the Yellow Pages. Note the ones you like, and emulate them. Note the ones you dislike, figure out what it is that you don't like, and avoid the same mistakes. Don't put too much writing in too little space. Clutter is unattractive to the eye, and people will not take the time to read your ad. Don't waste valuable space with silly illustrations. Give brief, attention-grabbing information: "We are the only store in town where you can buy live giraffes." "We repair all brands and types of geiger counters." "Same day service." If you want people to come to your location, list the days and hours you are open. If the address is hard to locate, give brief directions: "Between 6th and 7th, right across street from the roller rink."

Review the proofs of your ads carefully. Misspelled words and poor grammar will send an unprofessional image to people. One typo in your telephone number will make your listing worthless, or worse: people will call and think you are out of business. Proof, and proof again.

Pick your Yellow Pages category carefully, or consider listing yourself in more than one category. How many times were you unable to find a business in the Yellow Pages because you could not figure out how it was listed? Check to see how similar businesses to yours are listed.

Some businesses have no real use for Yellow Pages advertising. Many manufacturers and wholesalers, businesses that do specialized work for a limited number of customers, mail order and Internet businesses, businesses where you already know all your customers, and businesses that will not be seeking customers locally, have no reason to spend money on a Yellow Pages ad.

Before you run an ad, check with your suppliers about cooperative advertising programs. Your suppliers may help pay for your ad.

The term "Yellow Pages" and the familiar walking fingers logo are not trademarked, are not owned by the telephone company. Anyone can publish a Yellow Pages directory that may or may not be distributed widely. Be sure the Yellow Pages you advertise in are part of the telephone company, part of the local telephone book.

Insurance

Home owner's and home renter's insurance probably does not cover your home-based business, and does not provide liability protection if someone, visiting your home on business, is injured. If a customer, supplier, delivery person, employee, contractor, or any business-related person is injured, you may wind up with a lawsuit and medical expenses. Your insurance carrier may not only refuse to pay a claim, the insurance company may terminate your coverage.

Don't keep your home business a secret from your insurance company. Talk to your insurance agent about your home business. If you use a separate building, such as a garage or barn, for an office or storage or other business use, mention this to your insurance agent. Some policies cover only the residence itself.

For home-based businesses independent professionals, there are two types of home business insurance available to you: endorsements, and in-home business policies:

Endorsements: If your business is a small office type of business, low income, no employees, few if any customers coming to your office, and a low dollar value for equipment and inventory, you may be able to add an endorsement (also called a "rider") to your existing home owner or home renter policy. The additional premium is usually low. Such an endorsement usually covers liability, damage to the building, and a small amount of coverage to business assets. For many small Internet businesses, this endorsement may be all the insurance you'll ever need.

In-Home Business Policies: If your home business is a primary source of income, or if you have employees or customers coming to your house, or if you have valuable equipment or inventory you want to insure, you probably will need what's called an "In-Home Business Policy." This is a separate policy from your regular homeowner policy. It offers coverage for businesses that exceed the limits on homeowner endorsements. In-home policies often include liability coverage, damage to the building, coverage of business assets, and sometimes business interruption insurance, which will pay you for lost earnings if you are unable to operate your business because of damage to your home. These different types of insurance are covered in more detail in Chapter 11: Insurance. You will need to purchase regular homeowners insurance in addition to the in-home business policy.

Where to Find Insurance

If your current home insurance company is not receptive to your needs, look elsewhere. Some insurance companies do not want to insure home businesses, but some insurers are eager to insure home businesses. Trade organizations and professional societies sometimes offer home-business insurance.

Read your insurance policy. Don't just accept the insurance agent's word, verify it. If the language of the policy is confusing, or if it seems to contradict with the agent told you, take the policy to your agent and sit down and discuss it. Your home, your business, and your money are all at stake. Know what is covered.

Federal and State Homework Laws

If your employees work at their *own* homes (not at the employer's home), the U.S. Department of Labor's Fair Labor Standards Act, and several state "homework laws" restrict some businesses from hiring employees and require the employer to be certified by the Department of Labor. Contact the U.S. Department of Labor and your state's Department of Labor for details.

Income Tax Laws

When it comes to reporting and paying income taxes, the Internal Revenue Service treats home businesses just like every other business. Everything in the Tax section of the book applies to home businesses. Home expenses that are part business and part personal should be prorated, and the business portion deducted.

There are a few tax laws that apply only to home based businesses.

Telephones

Tax deductions for a home telephone are limited. You may not deduct the basic monthly rate for the first telephone line into the home. For tax purposes, it does not matter to the IRS how the phone is listed, business or personal. The basic rate for the first line into your home is not deductible even if it is listed as a business phone.

Expenses beyond the basic rate, such as business-related long distance calls, optional services, and any special business equipment, are deductible. Any additional lines into the house after the first line are fully deductible, no matter how listed, if used exclusively for business.

Commuting Expenses

The IRS does not allow a travel deduction for commuting. Regular commuting mileage, home to work and back, is not deductible. Home business owners do not commute, so this is not a problem, except for one fine point in the law.

If you drive around town visiting clients, the IRS considers the trip to your first client a commute, not deductible. The same goes for the trip home from your last call of the day. Any other local business travel is deductible.

There may be a way to avoid this loss of a deduction. If you go to your home office and do some work before you visit your first client, most accountants feel that you already did your commute (to your home office), and that your first client visit is deductible. Ditto for returning home after visiting your last client, if you return to your home office to work before quitting for the day. Pretty picky rules here, I admit. Part of the secret to success in business is (1) knowing the rules, and (2) knowing how to break them.

Moving Expenses

If you move to a new home, the portion of the moving expenses attributable to the business is fully deductible.

Landscaping and Lawn Care

For years, the IRS has ruled that landscaping and lawn care are not deductible for home-based businesses, even if done solely to enhance the image of the business. The only exception to this rule has been for home-based landscapers, if they are using the landscaping to demonstrate or advertise their services. The Tax Courts have overruled the IRS on this issue several times, and the IRS is considering a rule change. You should check with your accountant.

Michael Karna owns Karna Construction Company: "I have a truck with an advertisement sign and ten feet of cedar boards with a mahogany trim on both sides. This truck, along with my house, is gray and red. I also have a huge dog that comes to every project with me. Everyone remembers me by my truck and my dog. My business is run out of my home. For a display, I completely remodeled my kitchen with every kind of cabinet, two sinks, an island with a cook top, a big archway that leads into the dining area and also built a deck behind the kitchen. It has helped sell quite a few kitchens, plus we enjoy the luxury."

The "Home Office" Deduction

This is the biggest and most problematical home-business tax law. This is one of the few tax laws that you really should understand thoroughly. A lot of money—your money—is at stake.

The term "Home Office," for this important tax law, refers to any home business space—office, workshop, studio, warehouse, store, showroom, etc.—and the expenses directly related to the space including utilities, insurance, mortgage interest, property taxes, home repairs, etc. The term "home" includes a house, apartment, loft, condominium, trailer, mobile home, or boat (if you are living on it). The term also includes any separate structure that is part of your residence such as a garage, shop or other building.

In order to deduct your home office expenses, you must meet some very specific rules. Failure to qualify for the home office deduction doesn't prohibit you from operating your business out of your home. It only means that one possibly large expense is not deductible on your federal income taxes. You can still deduct all legitimate business expenses other than those directly related to the business structure itself.

These rules apply to sole proprietors, partners, owners of S corporation, and members of LLCs.

C Corporations: The home-office rules do not apply to C corporations. You can skip this entire chapter. If you own a C corporation and work out of your home, you have two ways to deduct your office expenses. You can take a personal tax deduction as an employee business expense, if you are eligible and if you itemize deductions on Schedule A of your 1040 return. Or you can lease the office to the corporation, at which time you as an individual have rental income to report on your personal tax return.

Regular and Exclusive Use

To be eligible for the home office deduction, a specific part of your home must be used regularly and exclusively for business. It can be a separate room or even part of a room as long as it is used for the business and nothing else. Period. No television in the room. No personal paperwork at the desk. (No games on the computer?) The business area can't double as a guest room, or kid's play room, or anything else, even when you are not working.

If you are using part of a room for your business, block it off with a partition, or a bookcase or file cabinet. This way you have a clean delineation of where the business space begins and ends. Should you ever be audited, you can much more easily defend you home-office deduction.

One exception to the exclusive rule: If your home is your sole fixed location for a retail sales business and if you regularly store your inventory or your samples in your home, the expense of maintaining the storage area is deductible even if it isn't exclusive use of the space.

Child care and day care businesses: The home deduction is allowed only if your business is officially licensed as a child care or day care business. If a room or rooms, or the entire house, is used for day care each business day, the IRS considers it used for the entire day. No need to prorate it for hours of use. If, for example, you operate five days a week, you can deduct 5/7ths (5 days out of 7) of the area used for business.

Lodging businesses: If you operate a separate hotel or inn on your property, it is not considered a home business. You do not have to meet the "home office" rules.

If you operate a bed and breakfast, boarding house or rooming house in your home, you may be able to take a full deduction for the home, depending on the circumstances. You should talk to your accountant.

"Principal Place of Business"

In addition to the Regular and Exclusive Use rules, your home office must meet at least one of the following three requirements:

1. The office must be your principal place of business, defined by the IRS as "the most important, consequential, or influential location," with the main emphasis on where you meet with customers or clients. A second, but less important guideline is where you spend the most time.

2. The office must be used regularly (not just occasionally) by customers, clients, or patients, or to generate sales.

3. The office must be the sole fixed location where you conducts substantial administrative or management activities for the business: where you do your paperwork, or your research, or ordering supplies, or scheduling appointments. You don't have to do all of your administrative or

management work at home. The great bulk of it must be done at home and nowhere else.

If your business is also operated out of another location such as a store, you are still eligible for a home office deduction, in addition to the cost of renting the store, if the home office meets the above requirements.

You can have a separate "principal place of business" for each trade or business you operate.

What's Deductible

Deductible home-office expenses include a percentage of your rent if you rent your home, or a percentage of the depreciation if you own your home; and an equal percentage of utilities, garbage pickup, property tax, mortgage interest and insurance. Home repairs, such as a new roof or furnace, are partly deductible.

The best way to figure percentage of the home eligible for the home-office deduction is to measure square footage. If 20% of the square footage is used exclusively for business, then 20% of the rent can be deducted, or 20% of the cost of the house (land excluded) can be depreciated, and 20% of home utilities, insurance, taxes, maintenance, etc. can be deducted.

Business owners can calculate business use of the home based on a room count, but unless all rooms are the same size, you will not get an accurate percentage to deduct. You may be cheating yourself, or you may be cheating the IRS, by saying one room in five equals a 20% deduction.

If the business uses a larger percentage of the utilities, you can deduct the actual percentage used by the business. If, for example, the business space is 20% of the home but the business uses 40% of the utilities, you deduct 40% of the utilities and 20% of the other related expenses.

If your homeowner's insurance includes special coverage or additional premiums just for the business, the business coverage is 100% deductible as a business expense. The balance of the homeowner's insurance, the coverage that applies to the entire home, is prorated, based on the percentage of the home used for business.

You can take a 100% deduction for decorating and for cleaning the office area, and for furniture, equipment, and office machines for the office. If you install a security system, you can deduct or depreciate the full cost if the system is just for the business area; or you can deduct a percentage of the cost if the system is for the entire house.

Tax Trap For Homeowners

If you are eligible for the home-office deduction, you will run into tax complications when you sell your house. Any depreciation you were allowed must be "recaptured." This means that you add up all the depreciation you were eligible for during all the years you had a home office—*whether you took the depreciation or not!*—and pay tax on that depreciation when you sell the house. The additional tax, however, which you don't have to pay until you sell the house, is more than offset by the current tax savings (in both income and self-employment tax) if you take the deduction.

Another warning: If your home business is located in a separate structure on the same property—such as a detached garage, barn, even a structure specially built to house your business—when you sell your home, this structure is not eligible for the tax exemption homeowners get when they sell their homes. Any profit on the sale of the separate business structure is taxable. This is in addition to any tax on depreciation recapture. This quirk in the law applies only to separate structures, not to a home business located inside your main residence or in an attached garage.

If you own your home, talk to your tax accountant when you first start your home business. Find out if it will be to your advantage to claim a home-office deduction.

If you decide not to claim the home-office deduction, arrange your office so that it does not qualify for the deduction, such as using the business space at least a small part of the time for non-business use. That way, you won't be eligible for the deduction, and the IRS depreciation-recapture rules and profit-on-sale-of-home rules will not apply to you.

Remember, the goal is to work at home, not to feel like you live at work.
—*Jacqueline Lynn, Business Start-Ups Magazine*

Business Loss

If your home business shows a loss, some of your home office expenses are not deductible this year. You deduct regular business expenses (other than expenses for the office space itself) and you deduct interest and property taxes on the office (assuming you own the home) regardless of profit or loss. But the remaining home office expenses (rent or depreciation, insurance, utilities, building maintenance, etc.) are deducted this year only to the extent there is no loss.

For example, assume your home business generated $20,000 in sales this year. Your expenses, not including the home office, were $18,000. The home office portion of rent (or depreciation), insurance and utilities came to $4,000. The home office portion of interest and property taxes was $800. Your allowable deductions are computed this way:

Total sales	$20,000
Expenses (other than office expenses	(18,000)
	$ 2,000
Home office portion of interest and property taxes	(800)
	$ 1,200

Only $1,200 of the additional $4,000 in office expenses are deductible this year. The remaining $2,800 can be carried to a future year and deducted then, again as long as there is no loss.

A second example: Let's say sales were $20,000, non-office expenses were $18,000, home office portion of property taxes and interest came to $3,000, all other home office expenses were $4,000. Now the calculations look this way:

Total sales	$20,000
Expenses (other than office expenses)	(18,000)
	$ 2,000
Home office portion of interest and property taxes	(3,000)
LOSS	$(1,000)

Since you are already showing a loss, none of the additional $4,000 in home office expenses are deductible this year. The $4,000 is carried to a future year. The interest and property taxes are deductible even though they result in a loss.

The carry forward of this year's expenses (if you have a loss) applies *only* to the home office expenses such as rent, utilities, insurance, etc. The carry forward does *not* apply to interest and property taxes on the home office, nor to any of your other business expenses. These expenses are deductible only the year incurred.

If you do wind up with a loss, although you cannot "save" the extra expenses until next year, you can apply the loss to reduce other years' taxes. This is explained in the Chapter "Net Operating Losses" in the Tax Section.

The Home Office Deduction and IRS Audits

There is a widespread fear that taking a home-office deduction will greatly increase your chance of being audited by the IRS. This is a home-business myth that's been repeated over and over. It is not true.

As I mentioned in the Tax section of the book, the home-office deduction itself does not increase your chance of an audit. A large home office deduction coupled with low income will, yes, increase your chance of an audit, the IRS being suspicious that maybe this isn't really a business. But even then, you odds of being audited are under 5%. If you are entitled to a home-office deduction (and if you won't have problems with the tax trap explained above) I suggest you take the deduction. If the U.S. Government in its wisdom is allowing a deduction, you in your wisdom should take it.

Claiming the Deduction

A sole proprietor takes the home-office deduction on Schedule C. You also fill out Form 8829, "Expenses for Business Use of Your Home." If you are a partner in a partnership, an owner of an S corporation or an LLC, you, the owner of the business, get a deduction for your home office, not the business itself. The deduction goes on Schedule E of your 1040 tax return. For more information, see the IRS Publication #587, "Business Use of Your Home."

My home is corporate headquarters. The nerve center of our company is the laundry room. It houses the company's fax machine, alarm system, credit card processing equipment, washer, and dryer. At night, with all the lights flashing, it looks like the deck of the Starship Enterprise.
—Glen Paul, Founder, QwikQuote Development

A warning: Some business owners rent their home office to their business and take a business deduction for the rent expense. Not a good idea. This can be a tax trap, and cost you unnecessary extra taxes. Do not rent your home to your business without first talking to your accountant.

"This Is A Business"

People who work in an office, a store, warehouse, or any out-of-the-home business location, are working in an atmosphere that is totally business, totally a workplace. The only other people they are in contact with during work hours are co-workers, customers and suppliers. It is an atmosphere conducive to work: you go to work, get your work done, and then you go home.

People who run businesses out of their homes often do not have that clear-cut distinction of a work-space versus a home-space, and work hours versus personal hours. If you have a family, particularly if you have young children not yet in school, the distinction blurs even more. You may set up a separate office, put it in a spare room or the basement or garage, and you may say, "10 to 4 is work time, period," but you will find again and again that others are not cooperating as much as you'd like. "Keep an eye on the kids for an hour, will you, honey, while I run to the store." Friends call or stop by to visit during work hours. People who would never expect you to take a break in the middle of the day if you are at the office will think nothing of it if you are working at home.

What's the solution? Have firm rules that your work space and your work hours are to be honored—and then be prepared to have those rules broken regularly. Ever try to explain rules to a three-year-old? Or to a tired spouse who needs a break from the kids for an hour?

There has been more than one home business that relocated to a separate business location just to get away from the family and the constant interruptions.

Outgrowing The Home

The great majority of successful home businesses never leave home. The home-business owners manage to balance growth, making a living, and keeping a physically small space.

But many businesses finally decides that it's time to move out of the home and rent a commercial business location. Resistance from customers and clients, who don't feel comfortable working with a home operation, is occasionally a reason. Zoning problems sometimes cannot be solved. Growing families sometimes cramp the space. The need to put a clear distinction between your business and your personal life can be a powerful motivator to move the business out of the home.

The main reason most home businesses move out of the home is because the business grew to a point where the home could no longer hold it. More products to store, more room to work, more employees. Success is forcing you in a new direction. "Forcing" is hopefully too strong a word. Hopefully, your success is happily leading you in that new direction.

If you are, in truth, being "forced" to move when you'd much rather stay home, give serious thought to how you can restructure your business so that it can stay within the confines of your home and still be successful. Do you really need to add new products? Do you need more clients? Can you outsource some of the repetitive clerical work to another business, maybe someone working out of his or her home?

Before making a final decision whether or not to move out of the home, be sure you've figured all of the added expenses involved. Whether you bring in a single extra dollar or not, when you move the business out of the home, you will be paying addition expenses for: Moving costs. Rent or lease, and possibly rent deposits. Fixing up the new premises. Insurance. Utilities and telephone, including hook up fees and deposits. Security system. Outside cleaning and maintenance. City permits. Commuting expenses. And possibly other fixed costs.

Can your current income support those additional expenses? Or will you feel the pressure to have to bring in additional income that you may or may not be able to generate? You will have to deal with landlords, neighboring businesses, traffic and parking, neighborhood problems, civic responsibilities, the list sometimes seems endless. Are you sure you want to move out?

"Place" for most people is important, having a definite sense of structure, of belonging. Space is a way that people can psychologically divide their lives, so they have a life outside of their work. If you want your home office to be truly heavenly, make sure you can walk away from it.
—Sarah Edwards, Home Business Consultant

It takes discipline, and technology.
—Diane Valetta, Marketing Consultant, Chicago

Section Five
YOUR BUSINESS

"Mercy!" Scrooge said. "Dreadful apparition, why do you trouble me?"

The same face; the very same. Marley in his pigtail, usual waistcoat, tights and boots. The chain he drew was clasped about his middle. It was long, and wound about him like a tail; and it was made of cash boxes, keys, padlocks, ledgers, deeds, and heavy purses wrought with steel. His body was transparent; so that Scrooge, observing him, and looking though his waistcoat, could see the two buttons on his coat behind.

"You are fettered," said Scrooge, trembling. "Tell me why?"

"I wear the chain I forged in life," replied the Ghost. "I made it link by link and yard by yard. I girded it on of my own free will, and of my own free will I wore it. Is its pattern strange to you?"

Scrooge trembled more and more. "But you were always a good man of business, Jacob," faltered Scrooge.

"Business!" cried the Ghost, wringing its hands again. "Mankind was my business. The common welfare was my business; charity, mercy, forbearance, and benevolence, were all my business. The dealing of my trade were but a drop of water in the comprehensive ocean of my business."

—excerpted from "A Christmas Carol" by Charles Dickens

HOW TO BALANCE A BANK ACCOUNT

The balance on your bank statement will rarely agree with the balance in your checkbook. But you know that. What you may not know, if you've never balanced a bank account, is that the difference is almost always easy to locate and reconcile. The difference is due to one or more of the following:

1. Checks you have written that have not yet cleared the bank; called "outstanding checks."

2. Deposits not yet posted by the bank; called "deposits in transit."

3. Electronic deposits or withdrawals you have not posted to your checkbook; called "automated payments."

4. Interest earned or bank service charges you have not recorded in your checkbook and any return (bounced) checks that you still show as deposits; called "reconciling items."

5. Someone's error, usually yours; called "oops."

If you follow these procedures, balancing your bank account will take only a few minutes each month (hopefully):

1. Sort the canceled checks returned with the bank statement into numerical order. Some banks do not return cancelled checks, and some charge an extra fee to return checks. I suggest that if you can get your checks back, even if it costs extra, you ought to have them. You occasionally will refer to them, to prove to a vendor you did pay a bill, to see if you made a posting error, to prove a deduction for an IRS audit.

2. Match each canceled check (or, if you don't have the checks, the bank statement listing of checks) with the corresponding entry in your checkbook. Put a check mark (✓) next to your checkbook entry so you'll know the check has been canceled.

Compare the amount on the canceled check with the amount you wrote in your checkbook. Too many speedy check writers will write a check for $15.16 and post it in the checkbook as $16.15. It is known as "transposition" and is an occupational disease of even the best bookkeepers.

There will most likely be several checks you have written that have not cleared the bank yet.

3. If you have authorized automatic payments to be deducted from your checking account, these will show up on your bank statement but not in your checkbook (obviously: you didn't write a check). Hopefully you didn't forget the automatic payment was due the same day you ran your balance down to zero.

4. Some credit card companies, financial institutions, and large corporations are using electronic check processing (also called check conversion, electronic checks, or e-checks). When you write and mail them a check for a bill you owe, your check is processed electronically. The check is photocopied and then destroyed. The payment shows up on your bank statement, but the check will not be returned to you. Compare the electronic payments listed on your bank statement with the checks you wrote, and put a check mark in your checkbook next to the checks processed electronically.

5. Match your checkbook record of deposits with the deposits recorded on the bank statement. Check off (✓) the deposits in your checkbook. And again beware of transposition errors.

Unlike checks, deposits should clear the bank immediately. Electronic deposits usually take two business days, mailed deposits take two to three days. Credit card deposits take one to two business days, or longer if you have a delayed deposit agreement with your credit card processor. Any real lag in a bank recording of deposits may mean a lost deposit. Contact the bank at once.

6. Look for other charges on the bank statement: notice of a bounced check, check printing charge, or bank service charges.

If you get a bank charge you don't think is proper, call the bank and complain. Very often, the bank will cancel the charge. They would rather keep your business and your good will than get a $5 fee out of you.

Any interest earned will also show on your bank statement.

Once you've checked off everything on the bank statement, you are ready to reconcile. With pencil in hand and a blank piece of paper, or the back of the bank statement:

1. Write down your checkbook balance.

2. If you authorize automatic deductions from your bank account, subtract these deductions from your checkbook balance.

3. If you receive automatic payments or electronic payments, add these to your checkbook balance.

4. Add up the checks you have written that have *not* cleared the bank, the ones without a check mark next to them. These are your "outstanding checks." *Add* this total to your checkbook balance.

5. *Subtract* from your balance any deposits you have recorded that have *not* cleared the bank. These are your "deposits in transit."

6. *Subtract* from your balance any bank fees and charges on the statement.

7. *Add* to your balance any interest paid.

8. If you made any errors recording check or deposit amounts adjust your balance.

The final figure you come up with should equal the bank balance on the bank statement. It doesn't? Darn. Let's try to isolate the problem.

Repeat the reconciliation, and check your addition. If you don't have an adding machine, this may be a good time to read the chapter on adding machines in the Bookkeeping section; at least it will be a good excuse to get away from these numbers for a little while.

Still computes the same? When you checked off the canceled checks and the deposits, did the amounts all agree? Are you sure?

At this point, the error is 99% certain to be in your running checkbook balance. Sometime during the month, you wrote a check and recorded the correct amount but subtracted it incorrectly from the balance. Go back and re-subtract each check from the balance, check by check. You are bound to find the error.

No luck? Did you lose one of the canceled checks? Add up the number of canceled checks and compare with the total number of checks listed on the bank statement.

Still can't find the difference? At the bottom right hand corner of each cancelled check you'll see a computer-generated number. This is the amount the bank deducted from your account. This number should be the same as the amount of the check and the amount posted to your checkbook. You may find your error here.

What else? Examine the bank statement: the beginning balance should be the same as last month's ending balance. Was there a reconciling item on last month's statement you forgot to post to your checkbook? Did you balance last month's bank statement? (I'm still trying.)

I think that it is impossible to go through all these procedures and not locate the error. But if you've done the impossible, I suggest two more things: (1) Just put it all away for a few days and forget it. Later, when you're in a better mood, repeat these procedures, from scratch. Don't look at your old calculations; if they are wrong they will throw you off. AND IF THAT DOES NOT WORK, then (2) take your checkbook and the statement and the canceled checks and all down to the bank and get them to help you.

The one solution I failed to mention is the easiest: forget it. Assume you've made a mistake somewhere, correct your balance to agree with the reconciliation, and forget it. But that's just not my nature, so...

If you do have an error or if there are reconciling items such as bank charges, correct your books as follows:

Error in addition: Adjust the most recent checkbook balance up or down to correct the error. Make a note in the checkbook as to exactly what you are doing.

Error in check or deposit amount: Adjust the most recent checkbook balance and write a note of explanation. If you recorded a check or deposit incorrectly, make sure you didn't make the same mistake on your expenditure or income ledger.

Bank charges: Record them in your checkbook the same way you record a check, reducing your bank balance accordingly. Remember to post the charges to your expenditure ledger in Column Two—Supplies, Postage, Etc.

Automatic payments and electronic deposits: Record them in your checkbook the same way you record checks and deposits. Post the deductions to your expenditure ledger and the deposits to your income ledger.

Balancing your bank account every month is essential to your business. Your bank account is the lifeblood of the business, and you need to know how healthy and accurate it is. Balance the account as soon as the monthly bank statement arrives. Every day you delay, you've added more entries to your checkbook, meaning more reconciling items, more time spent balancing the account, more chances for errors.

Drive ahead, don't spare the steam, make all the noise possible, and by all means keep down the expenses.
—*P.T. Barnum*

BALANCE SHEETS

A balance sheet, also known as a "statement of assets and liabilities" or "net worth statement," is a listing of your assets, liabilities, and net worth (equity) at any given point in time. Balance sheets are required on some partnership and corporation tax returns. Most banks will ask to see a balance sheet when considering business loans. Audited corporate financial statements include comparative (current year and prior year) balance sheets.

Balance sheets are made up of three sections: (1) Assets—the property you own; (2) Liabilities—money you owe; and (3) Equity—the net worth of your business, the difference between the assets and the liabilities.

Assets

Assets are broken down into two categories:

Current: Cash, and assets that will be used or sold within a year. Current assets usually include accounts receivable (money your customers owe you), less an allowance for bad debts; notes and loans receivable (money owed to you other than regular credit accounts) due within one year; inventory, valued at cost or market, whichever is less; prepaid expenses (beyond a year) such as next year's insurance (current year's prepaid expenses are not included).

Other Assets: Cost of fixed assets such as equipment, vehicles, furniture and buildings less the accumulated depreciation; cost of land; intangible long-term assets such as patents; notes and loans receivable that will not be collected within one year.

Long-term notes and loans receivable that are payable to you in installments over several years should be split between "current" and "other." The amount coming due within one year should be shown as "current"; the balance should be listed under "other assets."

Liabilities

Liabilities are divided into similar categories:

Current: Accounts payable (your unpaid bills: money you owe your suppliers); loans payable due within one year; unpaid taxes; unpaid wages.

Long-term: Any loans or other liabilities due

Bear Soft Pretzel Co.
as of December 31

Assets

Current Assets

Cash		$375
Accounts Receivable	$140	
Less allowance for bad debts	($20)	
		$120
Prepaid insurance		$150
Inventory (at lower of cost or market)		
Pretzels--hot	$25	
Pretzels--stale	$1	
Flour, sugar, salt	$75	
		$101

Other Assets

Equipment, at cost	$2,300	
Less accumulated depreciation	($450)	
		$1,850
Total Assets		$2,596

Liabilities

Current Liabilities

Accounts Payable		$120
Loan payable, portion due within one year		$250

Long-Term Liabilities

Balance of loan payments		$750
Total Liabilities		$1,120
NET WORTH (owner's equity)		$1,476
		$2,596

---

after one year. Loans payable in installments over several years should be split between "Current" for the amount due within 12 months and "Long-term" for the balance.

You should include under liabilities any "contingent" liabilities you know about. Contingent liabilities are crystal-ball suppositions about the future: liabilities that may or may not materialize. If the IRS is auditing you or you are being sued, for example, and there is a possibility you will owe money, some dollar estimate of the liability should be included on the balance sheet. Contingent liability estimates should be clearly labeled as such and should be explained fully.

Balance sheets can be simple or quite complicated. A balance sheet prepared for your bank when requesting a loan need not be elaborate. The audited financial statements required of large corporations, however, include fully detailed and footnoted balance sheets. Any accounting textbook will include a chapter on balance sheets. An easy way to learn about balance sheets is to study the published financial statements that most corporations put out. You usually can get them free on request.

PROFESSIONAL HELP:
Accountants and Attorneys

This book should help you with most aspects of beginning and operating a small business without need of an accountant. But the time may come when your finances are getting a bit too complicated, or you may need help incorporating or setting up an LLC. Anyone buying a going business or a franchise should get an accountant's help. And then there's income taxes. It's a rare business owner who has the time and inclination to study and understand tax laws.

How do you find a good accountant? Locating a good accountant is like trying to find a reliable doctor: you have to ask around. The best people to ask are other business owners. It is essential to find an accountant with small business experience. It is not important what kind of small businesses the accountant works with, because small business tax law is pretty much the same whether it's a grocery store or a photo studio, a computer consultant or carpenter, a big storefront or a home business.

If you do not know an accountant and can't get a reliable recommendation, here are a few suggestions and warnings to help in your search.

Do not pick a name at random from the phone book. There is no way to know what kind of person you will get or how qualified he may be.

Stay away from the storefront tax operations, the ones that open shop every January and promptly disappear April 15. Most of the people who work for these chains have little experience, brief training, and are usually familiar only with Mr. and Mrs. Nine-to-Five and their typical tax problems. These part-time accountants are not trained to handle complex problems nor do they take the time to delve into your business finances looking for tax savings.

Choose an experienced tax accountant, and expect to pay professional prices. It is not necessary to hire a certified public accountant. CPAs may or may not be the best qualified, depending on their experience with small business taxes. There are also Public Accountants (PAs), licensed in some states; Enrolled Agents (EAs), licensed by the federal government (despite the ominous name, EAs are not IRS agents although some of them used to work for the IRS); and individuals who have no official license but who may be excellent tax accountants. Judge the accountant by his or her experience, how many small business clients he or she has, and whether you like the individual or not.

Talk to the accountant personally before you commit yourself. If he or she will not talk on the phone other than in vague generalities, call someone else. Does the accountant seem familiar with your situation and your problems? Most important, does he make sense to you? Beware of the accountant who talks arcane business jargon or IRS code sections. You need an accountant to answer questions, in words you understand.

Ask the accountant if he prepares your tax return himself or if he outsources or subcontracts the preparation to someone else. Some accountants send their clients' tax returns off to mass-production tax processing centers, sometimes outside the U.S. Do you want someone you don't know, or someone in another country, having access to your personal information, Social Security number, and financial records?

It's important to understand what an accountant can do for you and, just as important, what the accountant cannot and will not do for you.

A good accountant will prepare your tax return faster than you thought humanly possible, will know all of the tax options you have, and help you make the best choice. A good accountant will show you ways you might reduce taxes by restructuring your business, changing your bookkeeping, timing certain purchases and payments, or making other changes that will help you better deal with taxes. This is the accountant's area of expertise, and you should make the most of it—you're paying for it.

It is more vital than ever that you assume greater responsibility for your financial future. You ought not to rely exclusively on paid advisors. You should be knowledgeable enough to raise good questions and evaluate answers when you deal with a professional. The informed client gets the best advice.   —Tax attorney Julian Block

The most expensive professional is the one you don't hire when you should.
*   —CPA David Scully*

Tax professionals are held accountable for the work they do and the advice they give. They will not tell you how to break the law, and they don't want to hear about any illegal tax maneuvers.

Certainly you can and should ask honest questions—Is this legal? Is this deductible? Must this be reported?—but expect honest answers. Don't put the accountant in a situation he shouldn't be in; you may be causing trouble for yourself and for the accountant.

These warnings don't mean that you and your accountant shouldn't explore questionable areas of the law if you are so willing, and if the accountant feels you have legal ground to stand on. Some tax laws are straightforward; but many are ambiguous, subject to interpretation, honest disagreement, what we call "gray areas." Some laws are so new and convoluted, no one is quite sure how to interpret them. The best tax accountants know, from experience and from studying tax manuals and court decisions, how to handle those "gray areas" of tax law.

Finally, avoid an accountant who takes your numbers, plugs them into a computer program, hands you a return and a bill. Even if you don't know any questions to ask, your accountant should ask at least a few questions and put some personal thought into your return.

If an accountant prepares your entire 1040 tax return, only the business portion (Schedule C and related schedules) can be deducted as a business expense. Partnership and corporation returns are fully deductible.

Bookkeepers

Accountants are not bookkeepers, and at the rates they charge, you don't want them to have to do any of your bookkeeping. Don't show up with a shoebox full of receipts. Don't show up with unposted or incomplete ledgers that need to be added up. If you can't get your ledgers right, if you hate posting that three-month backlog of invoices, hire a bookkeeper. Bookkeepers not only charge a lot less than tax accountants, bookkeeping is what they do every day. To locate a bookkeeper, get a recommendation from your accountant or from other business owners.

Some accountants do offer bookkeeping services, at a much lower cost than their tax and consulting services.

Attorneys

Most small businesses don't need an attorney. Your accountant can handle any tax matter and can probably provide all the help you need in drafting most business agreements. You may need an attorney's help filing legal papers, incorporating or setting up an LLC, but I suggest you check with an accountant first. The accountant will know what requires an attorney's signature and what doesn't.

If you are being sued or are suing someone, this is beyond the accountant's domain. But your accountant can probably recommend an attorney who specializes in business litigation.

HUSBAND & WIFE PARTNERSHIPS

When a husband and wife operate a business together, the business may be a corporation, a partnership, a Limited Liability Company (LLC) or a sole proprietorship.

Each of these legal forms requires different paperwork, and each can result in differences, possibly major differences, in income taxes, Social Security, Medicare and fringe benefits.

It's basically up to the couple to decide how they want to structure their business.

If a husband and wife jointly own and operate a business and share in the profits and losses, the IRS says they are partners in a partnership (unless they incorporate or set up an LLC). The couple files a partnership tax return, Form 1065.

Instead of setting up a partnership, the couple could just as easily decide that only one of them, either the husband or wife, is sole owner of the business, and set up a sole proprietorship. See "The Easiest Option" below.

How a husband-and-wife business is legally structured can have consequences well beyond IRS rules and tax returns. In many states, income earned by one spouse belongs equally to the non-working spouse. People concerned about which spouse has legal rights to the earnings and assets of a husband and wife business, should talk to an attorney. Laws vary from state to state on this important issue.

Income Taxes

The income taxes are exactly the same whether the couple sets up a sole proprietorship or a partnership (assuming they file a joint return).

In a partnership, the couple will share the income, divided equally or divided according to some other arrangement in the partnership agreement. But for IRS income tax purposes, the couple combines their incomes, and pays one income tax on the total business profit.

In a sole proprietorship, the husband or wife can hire his/her spouse as an employee and deduct the wage as a business expense. The income tax the couple pays on their 1040 return is the same as if they were set up as a partnership.

Here's an example: Let's say a husband and wife set up a fifty-fifty partnership (each owns 50% of the business). The business earns a profit (before any draw or wage paid the partners) of $40,000 for the year. Each partner's share is $20,000. The partners file a joint return and pay income tax on the combined $40,000.

Now we'll change the example. The same business is structured as a sole proprietorship with the wife as owner and husband as employee. The husband is hired at a salary of $20,000 a year. The sole proprietorship earned the wife a profit of $20,000 (the $40,000 profit reduced by the husband's $20,000 salary). The couple files a joint return and pay income tax on the combined $40,000, the exact same amount of income tax paid by the couple operating as partners.

Self Employment and Payroll Taxes

You will recall that partners, sole proprietors and LLC members pay self-employment tax, which is Social Security and Medicare for the self-employed. Employees, including a spouse on the payroll, are subject to regular Social Security and Medicare payroll taxes. Payroll taxes and self-employment tax are different taxes, requiring different calculations and different forms.

A husband and wife who set up a partnership or an LLC will each pay self-employment tax on his and her share of the profits. A wife who sets up a sole proprietorship and hires her husband as an employee, will deduct Social Security and Medicare tax from his paycheck and pay an additional employer's portion. She also pays self-employment tax on her profit.

Using the same examples as above, a business earning $40,000: If the business is a 50-50 partnership, each spouse pays self-employment tax (and gets Social Security credit) on $20,000. If the wife hires her husband as an employee, his $20,000 wage is subject to regular payroll taxes, earning Social Security credit for him; and her $20,000 profit is subject to self-employment tax, earning Social Security credit for her.

Although a couple's income taxes are combined, their payroll and self-employment taxes are never combined.

Things change, as far as how much Social Security Tax the couple pays. when the total profit from the business is over $87,900.

Businesses making over $87,900: The Social Security portion of payroll taxes cuts off at $87,900 (2004 maximum. This goes up every year). Only the Medicare portion, which is a much smaller tax, continues above $87,900.

If one spouse is a sole proprietor and the other spouse is not on the payroll, the first $87,900 is subject to the maximum self-employment tax rate (15.3%). Any profit in excess of $87,900 is subject to a much lower rate (2.9%).

If both spouses are officially part of the business, either as partners or as employer-employee, both of the spouses are subject to payroll or self-employment taxes, each spouse to the $87,900 maximum. Together, they might pay a great deal more in Social Security and Medicare taxes than if only one of them earned all the business income.

Outside employment: A similar Social Security tax situation exists if one spouse has a high paying outside job and is also the sole proprietor and the only official person in the business. The business profit subject to self-employment tax will be reduced by the amount of outside income (explained in the Tax section under Self-Employment Tax), reducing the self-employment tax substantially. Again, this savings can only be realized if only one spouse has an outside job and also runs the business alone.

Some More Considerations

If the husband is an official employee of his wife's business, the business must keep complete payroll records on the husband, issue regular

MAY I HELP YOU, SIR?

payroll checks, withhold taxes, file payroll tax returns, issue a W-2 at year-end, and comply with state regulations as well. A spouse-employee is not subject to Federal Unemployment tax.

How about one spouse hiring the other as an outside contractor? What you've created are two separate businesses, two sole proprietorships requiring two Schedule C tax returns. Both spouses pay self-employment tax.

The Easiest Option

Things can be a whole lot simpler than this. The wife can set up a one-person sole proprietorship. The husband can "help out" in the business but not be on the payroll nor otherwise officially included in the business. There is nothing wrong with this arrangement; it is perfectly legal.

Under this arrangement, the husband does not earn a wage. He is not subject to federal or state payroll taxes, and he pays no Social Security or Medicare taxes. No paperwork is required. Any "payment" the husband gets is just money withdrawn from the business. The wife is not allowed a business deduction. Her profit and her taxes are figured as if the husband earned no wage.

This arrangement is by far the least expensive way to set up a husband and wife business. The money the couple saves in payroll costs, Social Security and Medicare taxes, and accounting fees can be substantial. The drawback is that the husband receives no Social Security credit in his own name and is not eligible for employee fringe benefits. The husband would also not be allowed any deductions for travel should he accompany his wife on business trips.

This "unofficial" status is for tax purposes only. If the husband's name is on the bank account, he could write checks that his wife could deduct as business expenses. The husband probably could sign legal documents such as contracts and purchase orders, which would be binding on the wife's business.

In determining how to set up a husband-and-wife business, much more than the taxes and the paperwork needs to be considered. The structure of the business itself can affect the feelings the couple have toward each other, how well they work together, and (alas) how difficult and how fair a divorce might turn out. This could be a particular problem if one spouse is not on the payroll or "officially" part of the business.

One very astute woman pointed out to me, "An unpaid worker is generally an unappreciated worker, causing resentment and possibly a great deal of difficulty in a marriage. Tax savings should not be the number one priority in a husband/wife business arrangement. Mutual respect, sense of responsibility, appreciation, and cooperation are far more important than saving tax dollars." What's more, if the unpaid spouse had to look for another job, it could be difficult to establish a work history or job worth without some sort of salary history.

Employment Taxes, Workers Compensation Insurance, and Retirement Plans

Regardless of whether the business is a sole proprietorship or a partnership or whether a spouse is on the payroll on not, neither spouse is subject to federal unemployment taxes and neither is eligible for federal unemployment benefits.

Most states exempt husband and wife businesses from state unemployment insurance and from workers' compensation insurance.

Both spouses can participate in a Keogh, SEP, or IRA retirement plan.

Husband and Wife Corporation: If you incorporate your husband-and-wife business, the rules are different. Both spouses as owner-employees of a corporation are subject to the same payroll taxes as regular employees. You are eligible for company-paid fringe benefits, and you can set up a corporate retirement plan for yourselves (which is different from a Keogh plan).

Limited Liability Company (LLC): A husband and wife in an LLC would be taxed the same as a husband and wife in a partnership.

Two Separate Businesses

If a husband and wife each operate their own businesses, where two complete and separate businesses exist (possibly side by side), each spouse is a sole proprietor, each with his and her own set of ledgers, permits and licenses, and Schedule C tax returns. The husband pays self-employment tax on the profits from his business, and the wife pays self-employment tax on the profits from hers. If the couple files a joint tax return, the profit or loss from the two businesses are combined for figuring income tax.

If the two businesses share any assets, share an office or other business space, or share any business expenses, the expenses and depreciation should be divided between the two businesses, 50-50 if owned equally by both. It is not important which business actually writes the check or which has the equipment or lease or invoice in its name. Just be sure that each business records its share of the expense in its own ledgers.

A Northern California business that provides consulting services is owned and operated by a husband and wife, but the business is in the wife's name only. When I inquired why they structured it that way, the wife answered, "Many of our clients are women who prefer to patronize businesses owned by women. It brings us more work."

MULTIPLE BUSINESSES
(More Than One Business)

At one time, I owned three different businesses, all quite different, and all at the same time. It is not unusual for one person to have multiple income streams, to own and operate more than one business at a time.

How you set up the businesses, the bookkeeping, licenses and permits, and file tax returns depends on how you structure your businesses.

If your businesses are sole proprietorships, you have two options: (1) You can set up completely separate businesses, separate ledgers, separate permits and licenses, separate tax returns. Or (2) you could combine the businesses into one business, with one set of ledgers, one tax return, etc.

The IRS requires you to fill out a separate Schedule C tax return for each sole proprietorship you own. But the IRS lets you decide whether your ventures are separate businesses, or just parts of one business, requiring only one Schedule C.

Your income and self-employment taxes will be exactly the same whether you have one or multiple sole proprietorships. The time and expense of filling out more than one tax return might be significant, especially if you hire an accountant, who will charge you for two Schedule C forms instead of just one.

If you have only one business, you need only one business license, one DBA, one insurance policy, one bank account, one payroll, and only one form—and one fee—for whatever government agencies are making demands on you. If you have more than one sole proprietorship, you may have to get two or more of everything.

If you have more than one business, the IRS requires that you keep separate ledgers for each business. If you have only one business with several different "parts" or "divisions," you need to keep only one set of ledgers.

If you want, you can easily separate the different parts of your business, using different columns in the ledgers, to separately account for each business-within-the-business; or you can lump them all together.

Although it is easier and less expensive to combine business, the most reliable way to really know how each business is doing is with separate ledgers for each business. This way you can be much more objective about the success of each business. If you ever want to sell one of the businesses, you will have separate books to show a buyer. If you want to get a loan on one of the businesses, particularly the one that is more profitable, the ledgers for that particular business will paint a better picture.

If you do set up separate businesses or separate ledgers for different parts of your business, shared expenses that apply to both businesses, (such as office space, computer, telephone, employees working for both businesses) should be prorated between the businesses: 50-50 or any other split that reasonably approximates usage.

Partnerships, Corporations, and LLCs

If any of your businesses are partnerships, corporations or Limited Liability Companies, each business must be accounted for separately, each with its own ledgers, bank accounts, licenses, and tax returns. That's not only the law, but a protection for the owners of the businesses should legal or tax problems occur.

You can have multiple divisions within one partnership, corporation, or LLC, in much the same way you would set up multiple divisions within one sole proprietorship.

James Robertson was a highly respected publisher and book crafter, who lived in Covelo, California. He was the person who gave this book the title 'Small Time Operator': "You can make a thing—a book or a house or a camera—in such a way that it commands respect. I hate to think that the only people who care about the way things are made are a couple of oddball craftsmen out in the woods. The culture needs the attitude of making things with purpose, attention to detail and a certain kind of love."

IMPORTING AND EXPORTING

Importing and exporting involve an entire world of international laws, special tax incentives, international trade procedures, licenses, duties and tariffs, and various "middlemen" such as agents, brokers and freight forwarders that domestic businesses never encounter. You should be familiar with U.S. Customs and U.S. Commerce Department laws. You need to learn about standard payment terms, currency conversion, the stability of foreign currencies, shipping terminology, and shipping methods.

IMPORTING

Most of the people who get started in small-time importing are travellers on a trip or vacation overseas. They discover some handcraft or clothing that's attractive and inexpensive, or some clever invention or electronic marvel. They see some business potential in the products, and start figuring out how to bring the products back to the U.S. And "figuring out" is something you really should do carefully.

Customs, Duties, Quotas

You can't just buy a few cases of whatever sparked your imagination, and expect to bring it back to the U.S. without going through a maze of rules, customs, and duties. It is critically important that you have your paperwork in order. If your paperwork isn't done properly, Customs can confiscate and even destroy your merchandise. The U.S. Customs Service has a book thicker than the New York City telephone directory, listing quotas and duties on hundreds of different products from dozens of different countries.

Some imports are subject to quotas: so many pairs of men's shoes from Honduras per year, for example. Many countries have formal agreements with the U.S., called "quota visas," limiting the quantities of each item they are allowed to export to the U.S.

Many imports are subject to duties, which are taxes you the importer must pay before Customs will release your goods to you. Duties vary, from insignificant amounts on handcrafts and electronics, to approximately 34% on clothing and textiles, and on up to as much as 90%, 100% and even 110% of your cost on some restricted items from restricted countries.

Politics, and things like "most favored nation" status play a major factor in determining how easy and how expensive it is to import different goods from different countries. Strong U.S. industries like clothing manufacturers fight imports, so the duties on clothing are much higher than those on, say, handcrafted items and other goods that are not made in the U.S. by large, influential corporations.

Certain types of goods—chemicals, products made from animals, vehicles, agricultural and food products, products made with poisonous materials (such as lead based paints), goods made using child or indentured labor—are often restricted, subject to special regulations.

Shipping

Beyond Customs regulations, the most important consideration is shipping. How will you get your merchandise into the U.S.? Will you bring it back with you on the plane? Will you ship it air cargo? Can you send it by sea mail, where the Post Office delivers it to your door and collects duties when it arrives? How cooperative and reliable are the shippers and postal agencies in the exporting country? A friend of mine, an experienced importer who regularly travels overseas, always says that the first step is to ask, "How can I ship it?"

You can get more help from the U.S. Customs Service, or from a licensed Custom House Broker. Customs brokers are in business to prepare and expedite your paperwork and to help get your merchandise through Customs. You can locate them in the Yellow Pages of any major port city, or through a trade organization.

Finding Goods to Import

If you don't like to travel, you can often find goods to import by going to trade shows and gift shows. Most industries have large annual or semi-annual shows where manufacturers and distributors, including those from foreign countries, exhibit their wares. Sometimes you can close a deal and arrange all the details of shipping right at the show.

Be sure to examine actual goods before you order. I've heard of importers being very unhappy with merchandise ordered from specifications and illustrations.

One reason many people are attracted to importing is because goods manufactured overseas are so inexpensive compared to U.S. made goods. Part of the reason some products are so cheap is because workers in some parts of the world are paid criminally low wages and required to work long hours in dangerous and unhealthy work places.

So, don't hesitate to look for a great deal, but as Jiminy Cricket said, "...always let your conscience be your guide."

EXPORTING

Export regulations are entirely different than import regulations. Exporters don't have to deal with U.S. Customs duties or quotas. The U.S. government encourages exports and is eager to help you sell overseas.

Export Licenses and Documents

Most businesses can export goods without any formal permission. An export license is usually not required. Licenses are required for certain "strategic" goods (usually those with military uses), and goods shipped to certain "restricted" countries. You may have to prepare a Shippers Export Declaration (SED).

More information is available from the Bureau of Export Administration (the BXA), which is part of the U.S. Department of Commerce. On the Internet: www.bxa.doc.gov.

Contact one of the Small Business Administration's U.S. Export Assistance Centers. There are seventeen Export Assistance Centers across the U.S. They offer not just advice, but through the Export/Import Bank (located at the same offices) banking and insurance assistance. To find the nearest office, call 1-800-U-ASK-SBA. On the Internet: www.sba.gov and www.exim.gov.

Export Assistance Centers offer loan guarantee programs similar to SBA loans. These are short-term working capital loans only, and only available to businesses that have been in business at least a year. This is not start-up money. You must first have a contract or purchase order from an overseas buyer to get these loans.

Letters of Credit

If an overseas buyer decides not to pay you, it may be difficult for you to collect what's owed you. Many exporters require an "irrevocable letter of credit," where the overseas buyer's bank guarantees payment.

A letter of credit is like a contract. The wording should be precise, particularly the details of what's being shipped, the time deadlines, and the point where ownership passes hands. If the letter of credit specifies an exact weight or an exact count, or specifies a firm shipping date or a firm delivery date, the exporter could lose everything if he is off by a pound or a day. If the letter of credit states that payment is due when the goods are safely in the customer's warehouse rather than when the ship leaves port, the exporter may never get paid if the ship sinks, if the foreign customs inspector rejects the shipment, if the customer claims the goods are damaged or are not what was ordered.

Many exporters obtain export or marine (cargo) insurance, which can be purchased just for one shipment.

Exporting often requires travel to foreign countries and a knowledge of other cultures, customs, tariffs, foreign import regulations, and shipping options. If you will be taking product samples or promotional materials out of the U.S., check the duty requirements before you depart.

Like importing, you can avoid all the international headaches by going through intermediaries, freight forwarders, export brokers or others who will either arrange the paperwork for you or buy your products and then export them themselves. You can locate these people by asking other exporters or through a trade organization.

The Commerce Department's Export Counseling Division, Washington D.C. 20230, can help you find overseas buyers, explain shipping options, and even help you get paid. The Commerce Department and the SBA sponsor seminars, trade shows, and overseas trade missions where you actually visit potential overseas customers.

For more information, call 800-USA-TRADE. On the Internet: www.doc.gov.

Trade between countries is a net positive. People don't kill their customers.
—Randy Kirihara, Bloomington, Minn.

BUYING A BUSINESS

Buying a going business is certainly a fast way to jump right into the deep water. But such a purchase will require careful research. You should take your time considering this major commitment. (This chapter is not about franchises or business opportunities. They are in a separate chapter.)

Why buy a business someone else started? When you start your own business, it can be a year or more before it produces enough income to pay yourself a wage. When you buy a going business, you have an immediate income stream.

Another reason for buying is that someone else has done all the hard work: identified a need, set up the business, found the customers, worked through all the problems, and proved that it can be successful. Anything that can go wrong probably already has.

A third reason for buying is availability of financing. Investors and bankers are much more receptive to an "acquisition." A proven business is much less risky than a brand new, untested one. Quite often, the assets of the business you are buying can be used as collateral on a loan. Sellers often help with financing as well.

Finding a Business For Sale

How do you find out what businesses are for sale? There may be a For Sale sign on the business or an ad in the newspaper. There are business-for-sale listings on the Internet (hundreds are listed on eBay).

But most likely, you will have to ask around. Bankers, accountants, local business people, and people active in community affairs are likely to know who has a business for sale.

I know of businesses that sold just because someone walked in and asked the owner if he or she had any interest in selling.

Real estate agents and professional business brokers will know about businesses for sale. But when an agent or broker helps put a deal together, they collect their fee, usually a percent of the sale price, which will increase the price of the business. Keep in mind that brokers and agents are working for the seller and get paid only if the deal goes through. Don't rely on them for advice or anything other than just locating the business.

Is This The Right Business For You?

If the business you want to buy is successful, busy, rolling down the track like a fast freight, are you—the new owner, manager, clerk, employer, bookkeeper, and trouble shooter—ready to handle such an enterprise? Do you have the experience and the knowledge to jump right on and keep the business rolling smoothly? Or will your on-the-job training cause disruptions in the operation, possibly displeasing customers enough to lose them?

If the business depends on the owner's personality, or on the owner's training and experience (such as repair shops and service business), taking over that business and keeping the customers might be difficult. Customers get used to certain stores. Many customers are there because they like and trust the person who owns the business. And now, here you are, a new owner who they don't know. They've come to expect a certain level of competence, service, convenience, courtesy, from a store they frequent. They expect certain merchandise to always be in stock—the former owner always had it in stock—or they expect a service to be performed within a time period they are accustomed to. If you can't get in sync with the way the business is already running, if you can't get a personal relationship with the customers, almost immediately, the customers may have little patience for you.

Quite often, the buyer of a business will train with the seller, the two working in the store together for a period of time, so that the transition is smooth. Discuss this during negotiations with the seller, and whatever decision is made, include it in the written purchase agreement.

Is This Business Worth Buying?

Who owns the business? If it is a sole proprietorship, there is one owner, and that is who you want to deal with. If the business is a partnership, corporation, or LLC, be sure that the person you are dealing with has written authority from all owners to negotiate and close a deal.

Why does the owner want to sell? Is she or he simply tired out? A lot of business owners, particularly in retail businesses, wear themselves out after five or ten years, working every day. They just want to quit, take a rest, do something else. Is the owner old or ill, and wants or needs to retire? Is a divorce forcing the sale? Is the owner in some sort of trouble and needs the cash? Make sure the trouble is not directly related to the business, and be sure to get legal help with this. Is the business starting to fail? Does the owner know some troubling future prospects for the business—problems with the neighborhood, or a big-name chain store about to move in, or some other upcoming development that will be detrimental to the business—and wants to bail out? Is this type of business growing, or possibly a fad or trend on the wane?

How profitable is the business? Ask to see the ledgers and tax returns for the last few years. Tax returns are an excellent source of information since no one tends to overstate income or profit on a tax return. You should understand, however, that many sellers are not likely to show you financial information until they get to know you a little better, until they get a feel that you are serious about this particular business. They don't want to see their figures and tax returns floating around the countryside. It may help you to first open up to the seller, let the seller know about your own background, your financial condition, how serious you are.

When the seller finally does show you the ledgers and tax returns, be sure you know how to interpret them. If you don't understand the numbers, hire an accountant to help you. Do the numbers make sense? Income shown on bank statements, sales tax reports, ledgers, and tax returns should have some correlation. Don't pay an inflated price for revenues the owner claims he has been hiding from the tax man.

Are the profits on the increase, or on the decline? Is there enough income to provide you a living wage and to eventually pay off the cost of buying the business? Don't forget that the profit from a sole proprietorship or partnership will not include any salary for the owner. The profit *is* his salary. If it's a corporation, how much of a salary is the owner taking? If the business has a hired manager or employees who won't be needed if you buy the business, eliminating their salaries may improve the profit figure significantly.

If the business expenses include travel for the owner, fringe benefits, or other legally deductible but unnecessary luxuries, eliminating these from your expenses will paint a more attractive (and accurate) profit figure.

Be sure to figure in income and self-employment taxes. Taxes will reduce the profit figures considerably.

Equally important to profit is cash flow. Be sure the business has enough cash regularly coming in to pay the bills and to pay yourself a salary. Cash starved companies fail quickly.

Is the business in a good location? Can you assume the lease? How many years are left on the lease? To buy a business with no lease or a short-term lease means that the landlord can, on a whim, evict you, triple the rent, Lord knows what. Find out if there are any city plans for rezoning that may affect your location.

What is the condition of the assets? Is the building in need of repair or remodeling? Is the equipment in good shape, or will it need to be repaired or replaced soon? Is the computer system functioning smoothly? Will you have to sink a lot of money into the business to fix it up the way you want, or possibly to meet a building or health code requirement? Building inspectors sometimes tend to leave old businesses alone but suddenly notice all sorts of code violations when a new owner takes over.

What is the competition like? Is it growing? Are the competitors doing better than this store? Can you determine why?

How reliable are the suppliers? Are any closing their doors, moving away or making other major changes? If you will be dependent on the same suppliers, talk to them and make sure they'll do business with you.

Major customers. Does the business depend on a handful of customers or a major contract with one customer? If so, contact the customers to ascertain if they plan to stay with you.

Will you inherit obligations or problems? Are there outstanding guarantees or warranties to customers that you will have to honor? Contracts with customers or suppliers that you will be required to fulfill? Lawsuits or threats of lawsuits? Obligations to current or former employees? Contamination problems you might inherit?

The present owner of the business can probably answer all of the above questions, though you shouldn't expect unbiased answers. If you spend some time and study things closely, you will most likely find your own answers to the questions.

Observe the store, the customers, how much business is being conducted. Does what you see relate to the sales figures in the ledgers? Walk around the neighborhood, see for yourself if there is any nearby competition, and how well they are doing. Talk to other business owners in the area, particularly close neighbors. Tell them your plans and ask their opinions. I guarantee you will get an earful of valuable information.

Customers and suppliers are another vital source of information. Try to locate former customers and suppliers. I'm sure they can tell you a *lot* about the business. So can the employees; if appropriate, talk to them.

You should become Sherlock Holmes with the present owner's figures. If this is a sales business, check month-to-month purchases as some indicator of how fast the inventory sells once it's in stock (called "turnover"). It may indicate if the business has seasonal cycles—slow at one time of year, busy at others.

Check the inventory carefully. It may be much larger or smaller than the owner tells you, and it may be damaged or obsolete or simply unsalable. How much dust is on it?

Be suspicious of any recent legal fees or any unusual, large transactions. What were they for? If you see loan or interest payments, ask about them. If you won't be assuming a loan, you won't be making those payments.

How Much Should You Pay?

Finally you come to the most difficult question of all. Despite what the seller may tell you or what the textbooks say, there are few real guidelines and no reliable formulas when it comes to such a large, unique, emotion-laden transaction as the purchase of a going business. The bottom line, always, is that a business is worth no more than what a buyer will pay for it. The seller may *have* to sell this business; but you, the buyer, do not have to buy it. It is up to you to determine what you are willing to pay for it, and then find out if the seller will accept your offer.

You should realize that the seller has probably never sold a business before, certainly not this particular business. He probably knows what the business is worth, but he really has no idea what he can expect to get for it. A business is not like a used car, or even a house, when it comes to figuring out what price it will fetch. Comparisons are difficult, and prospective buyers are usually few. So, the seller is in the dark himself when setting a price. Quite often, the asking price is no indication at all of what the business will actually sell for. Businesses will often sell for half or even a third of the asking price.

The actual value of the inventory and equipment—what the present owner can sell it for if the business is closed and liquidated—is usually the bottom-dollar value of a business. A surprising number of businesses actually sell for close to this amount. So, first determine this value. The seller's original cost is a guideline, but consider age, wear, damage, and possible obsolescence.

Then, you can be sure the seller will want, on top of the value of the assets, additional money because the business is successful, established, earning a profit. Some people call this intangible value "goodwill," and they attempt to put a price on it, some dollar figure they pull out of the air (which is probably why this is also called, in business jargon, "blue sky"). Often, the seller will ask for the equivalent of one or two years' profits. Again, throw out the formulas. It is entirely up to you the buyer to decide if you want and can afford to pay for some or all of this "blue sky."

Many small businesses are bought on the installment basis, with the seller extending most of the credit. It is usually to your advantage to have the seller help finance the business, as he or she is much more likely to want to help you be successful. Most sellers, however, would greatly prefer to get the cash and be done with it, and are usually willing to reduce the price considerably if you can finance the purchase yourself.

Keep in mind that the purchase price of the a business is just a start. You will still need money for working capital (day to day expenditures, overhead, new inventory, etc.) and possibly for repairs, remodeling or sprucing up.

When you consider buying a going business, consider how much it would cost to set up, from scratch, a new, similar business at a different location. Why buy someone else's expensive business if you can start your own a lot cheaper?

Purchase Contract

Once the buyer and the seller agree on the purchase price and payment terms, you will probably need an experienced accountant's help to draft the purchase agreement. Everything should be in writing. The precise legal wording can affect how the sale is taxed, how the assets are valued for tax purposes, and how much of the purchase price will be deductible.

You, the buyer should be careful that you will not unknowingly inherit old business debts, liabilities, lawsuits, or other problems you should not be responsible for. Make absolutely sure all creditors are notified that the business is being sold, and that old liabilities will not be the responsibility of the new owner.

This is particularly important if you are buying a corporation. If you buy the corporation's stock, you are the new owner of an old business, a business that may have old legal and contractual obligations that you may be stuck with. Often it is better to purchase the assets, the lease, the business name and whatever else goes along with the deal, from the old corporation rather than buying the corporation itself. A buyer often gets a much better tax break by buying assets instead of the corporation itself. As you can see, this will require the help of an accountant or a lawyer.

You will want a non-compete clause, so the former owner doesn't turn right around and open a competing business down the street.

Tax Deductions

The costs of investigating and buying a businesses come under a variety of IRS rules. Costs incurred before you pick a specific business you want to buy, such as travel and general research, are usually not deductible at all. Once you are trying to purchase a specific business, the costs you incur are considered "capital" expenditures, and are deducted over a period of years according to the "Start Up Expenses" rules explained in the Tax section. If you do not finally buy the business, you have what's called a "capital loss" that may be deductible.

It's easy to find a lousy firm you can afford.
—Larry Hammons, Rational Technology Inc.

FRANCHISE BUSINESS

A franchise is an individually owned business operated as though it was part of a large chain. Midas Muffler, McDonalds, and H&R Block are examples of well known national franchises. Under a franchise, services and products are standardized. Trademarks, advertising and store appearance are uniform.

With a franchise, your own freedom and initiative are limited. You lose a lot of autonomy, a lot of the feeling of being your own boss. The name on the store is not yours. But a well known franchise gives you instant recognition. The goods and services are proven and trusted. Or as an old Holiday Inn ad read, "No surprises here."

How Franchises Work

Most franchises work this way: For a fee, the supplier (the franchisor) gives you (the franchisee) the right to use the franchisor's name and sell its product or service. The franchiser provides, and requires you to follow, a marketing plan. The franchise agreement may require you to purchase your supplies or equipment from the franchisor, at their prices, even if you can get better prices from local suppliers. You may have to pay the franchisor a percentage of your gross sales (a percentage of your total sales before deducting any expenses) whether you are making a profit or not. You may have to pay part of the franchisor's advertising. There may be marketing fees, training costs, national office overhead charges, charges for contract renewals. Franchisors may even dictate what prices you charge.

There are hundreds of franchise companies, some well known but some completely unknown, some with a good, profitable history, and some struggling like any other business.

Many franchises offer what they call a "turnkey" operation, a complete ready-to-run business (all you have to do is turn the key in the door) that includes training and management support. But don't let the ready-to-run concept fool you. A franchise is not a paint-by-numbers business. It will be just as difficult and just as much work to run as a non-franchised business.

Franchisors help with financing. Franchisors have their own loan sources; a few even own their own finance companies. But be warned: a franchisor will require you to put up a chunk of your own money, and they may want a second mortgage on your home to guarantee the loan. Just because it's a franchise, even a well-known franchise, there is no guarantee that you will be successful. If you can't make your payments, the franchisor will not hesitate to foreclose and resell the franchise to someone else.

Investigating a Franchise

Investigate the franchise—thoroughly. This may be a lot of work, but you are making a large investment, you'll be signing legal contracts. Now, before you sign anything or pay for anything or commit your future to anything, is the time to learn all you can about this venture.

The Federal Trade Commission requires franchisors to give prospective franchisees a copy of what's called a Uniform Franchise Offering Circular. This UFOC includes information on potential earnings (though these numbers are easily manipulated and should not be trusted), the costs, the company's history and financial standing, and terms of the agreement. The franchisor must give you a copy of the UFOC at least ten business days before you sign any contract. But you should get and study the UFOC long before those last ten days, before you've got so much time and money invested in researching this franchise. (Gasoline companies, auto manufacturers, and some franchises offered to experienced business people are exempt from this law.)

When you investigate a specific franchise, try to get a complete list of all of their franchisees and contact as many as you can. Find out how they are doing and what they think of the franchise. Ask each franchisee, "If you had to do it over again, would you invest in this franchise?"

Are there any lawsuits against the franchise? The Federal Trade Commission can tell you if any complaints have been filed against the franchisor. Contact the people who are suing the company and get their side of the story. Ask the franchisor for a list of former franchisees, call them up, and find out what happened to them. Also check with the Better Business Bureau.

Be particularly wary of franchises that are stagnant or shrinking, those with a high turnover of franchisees, and those with a small net worth. These signs may indicate trouble.

The Franchise Agreement is a binding, legal contract. Once you sign it, you are committed to it. The Agreement gives you certain legal rights, but keep in mind that the Agreement was written by the Franchisor, who's first goal is to look out for his own interests.

Study the terms of the franchise agreement. If you do not understand the wording, get help from a competent person who can explain the terminology. Get clarification, in writing, from the franchisor.

Some franchise agreements are negotiable. If you don't like the terms, percentages, restrictions, anything, propose changes. Some important issues that many franchisees face:

1. Will you have any flexibility, any of your own input, in operating your franchise? Or will you have to follow the franchisor's "formula" exactly?

2. Will you have territorial rights, and for how long? Territory (called "encroachment" in the contracts) is a major issue with retail franchises, and one of the most common rifts between franchisors and franchisees: How many Subway, or Burger King, or Jiffy Lube franchises in your town, or within so many miles of each other?

3. Can the franchisor sell directly to consumers in your area, or by mail order, on the Internet, or inside a Wal-Mart, competing directly with you?

4. Will you be allowed to sell or advertise on the Internet? Some franchisors restrict what you can do on the Internet, even down to domain names you can or cannot use.

5. How much of the company's advertising money will be spent in your area?

6. Can the franchisor cancel your franchise, and essentially put you out of business, if the franchisor chooses to do so? Is the agreement binding for the life of your business, or can the franchisor revise it, possibly to your detriment, in a year, or five, or ten? Will you be required to meet sales quotas, and what happens if you don't?

7. Can you sell your franchise to someone else if you want out of it? Does the franchisor keep a list of franchisees who want to sell their businesses? If you leave the franchise, can you start a similar (competing) business of your own?

Just like starting any business, do your own market research. Even if you are convinced you are buying into a franchise that is well structured and well managed, make sure there is a local market—customers—for the product. Even famous franchises have stores and franchisees (individual store owners) that fail.

Once you've done all the investigating you can do on your own, have a lawyer or an accountant review the agreement with you and explain to you *exactly* what you're getting into.

Give serious thought to whether a franchise is the best route for you to start a business. Certainly, a restaurant on the interstate called Subway will do better than one called Ralph's Diner. A Best Western will be more inviting than Ralph's Motel. But if you're starting a local business, will your print shop, video store, cleaning service, real estate office, or even hamburger stand, be more attractive as a franchise instead of as a locally owned, independent business? How important is a famous name and slick national advertising?

People will quickly get to know you and your business either way, and it will succeed or fail depending on your service and quality and prices. Why pay the fees and tie yourself to a franchise if it offers no discernable benefits?

There are many directories, magazines, and Internet sites that list details about hundreds of franchises. Also contact the Federal Trade Commission, Washington D.C. 20580. www.ftc.gov.

"And we'll leave the light on for you..."

People confuse being a franchise owner with being an entrepreneur. And frankly, we've taken a lot of the fun out of being an entrepreneur.
—*Don Dozier, American Fastsigns (franchisor)*

If you're the kind of person who likes to do things your way, then Breadsmith, or any franchise for that matter, isn't for you.
—*Dan Sterling, founder, Breadsmith (franchisor)*

The franchise idea, you have to answer to other people. That's what we were trying to get away from.
—*Kim Howell, owner, Just For Fun Sports*

"Business Opportunities"

Like a franchise, a "business opportunity" is someone else's idea, system or distributorship to set you up in your own business. Unlike a franchise, a business opportunity is not a retail store or a famous name. There is no protected territory, no national advertising, little or no management support. But a business opportunity costs much less than a franchise, allows you to run your business any way you please, and does not collect royalties or ongoing fees.

Business opportunities are often some sort of business "kit," such as a cleaning or repair system, vending machines, sales carts, customized novelty items. There is usually a one-time purchase of equipment and instructions, and then a catalog of wholesale inventory or supplies.

Some business opportunities are only a mail-order or multi-level (direct-selling, or networking) distribution plan, where you buy a bulk purchase of vitamins, or cosmetics, or some wonder cleaner, and then try to talk your friends into buying these products from you.

Unlike franchises, there is no federal oversight of business opportunities, no equivalent of the Uniform Franchise Offering Circular (UFOC). About half of the states have some regulations on business opportunity sellers. Ask the company what states they're registered in, and ask to see any disclosure statements. Research the business opportunity as you would research a franchise.

If the opportunity company goes out of business, will you be able to locate other suppliers to provide the supplies, inventory and equipment you need to keep your business alive?

Some business opportunities are legitimate and practical, and some are not. Use your good common sense, and do your market research.

"Make $1,000 a week, at home, in your spare time, stuffing envelopes!"
—*magazine advertisement*

FREELANCERS:
Professionals, Consultants, Artists, Writers, Photographers, and Designers

Freelancers—professionals, consultants, artists, designers, and other self-employed individuals—are in business for themselves, like all other business people, no matter how reluctant they are to deal with it.

Freelancers are sole proprietors unless they incorporate, form a partnership or LLC. Freelancers are responsible for their own business records, licenses, tax returns, and everything else covered in this book.

Freelancers should read the chapter on "Independent Contractors" in the Growing Up section. Many freelancers fall into this category.

Royalties

If royalties from creative effort, such as writing, design or art, are a regular and ongoing source of income for you, they are considered self-employment income, handled the same as any other business income with regular business deductions. These royalties are reported on Schedule C (if you are a sole proprietor), and subject to regular business taxes including self-employment tax. This also applies to licensing fees, assignment of copyrights or any other similar income.

If royalty income is only occasional or a one-shot, it is not considered self-employment income. It is reported on your 1040 tax return as Other Income. It is subject to income tax but not to self-employment tax. You can deduct some of the related expenses on Schedule A of your 1040, but only if you itemize deductions.

None of your royalties should be reported on Schedule E even though Schedule E says it is for royalties. The only royalties that go on Schedule E are royalties from coal, oil, gas and other natural resources.

Advances

Freelancers sometimes get cash advances, deposits on work to be performed, advances on royalties. How are these handled? You should first read the chapter "Cash Vs. Accrual Accounting" in the Bookkeeping section. If you use cash accounting, as many freelancers do, the money is considered earned income, subject to taxes, when you receive it. If you refund all or part of it at a later date, you reduce your income at that time (similar to making a sales return).

Accrual basis businesses recognize income when it is earned, not when cash changes hands. Any advance not yet earned is not taxable income until you do the work. This sometimes becomes a problem at year-end, if you have received an advance for work partially completed at December 31.You will have to report at least part of the advance, to the extent earned, on your tax return. This calculation may require an accountant's help. By the way, if a writer's advance on royalties is not refundable—you keep it whether the book sells or not—for tax purposes, it is not considered an advance. It is current earned income, currently taxable.

Reimbursed Expenses

If you have out of pocket expenses that you add to your billings, these reimbursed expenses should be included as part of your total income. You get to deduct the actual expenses on your tax return, so the net effect for taxes is zero.

Tuli Kupferberg

PRICING

There is no simple, one-size-fits-all answer to the question every new business owner asks: How to price a product or service? There is no magic formula, no industry standard, no single markup percentage that works for everybody.

Cost Factors

For sales and manufacturing business, the first consideration, when setting a price, is what your inventory costs you: the products you sell, and the parts and materials that go into products you make or repair. These are your "direct costs" of doing business (also called "variable costs" because they vary with your sales volume).

Other important, but often overlooked factors, are your fixed costs and your overhead, the dozens of large and small expenses you pay whether you are generating income or not: rent, utilities, phone, insurance, office supplies, permits, advertising and promotion, sales expenses, payroll, and the cost and maintenance of your furniture, tools and equipment. These costs cannot be tied directly to a product or service, but you need to factor them into your pricing.

Taxes—federal and state income and self-employment—should be figured into your pricing. These taxes depend, of course, on how much of a profit you earn, making them difficult to calculate in advance, but they are significant costs, anywhere from 15% to 40% of your profit.

So, the first step in pricing is to know your true operating costs. If you cannot recoup these costs from sales, you are in a situation commonly known as "going broke." Sounds pretty basic, right? You'd be amazed how many new businesses lose money because they never consider all the obvious and not-so-obvious expenses.

Profit Factors

How much do you mark up a product or charge for your services to bring in enough income, above and beyond your costs, to pay you for the time you put into the business, to pay you a living wage, to make it all worth doing?

There is no "official" answer. Only you know the answers to these questions.

How Much Can You Charge?

What are your customers or clients willing to and able pay? What are other businesses charging for similar goods and services? And what are they offering for that price?

You may or may not be able to charge more than what other businesses are charging. Factors such as how good your product or service is, how reliable you are, how important you personally are to your customers (such as being a highly regarded auto mechanic), or some other important consideration—a hassle-free, money-back return policy—may allow you to charge more than the business down the street.

Where you will be marketing your goods? If you sell to wholesalers or retailers, they have to get a good enough price from you to be able to mark-up the goods themselves, typically another 40% to 50%.

You also don't want to make the mistake of underpricing yourself. You can actually charge too little for a product or service, and make people suspicious that you have a cheap (that is, lousy) product, or that you are not experienced enough to charge a fair price for your services. Business consultants often refer to this as "perceived value": your customers not only want to get value for their money, they want to feel (perceive) they are getting value for their money. Price is a big part of this perception: The price of a product tells consumers what to expect in terms of quality and value.

For many small businesses, the secret to success is not charging the lowest prices they can; but instead charging a higher price and offering something extra—a better service, a friendlier or more elegant atmosphere, whatever it takes. Face it, you can't compete with the Wal-Mart. The secret is, don't even try. Consumers are willing to pay more, in fact they expect to pay more, for quality and value. Ask yourself how much you'd pay for the same product or service.

People selling services (selling their time) might charge by the hour or by the job. If you are a fast worker, and you have a good idea how long a job will take, charging by the job might earn you quite a bit more. It takes the pressure off your customer, who knows in advance exactly how much it will cost, and doesn't have to worry if you're taking an extra long lunch hour, or feel the need to secretly keep track of your time.

If some of these factors seem difficult or downright impossible to calculate, don't be discouraged. That's the way it is for most new businesses. You don't know many of your costs when you are getting started, and you certainly have no idea of the volume of sales or number of hours you'll be working. It is yet one more reason to try to start a new business on a small, part-time basis and to learn as you go.

Pricing is an inexact science. Some business people work hard at the numbers, keep track of the hours, and try to arrive at a logical formula that works all the time. Retail stores often decide on a flat mark-up for every item or for every item in a certain category (sometimes called "cost-plus pricing"). Some people simply charge what everybody else is charging, and hope it will be profitable. Some tradespeople, craftspeople and even some professionals "eyeball" your car and your clothes, or feel out how price-conscious you are, before quoting a price or an hourly rate—the old sliding scale. Don't be afraid to experiment; that's about all you can do anyway.

Different pricing for different customers, however, may backfire on you. If someone paid you $20 an hour and later learns someone else got you down to $15 an hour, you will have one angry customer on your hands. But you can offer first-time discounts, off-season discounts, repeat business discounts, limited-time-offer discounts.

And what about friends who want a "deal"? Some people automatically give their friends 10% or 20% off. Some people let their friends know that this is their living, their survival, and already offer the best price they can.

Federal Laws on Pricing

The federal Robinson-Patman Act prohibits companies that sell wholesale goods from discriminating between customers by offering price discounts or other special terms to one customer but not to another.

This law applies only to wholesale goods (parts and finished products sold other businesses for resale). It does not apply to retail goods, and it does not apply to any services, consulting, repair work, contracting, etc.

The Sherman Anti-Trust Act forbids competing companies of any size from entering contracts or other agreements, written or verbal, "in restraint of trade." That means it is illegal to make deals with your competitors about what price you'll charge. This law doesn't prevent you from raising or lowering your prices to match or beat a competitor's price. You can do that any time you want, you just can't consult with the competitor about it.

Business owner Sam Leandro: "The price of a product tells consumers what to expect in terms of quality and value before they even buy it. Consumers are willing to pay more for quality and value. Not only willing, they expect to pay more."

Business owner Glenn Kabler: "I just don't understand why, if I pay a dollar for something and try to sell it for $2, people turn away. If I sell it for $5, I get bombarded with business."

Watercolor artist Grady Harper: "One of my large paintings just never would sell even though it seemed to be the main attraction in my exhibit at all of the shows. After reading a pricing article, I decided to follow the #1 suggestion concerning top pricing secrets. I increased the price from $325 to $750. It was purchased after being on display only a few hours."

Dean Ritz, consultant, Washington DC: "I raised the price with each job until someone balked. Then I knew I had reached the appropriate level."

Sanat Sivdas, Key West, Florida: "In this country, yoga classes that charge a lot attract more pupils than classes that are free. In this culture, it seems, price equals overall value. It's taken me three hard years of offering free yoga classes to realize this. I'm moving to India."

TRADEMARKS, PATENTS & COPYRIGHTS

Trademarks (including service marks, trade names and trade dress), patents, and copyrights are known as intangible property or intellectual property. You cannot see or touch them, but they exist and they are quite valuable.

The IRS calls patents, trademarks and copyrights "Section 197 Intangibles." Their costs cannot be written off the year incurred. They are written off over a period of years (except for trademarks purchased or licensed from another business). See "Depreciation" in the Tax Section.

TRADEMARKS

A trademark is a word, name, brand, slogan or expression, a symbol, shape, design or logo, a color or combination of colors, a unique sound, or some combination of these, adopted by a business to identify its goods and distinguish them from goods manufactured or sold by others.

No two companies selling the same or similar products or services can use the same trademark. The same trademark can be used by two companies selling unrelated products or services.

However, large corporations that own famous name trademarks, McDonalds for example, can often can stop all other businesses from using the same or similar trademarks. Even if some other McDonalds or MacDonalds or even "Big Macs" couldn't possibly be mistaken for the McDonalds fast food chain, McDonalds can invoke "famous trademark" protection (also known as "trademark dilution") to force other companies from using anything remotely resembling the word McDonalds.

There is an important distinction between a design or logo that identifies your products or services (which can be trademarked), and original artwork such as a poster or T-shirt design (which can be copyrighted but cannot be trademarked). If the artwork you are selling *is* your company's logo, then it can be trademarked *and* copyrighted. These are two different procedures with two different sets of laws.

You cannot usually get a trademark for your own name, or for a geographical name, such as "Northwest." You cannot trademark expressions already in common use, such as "Have a Nice Day."

You cannot trademark words that actually describe your product. A window manufacturer cannot trademark the name "Windows" for its windows, but, obviously, a software company can trademark the name "Windows." You can, however, combine words or change the spelling of words to get a trademark, such as "Dunkin' Donuts" or "Pfister Pfaucets."

You cannot have a trademark that is so similar to another trademark it could confusing people.

Another term "trade dress" refers to a product's appearance or packaging, how it's "dressed up." It is basically no different than a trademark. A third term "service mark" applies to services instead of goods, but the rules are the same. All references in this chapter to "trademarks" include trade dress and service marks.

Trademark rights are only for the trademark itself. A trademark does not prevent others from making or selling the same or similar goods.

Trade Names

There is a distinction between a trademark, which identifies your products, and a trade name which identifies your company.

For example, a company called General Motors (a trade name) sells a product called Cadillac (a trademark). Sometimes the trademark and the trade name are the same. A company called Ford (a trade name) sells a product called Ford (a trademark). You can have a trademark that includes the name of your business: A company called Intel (a trade name) has a famous slogan for its computer chip, "Intel Inside" (a trademark). Amd sometimes the name of the company is so identified with its products (such as Kelloggs cereal) that the name is easily trademarked even though it isn't the actual name of the product.

A trade name cannot be federally registered, although it does have some legal protection. However, an artistic rendition of a trade name, or a logo that includes the trade name, can often be trademarked.

Acquiring a Trademark

You acquire a basic trademark right, with limited legal protection, simply by creating and using your trademark. You acquire stronger and more easily defended legal rights to a trademark by registering with the U.S. Patent & Trademark Office, or your state trademark office.

Federal trademark registration gives you protection throughout the United States, but it is only available to trademarks that are used in interstate or international commerce. You must be doing business across state lines or your product must cross state lines in the normal course of business. Federal trademark rights are not international. The same trademark can be owned by other companies in other countries.

For businesses not involved in interstate commerce, state trademark registration gives you legal protection within your state but no protection outside your own state. You cannot get a state trademark if someone else has previously registered a federal trademark. Not all states offer state trademark registration.

If you have a federal trademark there is no reason to get a state trademark as well.

Registering a Federal Trademark

If you are not already using a trademark, you can file an Intent To Use application, which is good for six months, and can be renewed every six months for up to three years. This protects your trademark until you actually use it. The application and each renewal costs $100.

Once you are actually using a trademark, you apply for regular trademark registration. The fee is $325. This fee is in addition to any fees you paid with the Intent To Use application.

After you apply for a trademark, the Trademark Office will conduct a trademark search to see if anyone else owns the trademark. If it is already owned, you forfeit your application fee. You can avoid this problem by doing your own trademark search. The U.S. Patent and Trademark Office has a complete list of federal trademarks on their Internet site (www.uspto.gov) you can search at no cost. Or you can go to a public search library (ask the Trademark Office for locations), use an online service offering trademark searches, or hire a lawyer or trademark search company to do the search for you.

You should check trade directories, product catalogs and other business listings, looking for unregistered (but still valid) trademarks.

The initial registration remains in force for ten years, but you must file a Declaration of Use statement between the fifth and sixth years. The trademark may then be renewed every ten years, for as long as you like. For more information, write the Patent & Trademark Office, U.S. Department of Commerce, Washington DC 20231. Telephone toll free 1-800-786-9199. On the Internet at www.uspto.gov.

The familiar ® symbol means that a trademark or service mark is officially registered with the U.S. Trademark Office, and full legal protection has been secured. The equally familiar ™ symbol (or "SM" for "service mark") is a formal notice that you are claiming ownership of a trademark but have not registered it. The ™ or "SM" symbol can be used even if no federal trademark application is pending. Using this symbol, however, does not provide the full legal protection accorded a registered ® trademark.

Internet Domain Names

Trademark law extends to the Internet. Conflicts occur when someone owns a domain name (a web site address) on the Internet and someone else owns the trademark to that same name. Owners of registered trademarks can usually stop someone else from using the trademark as a domain name. But if the trademark is not officially registered, or if the trademark was registered after the domain name was claimed by someone else, or if the other party is outside the U.S., Internet policy gets unpredictable. The owner of a trademark may or may not be able to force someone to abandon their domain name.

Trademark owners, aware of this domain name problem, try to acquire ownership of all domain names that are the same as, or similar to, their trademark name.

But on the Internet, as in the physical world, you cannot trademark a domain name that is just your company name, unless the company name is identified with your product or service. Thus a domain name such as bellsprings.com (my publisher's web site) cannot be trademarked because it simply identifies Bell Springs Publishing. But you could trademark a web site called small-time-operator.com (other than the fact that I already own the trademark to that name

You cannot trademark a generic or descriptive domain name, such as aboutpinball.com (a site that sells pinball machine books), but a domain name with a unique expression probably can be trademarked: The site LouisianaTreasure.com,

which sells books about New Orleans music, is a registered trademark. Sometimes a web site is so well branded that its name is synonymous with its products or service. Thus, companies such as eBay, Google, and Amazon.com can easily trademark their domain names.

The overall design of your web site can sometimes be trademarked under the trade dress laws, but most web site designs are protected by copyright (covered below).

Protecting Your Trademark

If you don't use your trademark for two or more years, it is considered abandoned. Anyone can claim the trademark. Use it or lose it.

You should continually remind the public, in your advertising, brochures, web site, etc. that your name or "brand" is a registered trademark.

Trademark law requires you to police your trademark. If you find anyone using your trademark, object immediately. If you ignore the unauthorized use, or wait too long to complain, you could lose your trademark rights.

By the way, businesses that purchase trademarked goods to sell in their stores or web sites, such as a clothing store selling Levis jeans, sometimes are not allowed to mention the trademarked name or use the logo in advertisements, as ridiculous as that sounds. Before you invest in an expensive ad promoting some manufacturer's product, you may want to find out if they will object. It is their trademark, after all.

Now that you know all the work and money involved in getting a trademark, do you really need one? If yours is a small local sales or service business, and you plan to stay small and local, I don't think you need to protect your identity with a trademark. If, however, you are making a product that will get widespread distribution and get to be well known, at some point a trademark will be a good investment.

Protect Your Business Name

Whether you have a trademark or not, the best way to protect your company name is to make it well known and easy to find. Get listed in every business, trade, association, and phone directory that offer free listings (plenty do; don't pay for a listing). Get publicity. Make it as hard as possible for new businesses not to have heard of you. People don't maliciously steal business names, they just don't know you're there.

PATENTS

Patents apply to physical products such as inventions, to some designs, to new plant varieties, to some software programming, and to some computer and Internet business methods.

A patent prohibits others from making, using or selling your creation without your permission. A patent is an official legal notice that this is yours, you invented it, and you and only you have the right to market it, sell it, license it. Most patents are good only within the U.S.

A patent does not guarantee enforcement of your rights. The patent owner, not the government, is responsible for protecting a patent, through legal channels (i.e. expensive lawyers).

Many small, independent inventors obtain patents, and many are successful. But a patent is no guarantee of success. How useful your invention is, how commercial it is (how many people would make use of it), how easy or difficult it will be to produce, and how well you are able to market your invention are as important, if not more important, than the patent itself.

Types of Patents: The Utility Patent

There are three types of patents: the utility patent, the design patent, and the plant patent.

The most common patent is the utility patent. Utility patents are granted to the inventor of any new and useful process, machine, device, or composition of matter, or a new and useful improvement of such.

"Useful process" refers to a procedure for making something or performing a task. A "machine" or "device" is a man-made tool or thing, something that does not already exist in nature. "Composition of matter" refers to some sort of chemical or organic composition, such as a new kind of cookie dough. A "new and useful improvement" is different from anything else already invented, and not obvious to anyone familiar with the technology involved.

Utility patents are issued for software programs. A clever way of doing business on the Internet can be patented (more below).

A patent will not be granted on a useless device (the government's definition of useless, not mine), on printed matter, on an improvement in a device that would be obvious to a skilled person, or on a machine that will not operate. The government says it never has and never will issue a patent on a perpetual motion machine.

You are required have a detailed written description or drawings of your invention.

A patent will not be granted if the invention was made known to the public, was in public use, was described in a publication, or was on sale more than a year prior to filing the patent application. So, be sure to keep your invention private and confidential.

Design and Plant Patents

A design patent covers the appearance of a product—the way it looks, not the way it functions or is constructed. Design patents are similar to trademarks, and may not be necessary if your design is protected by trademark.

Plant patents are for new plant varieties.

Length of a Patent

A utility or plant patent is good for 20 years, starting with the date you filed for the patent. The 20 years includes the time it takes for the patent to be approved, which itself can take anywhere from several months to as much as three years. So the actual time your patent is valid may be a lot less than 20 years.

The 20 year period can be extended, in some cases, if the Patent Office takes more than three years to approve your patent.

A patent may not be renewed or extended. Anyone can use an invention after the patent expires. To keep a patent valid, you have to pay periodic government maintenance fees.

Design patents are good for 14 years.

Applying For a Patent

Applying for a patent can be a lengthy and expensive procedure. The government charges filing, issuance, and maintenance fees, and sometimes fees for printing and claims work. You may require help from a patent attorney or agent. But any dedicated inventor who is willing to study the laws, do the research, and struggle through the forms, will be able to patent his or her own invention at a fraction of the usual cost.

Inventors who are unsure that their invention justifies the work and cost of going through the regular patent process have two other options.

The inventor can file a Provisional Patent Application (a PPA), which is a temporary form of patent-pending. A PPA requires a lot less time, money and paperwork than a regular patent application, yet offers full patent-pending protection for one full year. By the end of the year's time, if things are looking promising, you can apply for regular patent-pending status. But you have to start the patent application process all over again.

The PPA itself does not lead to a patent. Should you decide to proceed with the patent, you are spending more time and money, because you took the additional step of filling a Patent Pending Application. But you do get an extra year's protection. You get the full twenty years, in addition to the PPA's year. The PPA is for utility and plant patents. Design patents are not eligible for the PPA.

Inventors who are not even ready to file a PPA can file what the Patent Office calls a "disclosure document," a written explanation of the invention signed by the inventor and submitted to the U.S. Patent Office, which will file and hold it for two years. The document does not lead to a patent, but does offer evidence of the date of conception of the invention.

"Patent Pending" / "Patent Applied For"

Products that have federal patent protection from the U.S. Patent & Trademark Office, are said to be "patented." A different term, "patent pending" or "patent applied for," means that a patent or a Provisional Patent Application (PPA) has been applied for but not yet received. It is a formal notice but offers little legal protection. Some people use "patent pending" even though they haven't applied for *anything*, either to try to scare off imitators or to impress customers. This is illegal.

Other Options

If filing for and obtaining a patent is a bit overwhelming or too expensive, there are other approaches. Many inventors simply produce and market their invention without a patent, run with it while it's hot, and not worry about someone stealing the idea. Particularly when you are dealing with rapidly changing technology, it's possible your product could become obsolete before anyone has time to copy it.

Many inventors sell or license their ideas to reputable manufacturing companies, companies that will patent the invention on behalf of, or in partnership with, the inventor. Should you approach such a company, have them sign a confidential nondisclosure statement before you show them your idea. Keep detailed, signed, and dated records of your invention.

Be wary of product development companies and invention marketing services, companies that charge you a fee to appraise your invention and make recommendations. Stay away from such companies unless you know them well.

Internet and Software Patents

The Internet has drastically changed the world of patents and patent law. Computer programmers are "inventing" on their computers, and the U.S. Patent Office is struggling to keep up with the technology.

The biggest, and most contentious, patent issues involve business software and business methods used on the Internet. For the first time in the history of the U.S. Patent Office, patents are being issued to companies that devise new, and mostly computer-programmed, ways of doing business.

Companies that have created software to navigate web sites, acquire customers, process orders, offer different pricing methods, and other variations of doing business on the Internet, are being issued patents for these processes. Very often, the companies are simply translating basic business practices into computer code, and getting patents on their systems. The companies obtaining the patents are aggressively trying to stop other businesses from using similar business methods on the Internet, or demanding licensing fees from the other companies.

If, for example, you set up a web site that uses a system for processing orders similar to one set up and patented by some obscure software company you never heard of, you may one day hear from some lawyer—if the software developer happens to find you, and if they feel you are worth their time and trouble. My guess is that, unless you grow very large, you are not likely to hear from anyone accusing you of using their patented system.

More Information

For more information about patents, contact the U.S. Patent & Trademark Office, Washington, D.C. 20231. Telephone toll free 1-800-786-9199. On the Internet at www.uspto.gov.

Inventor Marcie Hart, owner, Fat Dog Product Designs, Hesperia, Calif: "Inventors are a different breed of people. They have the ideas but usually don't want to be bothered with 'the rest.' They just want to get on with the next idea. I really don't think it's the patent process in itself that has given these inventors such a negative attitude. It's the work that's required AFTER the invention that has become so difficult. Inventors have been pretty much locked out of 'Big Business.' The opportunity for success is still there, it's just that the rules have changed. It's because of this 'lock out' that I chose not to beat down the doors of Big Business, but to open my own instead. Opportunity from a closed door. Rather ironic, don't you think?"

COPYRIGHTS

Copyrights protect the work of writers, illustrators, artists, designers, and composers. The work must be on tangible or electronic medium: paper, fabric, wood, metal, videotape, cassette, CD, computer disk, the Internet, etc. Published and unpublished works can be copyrighted.

What can be copyrighted? Literary, dramatic, musical and artistic works. Writing (with some exceptions listed below). Illustrations. Paintings. Slides and photographs. Movies and videos. Games (physical games and descriptions, not the concepts). Puzzles. Sculpture. Models. Clothing. Jewelry designs. Architectural designs. Choreography and pantomime. Sound recordings. Maps. Software (some software can also be patented). Ads, brochures and promotional materials.

What cannot be copyrighted? Ideas and concepts cannot be copyrighted. You can write about ideas and concepts and copyright the writing. A description of a machine could be copyrighted as a writing, but this will not prevent others from making or using the machine.

You cannot copyright: An improvisational speech. A performance. Lists of ingredients or contents. Math tables. Rulers. Standard calendars. Blank forms. Height or weight charts. Names. Titles. Short phrases. Slogans. Familiar symbols or sayings. (Although names, titles and phrases cannot be copyrighted, they can often be trademarked.)

Databases cannot be copyrighted: compiled listings of information such as addresses and telephone numbers, stock quotes, business trade directories, lists of magazines by subject, etc., are not protected by copyright.

The owner of a copyright has exclusive rights to print and copy the work, including the right to make photocopies or to scan it into a computer; to sell or distribute copies of the work; to put it on the Internet; to dramatize, record or translate the work; to perform or broadcast the work publicly. A song played on a jukebox in a tavern, or even performed by the local bar band, technically requires permission from the copyright holder.

The owner of a copyright may or may not be the creator of the work. The creator of a work should be cautious when selling some or all rights to his or her work. If a work is specially ordered or commissioned, rights to the work usually go to the person or company paying for the work, not to the creator. Be aware of "work for hire" laws, which automatically give all rights to the employer, none to the creator of the work. To be entirely clear and legal about copyright ownership, the creator and the commissioner of a work should stipulate in a written contract who owns the copyright.

Acquiring a Copyright

Within the U.S., copyright protection automatically exists from the moment a work is created. You are not required to put a copyright notice on the work, although the U.S. Copyright Office strongly recommends that you do: the word "copyright" or the symbol ©, the year, and your name. This will eliminate the possibility that someone will innocently reprint your work, thinking it isn't protected. For recordings, use the ℗ symbol instead of the © symbol. Some foreign countries also require the words "All rights reserved."

To receive maximum legal protection, a work (and all updated or revised editions) should be registered with the U.S. Copyright Office. You fill out a simple form, pay a $30 fee and send the Copyright Office two copies of the work. It's that easy.

A copyright is good for your lifetime plus 70 years; it's not renewable. You can copyright a work at any time.

For information & forms, write Register of Copyrights, Library of Congress, Washington, DC 20559. Internet at www.lcweb.loc.gov/copyright.

Artists: The Visual Artists Rights Act protects, in certain cases, original paintings, drawings, sculptures and some photographs from being altered or destroyed after the works are sold.

Copyright on the Internet

"The Internet is one giant copying machine."
—PC Magazine

Copyright laws are the same on the Internet as they are everywhere else. Your entire web site is protected by copyright law. But it is much harder to protect your copyright on the Internet, where anything and everything is so easy to copy, duplicate and alter.

Many people who "borrow" material from a web site do not fully realize that they are stealing. People think of the Internet as a place where everything is free, including your hard work. Quite often, just reminding your visitors that everything on your web site is copyrighted, and that copying is not permitted, will stop many of them from taking anything.

However, many businesses want people to download and print their web sites. The sites double as catalogs. People who download the web pages will have the pages to refer to after they log off the Internet—and can't find you again because they forgot your domain name. These businesses often put a small copyright notice on the web site but do not warn visitors not to copy the web pages.

If you find that someone has taken anything from your web site and put it on their own web site, you can send a "cease and desist" letter, notifying the infringer that such use is illegal,

demand that the material be removed from the infringer's web site, and suggest that failure to comply can result in legal action. Quite often such a letter is all you need to end the problem.

The tone of the letter can have quite an effect on the infringer's response. Being polite but firm is often more successful than being belligerent, rude or accusatory. A cease-and-desist letter does not commit you in any way to legal action, it can be a bluff. But be sure to keep a copy of the letter and any response, should you decide in the future to talk to a lawyer.

Technological Copyright Protection

Posting a copyright notice and reminding people not to copy your work will stop many people from downloading, printing and reproducing anything that catches their eye. But there are people who don't care and who will help themselves to whatever they want from the Internet.

You can purchase software or subscribe to an Internet service that will help protect the contents of your web site from unauthorized copying and downloading. Digital rights management, digital object identifiers, password access, encryption, digital watermarks, and lock-down technology are different terms for different ways to limit access and use of your site and its contents.

You can get software that searches the Internet for web sites that have taken content off your web site and placed it on their sites.

If you put photographs or illustrations on your web site, you can easily put a copyright notice that includes your domain name (something short, such as ©crystalroseart.com) directly on the photo or illustration. If someone borrows your work, the copyright notice will stay with the photo. People who view your work on someone else's web site, and like what they see, can use the information from the copyright notice to find your web site. In a way, it's a form of free advertising.

No technology will stop a determined hacker, but few web sites have to deal with such mad scientists. Just as most thieves can be deterred simply by locking a door, most web pirates can be thwarted with simple protection methods. There's plenty easy pickings on the web, no need for some reprobate to spend a lot of time trying to decode your site.

Protecting Your Copyright

You don't have to police your copyright, you don't have to be constantly searching for unauthorized use of your material, but if you find someone who is using your copyright without your permission, you have to act promptly. If you do not attempt to stop the unauthorized usage, you can lose some of your legal protection for the copyright. You don't have to hire a lawyer and go to court, but you do have to be persistent, continue to state your objections, and keep a record of your actions.

If you license rights to copyrighted material, as many photographers and cartoonists do, check on the licensee to verify he hasn't used your work after the term of the license expired or beyond the scope of the license. You are not required by law to monitor licensing usage, but act promptly if you find a violation. And in the case of a wayward licensee, be friendly and non-accusatory. This is not some crook who stole your work or an ignorant user who took without asking. A licensee has already paid you some money and might even pay some more.

CONTRACTS

Business dealings are more likely to be successful and free of disagreements, arguments, misunderstandings and lawsuits if they include a written contract.

This is especially true for someone providing a professional service or doing a multi-faceted project. The issues of who does what, when, and for how much, can get dicey without a written contract.

A contract defines your responsibilities and your client's commitment. A contract demonstrates business professionalism and weeds out insincere clients. A contract will protect you from the anguish and frustration of indecisive clients and people who continually change their minds and the extent of the job midstream. It gives your customers a sense of security. Sometimes the only proof you have of the extent of your obligations is your signed agreement. Contracts may help you get insurance or financing.

Don't think of a contract as a means to win, or to protect yourself against a lawsuit. The main purpose of a contract should be to clarify an agreement, to make sure all parties fully understand the agreement, not to set up the rules for a fight. Nor should contracts be used to keep crooks in check. If you don't trust the people you're dealing with, maybe you shouldn't be dealing with them at all.

Contracts should be understandable. No whereas's, heretofore's, or legal mumbo-jumbo. Avoid words like he, she and they; it's too easy to confuse who you're talking about. Use names, or "landlord" and "tenant," "seller" and "buyer."

Contracts should be simple and concise yet include full details. A good contract tries to answer all the questions before they're asked.

Contracts should be signed by both parties—original signatures, not faxed, not photocopied. Many lawyers suggest you sign in blue ink, so it will be easier to spot as an original.

If only one party signs a contract, it is still a legal contract. But only the person signing is bound to the agreement. The person not signing has made no legal commitment.

Some clauses a contract might include:

1. The duration of the contract.

2. A description of the products and services you are providing.

3. All deadlines.

4. Consequences of missing the deadlines or not completing the contract.

5. Amount, terms, and timetable for payment.

6. Conditions under which the contract can be terminated.

7. Wording to the effect that something of value is to be given, and something of value is to be received. This is legally known as "consideration", and it should be spelled out in the contract. A contract is not legally a contract unless there is an exchange.

8. If there will be out of pocket expenses, the contract should specify who pays the expenses, when and if they are to be reimbursed, and any dollar limit.

9. Limits to your liability.

10. Can any rights in the contract be sold, given or traded ("assigned") to a third party?

11. A statement that the contract cannot be altered orally. Any changes should be in writing, signed by both parties.

Contracts don't have to be formal, legal-looking documents. Formal contracts sometimes backfire, scaring off a potential customer. A simple letter of agreement, signed by both parties, is a valid contract and may be more appropriate in many situations. Signed purchase orders are valid contracts. An e-mail can be a valid contract (see "E-Mail" in the "Internet" chapter).

If your business is a corporation, partnership or limited liability company, it should be disclosed in the contract. Be sure to sign as a representative (President, etc.) of the business, not as an individual, not as "owner." Make it clear that the business, not you personally, is responsible for the contract. This will help limit your personal liability.

Avoid oral contracts. There's an old saying, "A verbal agreement isn't worth the paper it's written on." Although some oral contracts are legally binding, the problem is and always will be that everyone remembers the agreement differently. People's memories are mighty short. They honestly think they agreed to something completely different than what you think they agreed to.

Before I write up a contract, I make a list of the things I want to cover. I take a few days, to make sure I think of everything. I find it helpful to look at other contracts to see how other people wrote theirs. There are books of sample contracts you can buy (or check the library). Trade organizations sometimes have sample contracts. Friends in business might let you have copies of their contracts (with names and numbers scratched out). Your accountant may be able to get you samples of contracts. If you are using someone else's contract, make sure you understand every word. If the legal mumbo-jumbo doesn't make sense to you, don't use it, or re-write it so it does make sense.

A note to designers, artists and others whose work involves intellectual property (writing, artwork, computer programming, etc.): The contract should spell out who owns the rights to your work, and the extent of those rights.

Other People's Contracts

If you are asked to sign someone else's contract, it's a whole different ball game. Large corporate vendors and purchasers, government agencies, landlords, banks, leasing companies, professional consultants, and independent freelancers often have their own contracts ready for you to sign, and they probably had talented and expensive lawyers create them.

Make sure you understand and fully agree with every word. Don't be too embarrassed to admit you don't know the meaning of a word. Look it up or ask. Be on your guard; nothing in these contracts is superfluous. Every clause was carefully thought out, to give the best advantage and protection to whoever had the contract prepared. And look out for the word "indemnify." It means that, if there is a lawsuit, you agree to pay the other party's legal expenses.

Just because contracts are printed on fancy paper, are formal, technical, legal, and etc. and etc., they are not cemented in stone. You can take out your pen and change them, eliminate sections and conditions you don't agree to.

If the contract is important and valuable enough, get a lawyer's help if you feel unsure of yourself. Just don't sign it and hope for the best.

A Warning

I don't guarantee that the contract details in this chapter will make your contract legally binding. Your state may have contract laws and filing requirements, may require some precise legal wording, a witness or notarization. If a lot is at stake in a contract, have it examined by a lawyer. The purpose of a contract is to avoid legal entanglements. Once a contract winds up in court, everybody loses.

Groucho: Now here are the contracts. You sign at the bottom. There's no need of you reading them, because these are duplicates.

Chico: Duplicates?

Groucho: I say they're duplicates. Don't you know what duplicates are?

Chico: Sure. Those five kids up in Canada.

Groucho: Well go ahead and read it.

Chico: You read it.

Groucho: All right, I'll read it. Now pay particular attention to this first clause 'cause it's most important. It says, "The, uh, party of the first part shall be known in this contract as the party of the first part." How do you like that?

Chico: I don't like that part.

Groucho: What's the matter with it?

Chico: I don't know.

Groucho: Look, why should we quarrel about a thing like this? We'll take it right out.

Chico: Yeah, it's too long anyhow. Now, what have we got left?

Groucho: I've got about a foot and a half. Now, it says, uh, "The party of the second part shall be known in this contract as the party of the second part."

Chico: I don't know about that.

Groucho: Now what's the matter?

Chico: I no like the second party either.

Groucho: Well you should have come to the first party. I didn't get home til four in the morning. Now, uh, you just put your name right down there and then the deal is, uh, legal.

Chico: I forgot to tell you. I can't write.

Groucho: That's all right. There's no ink in the pen anyhow.
—Marx Brothers, from "A Night at the Opera"

HOW TO AVOID CROOKS
and How To Collect What You're Owed

There are a lot of con-artists in the world. Naive small business owners are particularly vulnerable, and every business, I suspect, gets "burned" once or twice. I am not talking about armed robbery or shoplifters or embezzlers. I'm referring to people who offer to buy from you or sell to you or some other business dealing, but are really trying to con you out of goods or money. Pretty quickly you start to recognize these kinds of people, and you learn how to deal, or not to deal, with people you are suspicious of.

In one business I helped set up, which sold books wholesale and retail through the mail, I developed some safeguards for the business that protected the business from the rip-off artists as well as from people who seemed suspicious but may in fact have been quite honorable. It is important that any procedures you set up appear to apply to everyone you deal with, so as not to offend people who may turn out to be valuable customers.

Here is how I suggest handling a new, untested and maybe untrustworthy account. The easiest way, of course, is Cash Up Front. We had a written sales policy, just a sheet of paper we handed out to most prospective (and unknown to us) dealers and wholesalers. It stated, "We request that your first order be prepaid." As an extra incentive, we offered an additional 5% discount for prepayment. Some people offer free shipping for prepayment. This may sound like the end of your problems, but of course it isn't. All rules are made to be broken, and you will find yourself dealing with people who, for any of a hundred reasons, cannot or will not prepay (maybe they don't trust *you*). Do you do business with them anyway? Do you take a chance? Sometimes that's what business is all about.

Minimize your risk. Like the cardinal rule of gambling, don't ship more than you can afford to lose. Tell them you will send them one case of whatever-it-is, so they can "try it out and see how it does"; and as soon as they use it up or sell it or whatever it is they're doing with it, *and* pay for it, you will be more than happy to ship some more. Emphasize that yours is a small business, and thanks to a lack of red tape and bureaucracy, you can ship reorders very quickly

Here is a warning about shipping COD (cash on delivery). If the shipment is more than one package, make sure each package has a COD tag on it. Check with the post office or your shipper to find out how to mark the COD tags. We once sent a shipment of six cartons COD and put the COD tag, one bill for all six cases, on only one of the cases. They were shipped as one lot, marked 1 of 6, 2 of 6, etc. Well, two weeks later, the case with the COD tag comes back refused, and Lo And Behold, the other five cases do not come back. No payment ever came either.

When you get an order (not prepaid) in the mail from a company you don't know, call Directory Assistance and ask them if they have a listing for the business. No listing doesn't mean the company isn't legitimate (many home businesses are not listed) and, likewise, a business listing does not vouchsafe for it either, but it is an indicator whether you're dealing with reputable people. I am immediately cautious of a company without a business listing; we usually stuck to the written policy and demanded prepayment.

If you do get the company's telephone number, and the order is big enough to warrant a long-distance call, call the company "to confirm the order," maybe inquire how they want it shipped, tell them about your special prepayment offer, and definitely ask if you are going to get paid.

Establishing Credit

When dealing with someone for the first time and extending them credit, be very direct about being paid. Tell them you will be happy to extend credit, but you need their assurance that you will be paid. If you are dealing face to face, look the person right in the eye. And get the person to say, "Yes, I will pay this bill." Sometimes they'll say, "Well, this and that corporation extend us credit, we have an AA#1 Dun & Bradstreet rating, we are an established business, member of the Chamber of Commerce" and various and sundry impressive stuff that is of absolutely no value to you. Just repeat that all you need is their assurance you will be paid. It's a powerful "Yes" when they say it. Even crooks have a hard time going back on their word.

Collecting Past Due Accounts

If a bill goes past due, get on it right away. The longer you wait to try to collect it, the less likely you'll collect. Many people have little money, and they pay as they can until they just call it quits and disappear or file bankruptcy. You want to get paid before this happens, and squeaky wheels get the grease. Fax a copy of the bill. Write. Telephone once a week.

Be friendly and understanding, but be persistent. Don't be hostile or threatening—it will get you nowhere, and that's the truth—but be persistent.

Let people know they can make partial payments. Many people are unable to pay the entire balance at once, so they let the bill languish, unaware they can make partial payments.

And if it finally becomes apparent that you aren't going to get your money, just drop it and forget it. It's bad enough not getting paid, no sense twisting the knife in your own wound with anger and ulcers. If you've been "conned" there's really nothing you can do. The con artist has moved on. A collection agency, attorney, even the courts are not going to be of any help. Accept the fact that you won't recover the goods or your money, and be done with it.

Crooks on the Internet

Some businesses are much more vulnerable to online fraud attempts than others. Businesses selling high ticket items such as computers, cameras, and expensive jewelry, and businesses selling products people might be tempted to steal such as music CDs, are more likely to be targeted than businesses selling less expensive or less "flashy" items: books, hardware, stuff that does not attract thieves too much.

How you set up your fraud prevention depends on how your web site is set up to handle orders. If you process your own credit card orders, you always have the opportunity to examine the orders carefully before filling them. If a credit card processor handles your orders for you, you should talk to the processor about how you can screen orders before processing them.

Get complete information from customers, including e-mail address, a phone number, and both "bill to" and "ship to" addresses if different.

Possible indications of fraudulent orders include:

1. Unusual orders, large-dollar orders, and orders for a lot of items. Most people order one item or only a few items. Someone who orders one of everything may be suspicious.

2. Orders from foreign countries.

3. Orders with different "bill to" and "ship to" addresses.

4. Orders requesting overnight or expedited delivery. A thief won't care how much it costs to ship, since he doesn't plan to pay for it anyway.

5. Orders from unconcerned customers, such as not caring about color or size.

6. Orders that do not include the customer's phone number.

If you have a reason to be suspicious of an order, you can telephone your credit card company to verify a card member's name and address. You can call the customer on the phone to "confirm" the order. Not many thieves will give you a valid telephone number. But use the phone confirmation as a last resort. Many people,

people placing legitimate orders, may not want you calling their home or office. What if the order is a gift for someone in the family? (What if the order is a gift for someone not in the family?)

Going To Court

Should you take a non-paying customer to court? The answer depends on two important factors: (1) Can you collect if you win? Does the debtor have accessible assets such as cash or property, and will you be able to get the assets? Otherwise all you have is one more piece of paper that says the debtor owes you money, but you still don't get the money. And (2) Will your legal fees be more than the settlement? I know, it's the principle of the thing, but how much more money do you want to throw away?

Retail Customers

Retail customers are easier to deal with. People don't usually expect to get credit, and they don't usually ask. When we received a retail order in the mail, "Please send one book and bill me," we almost always declined. Even if the person is honest (and most are) it's simply not worth the time, the invoices, the ledgers, writing for payment, etc. We sent an order form and a note saying, "We request prepayment on all retail orders." The word "all" is important because it implies no bias or suspicion towards one person. And try to help the customer, because lack of trust cuts both ways. Offer an unconditional guarantee. "Cash refund if you are not satisfied for any reason at all." No explanations required. Be simple and straightforward; it always sounds the most honest.

We handled retail telephone orders differently. We took VISA and Master Card, and most of the people who called had those cards. But for several years, we did not take credit cards and we did bill retail customers when we got telephone orders. A long distance telephone call is a lot less anonymous than a postage stamp, and less likely to be used by someone who's trying to rip you off. We told every customer that we would mail the merchandise and a bill, and all they had to do was agree to pay when it arrived. They agreed every time, and they paid *almost* every time. Non-payment was rare. If they didn't pay, we

would send a reminder note in the mail, and then kiss it off. Not worth the $15. If you take large dollar orders, you may want a less risky policy.

No credit policy should be cemented in concrete. I would not hesitate to extend credit to most large corporations, government agencies or anyone whose title or company suggests that they are likely to pay.

For many types of small businesses, the "credit crooks" are actually rare. And after a few experiences, I tell you, you can spot 'em a mile coming. Something about them always tips you off: maybe their stationery, or lack of it; or the "hustle" in their voice; or their lack of knowledge how your type of business usually operates; or always a red flag for us, some stranger talking large quantities and big dollars.

In a way, it's kind of fun, too, sleuthing, feeling the people out—and what great dinner stories. Someday I'll tell you about the guy on the phone from Philadelphia, Mr. Cream Cheese my wife called him. He was a real *pro*.

Business columnist Bob Orbin: "You go to a coin-operated store to wash and dry your clothes. Then you go to a filling station where you pump your own gas. And on to a fast food restaurant where you carry your own tray. And what is it called? A service economy."

Author Tom Peters: "Why do customers switch from one store to another? 14% switch because of price, 15% because of the quality of the product, and 71% because of lousy customer service."

Businessman Larry Taylor: "Service isn't a department. It's a way of life."

J. Riga, owner, California Limousine Service: "It's not a limousine, it's a statement. That's how limousines work. I don't rent cars, I rent fantasies. Most customers aren't big shots but people trying to pretend they are. Our customers are sending a message that they have it all, if only for a night. Of course, if they had it all, they'd have their own limousines."

THE INTERNET

There are 36 million web sites on the Internet. 40% of those web sites—over 14 million sites—are owned by U.S. small businesses, self-employed individuals, independent professionals, and freelancers, many of them one-person and home-based operations.

Brand new businesses are being started and operated 100% on the Internet. No store, no shop, no public visibility, but genuine and successful businesses just the same, providing a product or a service, marketed and sold entirely on the Internet.

Small local businesses are getting national and international customers from the web. Established "bricks and mortar" businesses (businesses with a physical location in the real world) are using the Internet to increase visibility and sales. Professionals, freelancers, independent contractors, and tradespeople are creating web sites to communicate with old clients and attract new ones.

Catalog businesses are using the Internet to display their products. Full color catalogs, often prohibitively expensive when printed on paper, are much less expensive on the Internet. You can change products, prices, and descriptions (and you can correct mistakes) instantly. Your catalog never has to be out of date when it is on the Internet.

Business-to-business (b-to-b) auctions and marketplaces are an easy, inexpensive way to locate new customers, and especially to sell overstock, damaged goods, and outdated merchandise that you can no longer sell through your regular business channels.

eBay and similar consumer auction sites have converted hundreds of flea market entrepreneurs into Internet entrepreneurs. No more weekends sitting at a booth waiting for browsers to plunk down their money. List your goods on eBay, scan in a photo, state your minimum bid, and check back in a week. Instead of reaching a couple hundred people on a Sunday afternoon when you'd rather be at the beach, you'll reach thousands of people from all over the country, while you are at the beach.

The Internet lets you have multiple businesses, to change businesses on a whim. You can be selling antique typewriters one week, and then switch, overnight, to guitars. Or do both at the same time.

The Internet is especially valuable to businesses that sell unusual products, old and rare items, goods with limited interest. People looking for such goods are usually determined to find them. These people will take the time to search the Internet. If you are on the Internet, there's a good chance they will find you.

If you have a specialized niche or esoteric market (such as a business that sells unusual collectibles, or caters to a specialized group of hobbyists, or to people who love a certain breed of animal, or to fans of a certain kind of music, etc.) you can easily make your presence known. By focusing on one unusual area, you can easily become the specialist, the expert, the place a small but loyal group of customers will return to, and tell others about. This connection between seller and buyer was impossible before the Internet.

The Internet can bring you new business even if you do not have a web site. Your business can get listed in Internet directories, your products and services can get recommended by Internet sites. If you have a product to sell, you can find other businesses already on the web that want to offer your product, much like a large catalog might include your products in its pages. You can increase your wholesale business greatly by finding businesses on the Internet that might be interested in what you offer.

Market Research

Savvy businesses use the Internet for market research. You can easily study the web sites of competing businesses, see what they are offering, see what they are charging, see the newest trends, pick up some good ideas to use on your own web site.

If you are researching a new product you want to carry, or a new type of business you want to start, or a franchise you might want to invest in, or a company you might want to buy from or sell to, the Internet can probably provide more background information than anywhere else. For import and export businesses, the Internet is fast becoming the quickest way to find overseas customers and suppliers.

The U.S. Census Department provides a wealth of free demographic and economic information about communities all over the U.S. The Census is a marketer's dream come true.

Legal, Tax, and General Business Research

A problem every business has struggled with over the years, is obtaining accurate and current tax and legal information: What government agencies are making what demands on your business? What IRS laws have recently changed? Where can you get government forms and instructions, and where do you send them?

Every federal agency has a web site: the IRS, the Small Business Administration, the Patent and Trademark Office, The Copyright Office, The Department of Commerce, the Federal Trade Commission. These government web sites include information about all the laws discussed in this book. Many government publications are online, and you can download many of the forms you need.

Most state government agencies have web sites, with information about your state's employment laws, income tax laws, sales tax laws, consumer protection laws, and other regulations affecting businesses.

Many government agencies are allowing businesses to apply for business licenses, get permits, and file tax returns on the Internet. Instead of standing in line for half an hour at City Hall to get an application, you may be able to do all of your paperwork on the Internet.

You can get legal and business advice, absolutely free, from the many business periodicals, legal publishers, business consultants, CPA firms, and law firms that put their magazines, newsletters, and updates on the Internet.
Trade, professional, and small business organizations have web sites where people within your trade or profession discuss business, answer each other's questions, and share information. It's like a merchant's luncheon without going out to lunch, and you get to "talk" with people all over the country and the world.

Gathering information from the Internet, however, requires caution and skepticism. Information may be inaccurate or out of date. Just because a CPA or a well-known business journalist says something, it is no guarantee the information is correct or current. Be especially careful if you are researching a tax law. Tax laws change every year, often several times a year. A tax newsletter on the Internet could be months or even years old. If the information does not include the date it was posted or a year it applies to, do not rely on it. In fact, even if it is current, do not rely on it, at least until you can verify it from other sources or from a reference to an IRS publication.

Web Sites

According the U.S. Small Business Administration, over 50% of all small businesses and self-employed professionals have a web site.

Some businesses use the free web space that many Internet Service Providers (ISPs) include as part of their Internet access package. Most ISPs offer their customers a limited amount of space on the web to create and operate your own web site. The site, however, is hosted by the ISP, and only available to you as long as you are a customer of that ISP. The web address you get as part of the ISP package is not "www.your-business.com." The web address will include your ISP at the beginning of the address, something like www.yourISP.net/a mysterious string of numbers and letters here/your-name-way-back-here, a long and impossible to remember address.

Some businesses use a "mall" site that is part of a larger site such as Yahoo or eBay. Some of these mall services simply provide web access, some set up your site for you, some offer credit card processing and other business functions. But, like your ISP's free web space, you are operating within someone else's site, with restrictions that may be less than ideal. Your site may be saddled with the host's advertising, which can be irritating for you and your customers.

These low-cost web sites, however, let you try out your ideas without spending much money. You can always move your site later, to a new address, and keep both sites or refer people from the old site to the new one.

We've only begun to tap the vast potential of the web to enhance our lives, by which I mean buy stuff. You'll be able to order everything you see on the screen through your Internet account. This means that, merely by spilling beer on your keyboard, you could become legally obligated to purchase a helicopter.

—Columnist Dave Barry

Your Own Web Site

Most businesses that are serious about having an Internet presence have their own stand-alone web site (also called a domain or a URL which stands for Uniform Resource Locator): "www.yourbusiness.com". This domain name is 100% yours, and stays with you as long as you pay the licensing fees.

To get your own web site, start by choosing a domain name that no one else has claim to. Many businesses want to use their business name, a product name, a product category, or some other name that is easily identified with the business. But with over 38 million sites already on the Internet, this may be a difficult task. You may have to get very creative to come up with a name no one else has thought of.

If a domain name you'd like to own, such as www.mybusiness.com, is taken, you can try www.mybusiness.net, or www.mybusiness.org, or www.mybusiness.biz, or one of the other two-letter, three-letter, or four-letter designations used at the end of most web addresses. (These suffixes are officially known as "top level domains" or "TLDs.") Anyone can use .net or .org. or .biz, or several other TLDs, and each is a different web address, available to anyone on a first-come first-served basis. However, keep in mind that most people automatically type a ".com" after every web address. People may have a lot of trouble remembering that your site ends in ".net" or ".org" or another TLD.

When you find an available domain name, make sure that the domain name is not trademarked by another company. The owner of the trademark has the legal right take the domain name away from you. See the chapters "Business Name" in the Getting Started section and "Trademarks" in this section.

Multiple Sites / Multiple Businesses

Many businesses set up separate web sites for different products or different areas of interest. Specialized and niche sites often draw more viewers than general sites. People often have trouble focusing when they visit a web site that covers a potpourri of businesses or subjects.

Some people set up separate businesses, each with its own web site. One person may own two or three businesses, all run from the same loca-

tion, sharing the same mailing addresses and phone numbers, using a shared credit card account. See the chapter "Multiple Businesses" in the Getting Started section.

Domain Name Syntax (Rules)

Web site names obey the peculiar rules of web syntax. Almost all web sites start off with "www" (which stands for World Wide Web, or the "web" for short). For most web sites, you do not need to type in the www to access the sites. For example, typing bellsprings.com or www.bellsprings.com will get you to the Bell Springs Publishing web site (my publisher).

You cannot use blank spaces or ampersands. So when the bookstore Barnes & Noble went online, it became barnesandnoble.com. You can use capital letters but the Internet will ignore them. "MyBusiness.com" and "mybusiness.com" are the same domain name. You can glue several words together and have the awkward but possibly unique www.smithaddingmachinerepair.com.

You can put dashes or periods in your domain name, for example, "my-business.com" or "my.business.com." A domain name with a dash or a period is a completely different domain than the same domain name with no punctuation. (But none of your customers will remember where to put the dash or period).

Another possibility is "eMyBusiness.com" or "E-mybusiness.com" since people are already familiar with the "e" in front of site names. Any letter in front of your name will work, if people can remember it.

You can make up totally meaningless names out of real or made up words. But cute spelling gimmicks, such as "KuteeKlothes," often backfire, when no one, not even your regular customers, can remember how to spell your name. Finally, keep in mind that the Internet is global. You probably don't want your site name to mean "idiot" or "free sex" in Dutch.

Registering a Domain Name

Once you have a few ideas for your site's name, log onto any of the Internet domain name registrars. Registrars are Internet businesses authorized to issue web site addresses, and there are many of them. For a full list of registrars, log onto www.ICANN.org, the Internet Corporation for Assigned Names and Numbers. This is a non-profit organization authorized to license the registrars and to oversee the Internet.

Domain name registrars maintain a database of all domain names in use. You can log onto their site, and do your name research there at no cost. Simply type in the domain name you would like, and you will get an answer whether the name is available or not.

If your domain name is available, you can immediately acquire the name. You fill out an application on the Internet and pay with a credit card. The individual registrars set their own fees, usually anywhere from $10-35 per year. The domain name will be yours for as long as you want, just by renewing the registration every year (see "Domain Name Renewals" below).

All of Your Choices Already Taken?

If you cannot find an available domain name you like, you may be able to purchase a domain name from the person who already has the rights to that name. Information about many domain names—who owns them and how to reach the person—is accessible by doing a search on one of the many "whois" directories on the Internet (type in "whois" in a search engine).

Some registrars maintain a list of domain names being offered for sale by the name holders. And there is a lot of web site turnover. People let their registrations lapse. The "whois" information includes the date the registration expires for each domain name. You can check back to see if the name has been renewed.

Another way to try to get a domain name you want: Some registrars let you put a "hold" on a domain name that's already taken. You reserve the domain name with your credit card. If it becomes available, the registrar will try to get the domain name for you. Putting a domain name on hold does not guarantee that you'll get the name, as there may be several people who have put the same name on hold.

As you can see from the "whois" information above, who owns a domain name is public knowledge. When you get a domain name, your own name, address, phone number, and e-mail are accessible to anyone who wants to look it up. You can pay an extra fee to be "unlisted" (anonymous. However, no one verifies the names, addresses, or phone numbers people use when they register web sites; the information could be totally fake.

Domain Renewals

You can renew your domain name as many times as you want. As long as you renew before the current registration expires, you retain rights to the domain name indefinitely.

The registrar that handled your registration is supposed to notify you by e-mail when your domain name renewal is due. If you fail to renew, there is usually a 30-60 day "grace period," giving you the opportunity to reclaim your domain name, after which time the domain name goes back into the available list, up for grabs by anyone who wants it.

But do not rely on being notified. Know when your domain name is up for renewal, and renew the name by the deadline. Losing your domain name will be a first-class disaster. The responsibility is yours.

Web Site Hosting Services

Registering a domain name does not automatically give you a working web site. If you try to log onto your site, you will not be able to access it, or you may get a notice that your site is "Coming Soon" or "Under Construction." To get your web site online, you have to sign up with a web host (also known as a web server) to host your site.

A web host is a business that has your web site on their computer, along with hundreds or thousands of other web sites, and has a hookup to the Internet so anyone using the Internet can access your site. Actually, you don't have to have a web host. You could host your own site, instead of paying a web hosting service, if you had the necessary computer systems. But few small businesses have the time or knowledge, or care to invest in the equipment and training, needed to host their own sites.

The Internet has made shopping impersonal, to say the least. Customers really want to know there's someone on the other side of the browser. We try to respond personally to each customer. It's amazing how much people appreciate that.
—Richard Hooten, Americabilia.com

Many domain name registrars offer web hosting services. You can get a simple (but often nice looking) fill-in-the-blanks design that you can have up and running in less than an hour. Some registrars offer custom design and full web hosting services.

There are many Internet companies, in addition to the registrars, offering web hosting services, starting at just a few dollars a month, and going up in price depending on the features and complexity of the site. Many hosting services advertise in business magazines and on the web, or you can ask for recommendations from people you know who already have web sites.

Your web site depends on your web host. Investigate web hosting services carefully. Compare packages and prices. Don't sign a long-term contract unless you are completely confident about your host's ability to deliver what's promised. Your web site is yours, so if you do not like your hosting service, you can switch to another host without having to change your web address. Some important issues:

1. Be cautious if a web host registers your domain name for you, or if a web host offers you a free domain name. Some web hosting services register your domain name under their own name, and they control ownership. If you leave the web host, you may be shocked to learn that your domain name is not yours and that you cannot take it with you to a new web host. Be sure your domain name registration is under your name and is 100% yours.

2. Make sure the host is "transparent," invisible to your site's visitors. No ads, no links, no "hosted by" messages.

3. Pick a web host that looks like it has staying power, one with ample resources, not likely to close their doors without warning.

4. Ask about the web host's restrictions on your web site activities. Can the host cancel your contract if they do not like the content of your site, or if you attract too many visitors, or if you send or receive a lot of e-mail? Will the host charge you more per month if your traffic increases?

5. Ask about downtime and technical problems. Does the host have a poor record of breakdowns? Is the host monitoring its systems 24 hours a day? Does the host have a back-up generator if the power goes out? Is the host prepared in case of a technical emergency or a natural disaster?

6. Does the web host offer a secure system (called a "secure server") for credit card transactions and transmission of private data? Is the system flexible, with different options? This is an area of web hosting that requires careful examination on your part, if you plan to make sales over the Internet.

7. How is the host prepared to deal with hackers and other breaches of security? Does the host have procedures that keep unauthorized people from getting into your web site or obtaining technical information about your site? Does the host have insurance or a bond to cover you should a security lapse cause you or your customers financial loss or other problems?

8. Is the host located in a state that is trying to demand sales tax collections from the host's customers? See the "Sales Tax" chapter in the Getting Started section.

9. If you want to transfer to another hosting service, or if your hosting service goes bankrupt, will you be able to gain access to your site?

10. Don't choose a host that allows adult sexual content or bulk spam. These hosts are often blacklisted by search engines.

11. Read the fine print in the contract (sometimes called a "Terms of Service" or "Terms of Use" agreement). Every word in the web host's contract is there to protect the host, to limit its liability. Be very careful if the contract states that you indemnify the host against any problems caused by your web site. "Indemnify" means that you agree to pay the host's attorney fees and court costs if there is a lawsuit.

12. If you don't like your web host, you can usually cancel your agreement and find a new host, though you are not likely to get a refund.

Web Site Design

Anyone who has spent time on the Internet knows how many different designs there are for web sites. Your options are limitless. And yet, how many business web sites have you visited that you couldn't quite figure out what the site was doing there, what the business was trying to convey, if you could purchase anything from the company, or how? There are a lot awful web sites out there.

Entire books have been written, and entire

college courses are given, on web site design. Every business magazine includes articles on web site design.

I suggest that you study popular business web sites and successful web sites for your type of business. Note how these sites inspire customer confidence. Note how easy or difficult it is to navigate these sites, to get information, to place orders.

I am not a web designer, although like every other site owner, I've given it a try. I do not know web design software too well. I hired someone to do that for me. But I do know some important considerations when designing a web site:

1. People always have, and always will, judge you by your appearance. A good looking paint job helps to sell a car, a good looking cover helps to sell a book, a good looking web site helps to sell a business. Your site should look good and should look professional. An attractive, professional looking site instills trust in consumers who don't know you.

2. Your web site should download fast. People have little patience for slow loading web sites. Many people have old computers and slow modems, and these will make a slow loading site even slower. Large graphics, video, and other flashy software are a main cause of slow loading sites. A good web site designer knows how to code graphics so they load fast.

3. Make your site easy to understand, easy to navigate. The best web sites help people quickly find the information they want. People have no tolerance for confusing, complicated sites. People like sites that are "intuitive," that is, sites people can figure out without reading the instructions.

4. Avoid color combinations and background designs that make reading difficult. Many people have trouble reading dark type on a dark background, light type on a light background, and words typed on top of checkered or "busy" backgrounds.

5. Every page on your site should have a link to your home page. Quite often, someone using a search engine will find one of your pages but not your home page. Someone who is directed to the middle of your site by a search engine might get confused if your site does not make it clear on every page who you are, how to reach you, and how to find your home page.

6. Keep web pages short if possible, and keep the text narrow. People do not like to scroll down too far, and they hate having to scroll back and forth, and back and forth, to read lines that are too long for their screen. Some printers cannot copy wide web pages, cutting off part of the right-hand side of the page.

7. Do not underestimate the importance of good grammar, correct spelling, proper sentence structure, and all that other stuff you didn't learn in high school. People who know good English when they see it will be critical (and possibly distrustful) of a web site that uses poor English. Much more important, however, incorrect grammar makes sentences harder to read and harder to understand. Bad grammar often results in miscommunication. If you are not good at English composition, find someone to edit the content of your site.

8. Check your site from other computers using other operating systems, other Internet access providers, and other browsers, to see if the site works for everybody trying to access it.

9. Ask friends to "test drive" your site, navigate the entire site, and look for flaws, problems, things that might confuse people. Find someone who is not an experienced Internet user, someone who does not already know tricks for navigating web sites. If a novice web surfer can use and understand your site, you will turn many more visitors into customers. A huge percentage of visitors leave sites solely because the visitors cannot figure out how to use the sites.

10. Check your site regularly. Make sure your server has it up and running properly, make sure no error messages have suddenly appeared.

11. If you want repeat customers, change things on your site regularly, just as a retail store changes what's in the window. Let customers know what's new. Create an e-mail newsletter or develop an "Ask The Expert" column. Keep your site current; if you have a holiday theme, don't forget to take it down after the holiday.

12. Solicit feedback from visitors, and use that feedback to improve the site, making it easier to use, adding new features. Show your e-mail address prominently on your site and encourage visitors to contact you. Make sure the visitor can simply click on your e-mail address and automatically have a pre-addressed e-mail dialog box, ready and waiting (see "E-Mail" below). Check your e-mail regularly. A same-day reply will

increase the likelihood your visitors will become customers.

13. People often mistrust Internet businesses they don't know or can't contact. If you've been in business for a few years, or if you have credentials that sound impressive, brag a little, let people know about it. Include your telephone and fax numbers, and a mailing address, to help visitors feel confident that they are dealing with a legitimate business. If you list a toll free number, include your regular phone number for overseas customers.

14. Include your phone number or other contact information on every page of your web site. Some people print out a page from your site and then can't remember how to contact you.

15. Don't force people to register on your web site or give out personal information unless they are placing an order. If you ask for personal information, you will lose most of your visitors.

16. Buyers want to know up front how much an order really costs, including shipping. Too many sites don't show shipping charges until after the customer fills in the order form. If your customers have to fill out their orders before finding out how much shipping will cost them, you will lose many customers.

Starting With a Simple Site

If you are just testing the Internet waters, I suggest you start with a site that is simple and basic, something you can have up and running quickly, and expand from there. You can start with an easy-to-build web site, often called a "billboard," "brochure," or "static" site, where your visitors get to look at your site, contact you by e-mail, and place orders offline by mail or telephone. From there you can add online ordering, product searches, and other interactive options. Web sites can be designed and modified and remodified, constantly if necessary, until you hit on a formula that works.

Don't be afraid to experiment with your site. One great advantage that web sites have over printed catalogs and retail stores is the ability to try a new design or a new offer, with little cost, and see near-immediate results. What happens if you offer a 10% discount versus a 5% discount, or no discount at all? You can test your prices quickly, sometimes within a few hours, and keep revising your offers until you find out what

works. Try offering free shipping, and see if sales increase. What if you offer free gift wrapping? If you suspect that an offer of free gift wrap might boost sales, you can test that idea for a few days, and measure the results before investing in a truckload of wrapping paper.

Before you promote your site to the world, test and fine-tune it until you like what you see. Once you are satisfied with the site, include the web address on advertisements, business cards, stationery, etc.

Choosing a Web Designer

Everybody and her cousin, it seems, knows someone who is a web designer. You have lots of options if you are looking to hire an individual or a business to design a web site for you. You can hire someone who advertises nationally, someone who you never meet in person. Or, as I much prefer, you can hire someone local, who you can meet and work with, face to face.

Get recommendations from other businesses. If you work with a local ISP, they will know (or even have) people who design sites. A local computer shop, or the local college computer instructor, can usually recommend web designers. Some important considerations:

1. What experience does the designer have? Talk to other businesses who have used the designer and ask if they are satisfied with his or her work.

2. Look at the web sites the designer created. Do they look good? Do they load fast? Do they work well?

3. Do the major search engines find the designer's web sites and give them prominent listings? A good web designer knows how to design a web site so search engines find the site.

4. Will the designer create a site for you that you can maintain, change and update yourself without the designer's ongoing assistance?

Contracting With a Web Designer

All aspects of the design work should be discussed in detail, in advance. There are many variables when it comes to designing a web site, hours spent that may not produce the results you want, work that may require fine tuning or even starting all over. Don't be embarrassed to talk money, don't leave it to "we'll work it out later."

All of the details should be in writing, part of a written contract. If you leave the details to chance, chance is you'll wish you hadn't. Some things your contract probably should cover:

1. What the designer will create, how big the site will be, what will be included in the site, how long the work will take.

2. Cost and payment terms. Do you pay the designer a flat fee for a complete job, finished to your satisfaction, and paid when the job is done? That by far would be your best deal, but the designer may not care for such a contract that leaves him vulnerable to not getting paid. Do you pay by the hour, no matter how many hours are spent, no matter what the results are? Do you set a maximum number of hours? Do you pay a deposit? Do you pay in installments? When is payment due? What if you do not like the work? What if you want to make changes after the work is completed? Do you set deadlines for completing the work? What if the deadlines are missed?

3. Does your contract include an agreement for ongoing help from the designer, or for making changes to the web site, after the site is designed and online? Will the designer teach you how to maintain and update your web site yourself?

4. Your contract should state clearly that you own all of the rights to the contents of the site, the overall design of the site, and the programming used to create the site. This is a critical clause in the contract. If you do not establish your ownership right with a signed contract, the designer of your site can sometimes claim legal ownership of the contents and the programming. Don't let this happen.

For more information about contracts, see the chapter "Contracts" in this section of the book.

Know what your site is supposed to accomplish before you design the web pages. If you don't know what your site is for, your visitors certainly won't either. This may sound obvious, but you would be surprised how many commercial sites are out there that look like they have no clear purpose.

—James Dillehay, author, The Basic Guide to Selling Crafts on the Internet

Online Ordering: Shopping Carts

The most common way to take online orders is through what's called a "shopping cart." This isn't a cart at all, but a software system for taking credit card orders over the Internet. It's called a shopping cart because many web sites offer several different products. Each product you want to buy, you add to the "cart." Once you've loaded your cart, you "check out," which means you type in your name, address, credit card number, and all the other information the site requests and/or demands of you. When the order is complete, the customer clicks a final button to send the order.

Web hosts offer shopping carts as part of their web packages. While all shopping carts are similar, there are subtle but sometimes significant differences between the carts. Some allow more flexibility and customization than others. Some are more user friendly than others.

Internet buyers are quick to abandon a shopping cart that confuses them, that makes them work too hard to use the cart, or that asks too many unnecessary personal questions. Any shopping cart that demands personal information before the order is filled out is most likely to be abandoned.

A good shopping cart system will include an automatic follow-up e-mail sent immediately to the purchaser, confirming the order, thanking the purchaser for the order, letting the purchaser know when the goods will be shipped, and giving the purchaser a way to respond if something is wrong.

How The Shopping Cart Sale Works

When someone orders from your shopping cart, the order is automatically sent to you, or sent to your credit card processor, who then forwards the order to you. The order information the shopping cart collects travels over the Internet. This information can be read by anyone who can gain access to the information, legitimately or otherwise.

One way to protect private information from prying eyes is to use a "secure server." A secure server scrambles ("encrypts") the information into an unreadable code, so it cannot be understood until it is unscrambled. Encrypted information keeps thieves and hackers and unauthorized people from understanding the information should they be able to access it.

Most secure-server software encrypts information only while it is travelling, from your customer to you or to your credit card processor. The likelihood of someone grabbing your customer's information while it is travelling from the customer's computer to yours is highly unlikely, encrypted or not.

As soon as the information arrives, it is unencrypted. When customer information is on your computer hard drive, or on your web server's computer, it is a sitting duck for anyone trying to break into the computer. Should someone gain access to your computer or your web server's computer, the hacker could see (and steal) your customer's information. Again, this is an unlikely scenario.

Because secure servers encrypt information only during transmission, the protection they offer is minimal, almost worthless. But Internet shoppers don't know this. Internet shoppers think secure servers are secure. The shoppers look for the little padlock logo that tells them they are on a secure server, and they are much more likely to order from you if you have a secure server. Anything you can do to make your customers feel comfortable and safe when ordering from you, will be worth the effort.

I recommend, however, that you do not include a statement on your web site or shopping cart that customers' transactions and private information are 100% secure, because they aren't. Once you make such a claim, you are setting yourself up for problems if the claim proves to be untrue, even if it was not your fault.

Some web sites warn customers that they have no control over hackers. Some web sites require customers to agree not to sue the web site owner if the customers' information is stolen. This, of course, is unfriendly territory, likely to scare away customers. You may be best off just not saying anything.

E-Mail

If you want your business e-mail to look professional, be sure the service you use does not tack on an ad. Many of the free e-mail services put an advertisement on every e-mail sent. If all of your e-mails to your customers include a message like "Get your own free Hotmail account,"

that looks unprofessional. Prospective customers will be wondering if this is a real business.

E-mail is a double-edged sword. Because e-mail is informal by nature, people type things in e-mail that they'd never write in a letter, let alone say to someone's face. Once an e-mail is sent, there's no retrieving it. It's as good as cast in stone. E-mail, being so spontaneous and often not well thought out, has gotten some people in legal hot water. Lawyers often talk about "smoking gun" documents in legal cases. E-mail has become the #1 source of damaging evidence in many legal disputes.

Lastly, check your spelling. Most e-mail programs include a spel checker.

E-Mail and the Law

When you make a sales offer, or agree to a purchase, or make any other business commitment using e-mail, you have created a binding, legal contract, if the other party decides to hold you to it.

Think out your e-mail business dealings as carefully as you would a formal contract. Once an e-mail is sent, there's no retrieving it. As Stevie Wonder sang, it's "Signed, sealed and delivered...I'm yours." Consider holding the e-mail for a day before sending it, just to be sure you got everything the way you want it. Give it a fresh re-reading the next morning before sending it. Do not send anything by e-mail that demands security or might cause you a problem with privacy. Delete sensitive information as soon as possible.

E-Mail From A Web Site

I like web sites that let visitors e-mail your business directly from the site. The visitor does not have to log off the site, or type in your e-mail address, to send you an e-mail.

Most web sites use an e-mail address that includes the domain name of the web site. For example, if your domain name is www.buystuff.com, your e-mail can be sent to you@buystuff.com, or info@buystuff.com, catalog@buystuff.com, newsletter@buy-stuff.com, any-name-you-want@buystuff.com. You can have multiple e-mail names @buystuff.com.

All of the different e-mail names @buystuff.com are actually sent to one e-mail address, your regular e-mail address at your regular ISP. Even if your ISP does not host your web site, the e-mail is still routed to you through your ISP. This is known as an e-mail "alias." It is a seamless operation, invisible to the web visitor.

An e-mail address through your own web site has a professional appearance, and makes it easy for customers to remember your e-mail address. An e-mail address through your web site eliminates the problem of losing your e-mail address if you switch ISPs. The web site can direct e-mail from the site to any ISP you choose.

Links

Links from other web sites will bring more visitors to your site. A link is like a recommendation, like word-of-mouth publicity, and usually costs nothing.

Let me give you a real life example. My publisher, Bell Springs Publishing, publishes a pinball machine repair book, which appeals to a small but eager group of people. Bell Springs set up a separate web site just for that one book (www.aboutpinball.com). The publisher then went surfing the Internet, using search engines, and found several hundred web sites about pinball. Some were businesses, some were pinball organizations, many were individuals with small web sites dedicated to their favorite hobby. My publisher e-mailed every site she found, requesting a link. Many of the sites happily agreed. The links brought many additional visitors to the aboutpinball.com web site.

Links have extra benefits. Search engines often find a link to a web site rather than web site itself. It is effortless for a web surfer, led to a link, to click on the link and get re-routed to your site. Links from other sites also can boost your search engine rankings.

Legal Problems With Links

If your web site includes links to other sites, the links may cause you problems. Some web sites do not want to be linked to others, and strictly forbid it in the terms posted on their sites. Sites that are linked without their approval have been known to claim copyright infringement, or even trespassing, against the site offering the link. Sites that have legal requirements for entry, requiring visitors to click on an ap-

proval button, may claim breach-of-contract infringement if your link to their site bypasses the approval button.

Some sites are concerned that viewers will think the link is your site, and not their site. This is especially true if the link leads your visitors to a page within someone else's site and not to that site's home page. This is known as "deep linking," and makes it easy to mislead viewers as to who's site they are actually viewing. This is an untested and questionable area of law. But you don't want to be the one doing the test, and there is nothing to be gained by angering the owners of a site. Get and keep written permission to link a site.

Want to know more link-related problems? If you are linked to a site that has libelous, objectionable or illegal material on it, your site could be implicated. The courts sometimes rule that third party sites can be liable for contents of a linked site, if the third party knew, or should have known, that the linked site contained infringing or illegal material.

This "third party" liability is a rare situation, and easily avoided. This situation might occur only if you include a link to a "problem" site on your own site. It's always a good idea to periodically check any links you include on your site.

Generally, you are not held responsible for another site's contents if that site includes your site as a link. But if you find your web site listed as a link on someone else's web site that you find questionable or problematical, send an e-mail and request that the link be removed. Keep a copy of your e-mail should you ever be questioned about your connection to the problem site.

Protect Your Business

The more your business relies on technology, on networks, on the Internet, on any functions not directly within your control, the bigger your risk that some technological glitch can shut you down or do damage to your business operations, your records, your transactions, and your relations with your customers and suppliers.

I won't get into the usual nightmare list of possible disasters. I simply suggest that you sit down, right now while everything is working properly, and make contingency plans to protect yourself if the tech world you depend on causes you a problem or two.

You should have backup data for all of your business records, data that is not on the Internet and not on your hard drive, data you can get your hands on if the power fails, if the computer blows up, if your Internet Service Provider deep-sixes. And you should keep your backup data up to date.

Backing up your files is extra work, and it's a nuisance. But sooner or later you will lose something in the computer or on the Internet. Your backup is your insurance, and you write your own insurance policy on this one. It's up to you.

One possible problem you definitely should inquire about: What happens if your Internet Service Provider goes down? Does your ISP have a contingency plan? If the Internet is essential to your business, you may want to have an account with a second ISP, one you can log onto should you main ISP fail you. Same for e-mail. Having more than one e-mail account gives you some backup protection.

Internet Security

Nothing on the Internet is 100% secure. Web site owners should take as many reasonable precautions as possible.

Limit access to your computer. If employees or others will be using your computer, establish passwords that let people only into the areas you want them to be able to access. Change the passwords if an employee quits or is fired. Lock the door when you are not around.

Don't leave your Internet connection on all the time. A sitting, Internet-connected computer gives hackers lots of time to try to break in.

Do not store your customers' personal information on your web site. Once a transaction is complete, move the information offline. This way, should anyone gain unauthorized access to your site, there will be no credit card numbers and other private customer information to steal.

Have a back up copy of your web site in case your web host goes out of business.

Protect Your Privacy

The Internet is a very un-private place. Anyone can see your web site, and many people could wind up reading what you thought was private e-mail. Information you give to others over the Internet, even confidential information, can find its way to web sites, other businesses, individuals, and (uh oh) government agencies.

Internal Revenue Service auditors sometimes look at web sites of businesses they are auditing. The auditors get an idea of what the company does, how big it is. Auditors look for information on the site that might have a bearing on what the company reported on its tax return. (Isn't this a great way to end the chapter?)

Aaron Brown, Co founder, CRaider.com, New York, NY: "The Internet is smart and flexible, while big companies are mostly pretty stupid. While business is trying to take over the Internet, the Internet will take over business."

Mark Monaco, Partner, DiBruno Brothers Gourmet Foods, Philadelphia: "We took an intimate, personal retailer and made it work across four time zones."

Robert D. Hof, Business Week: "If you click past the famous brand names, you'll find thousands of small businesses you never heard of, quietly making a go of it online, providing welcome relief from the big brands. The small businesses thrive because they're focused on narrow niches they know really well, allowing them to provide intensely personal service."

Eric Rydholm, Motley Fool Corporation: "To succeed online you need to build a cult because you can sell a lot of stuff to a cult."

MANAGING and MARKETING YOUR BUSINESS

Volumes have been written on the subject of small business "management." I put the word in quotes because it is such an all-encompassing term. Just about anything you, the owner, do is labeled "management." And just about every study on small business failures blames over 90% of those failures on "poor management."

"Poor management" refers to everything from sloppy bookkeeping to lousy business location. If you sell clothing, and the fashions suddenly change leaving you with unsalable merchandise, it's labeled "poor management": you should have been aware of the market trends and should have made advance preparations to anticipate them. If you expected your business to show a profit the first year, but you wound up with a loss and not enough reserve cash to keep things going, that's another situation they call "poor management."

Management is an organic part of your business, interwoven into every aspect of business. It isn't like Step One—get a business license, Step Two—manage, Step Three—post the ledgers, etc. Management is something you can learn only by doing, but a few evenings spent with some good management reading won't do you any harm.

Almost every library in the country has at least ten books on business management. Some of the books are excellent, some are shallow; almost all of them go unread. An interesting SBA study of 81 small businesses showed that only one owner in 81 read any management literature. Most of those 81 businesses failed. There are thousands of defunct businesses, gone belly-up because of the same management errors repeated over and over again. I guess it's just human nature to want to learn from your own mistakes.

You will get the most value out of management books if you read them after you've had several months' experience in your new venture. You will understand much better what the books are discussing, and you will quickly spot the information most valuable to you.

Join the trade organizations for your type of business, and subscribe to the trade magazines. Many libraries have reference books listing dozens of trade organizations and journals.

The best management advice you can get, however, is from other small business people.

Business men and women, I find, love to talk about business. Business is a large part of their lives, and they love to share their experiences and their ideas. You can't get better advice at any price. No accountant or lawyer or college professor knows half of what the person who's doing it every day knows. Strike up acquaintances, get to be friends with business people, find out about the local merchant's organizations and attend their luncheons. Have a little fun, too.

Management is just common sense. As soon as you read or hear advice or a suggestion, you know instinctively that it's right. ("Why didn't I think of that?") If it doesn't hit you that way when you hear it, if it doesn't make total sense, don't rely on it. It's probably bad advice, for now anyway; but check back in six months or a year.

Marketing

Keeping a business successful requires ongoing marketing: promoting your business every day, trying to satisfy and keep the customers you already have and find new ones.

Marketing will always be experimental. Bounce your ideas off other people. Talk to everyone who is interested. Don't hire a consultant.

A common misconception is that marketing means advertising. Advertising is only one element of marketing. Advertising may or may not work depending on the type of business you have and how talented you are at designing ads. Word of mouth may be your best advertising, and that means always making sure you have satisfied customers.

Think like a customer. Forget how great your business is, and put yourself in the shoes of your customer. What would *you* want as a customer?

Sometimes, a business will take unsuspected detours as the owner responds to customers' needs. There are many businesses that began in one direction only to be forced by the rhythm of their particular business, and the needs of their customers, to go in another direction entirely.

One more suggestion: Take all complaints seriously. Most customers don't complain. ("How was the meal?" "Fine.") They just walk away and never come back. They don't say anything to you, but you can be sure they tell all their friends. If only one customer complains, you can figure at least ten others have the same complaint. If you can solve that customer's problem, not only will you keep that customer (and make him or her one of your best boosters in the bargain), you'll probably keep many of the others you would have otherwise lost.

Lara Stonebraker, Cunningham's Coffee: "It's important to keep your merchandise rotating in the store, constantly change the position of things. You'd be surprised how many people will say, 'Gee, you've got something new in,' when you know it's been sitting there for two years; you've just moved it from this shelf to that shelf. It has to be displayed in a coherent manner. You have to have all those things that are related together. And you have to give your customers an incredible selection. If you have espresso pots, you have to have them in nine sizes because people will not be inclined to buy if there is only a choice of two or three. Even if you stock only one of these odd-sized items that you know will not be selling, you still have to have it just to fill up your shelf, to give the impression that you have a huge variety.

"People will come to your store because they know you have a large selection. A lot of times I know that it's purely psychological, because I know that I will never sell a 12-cup pot and I know that I will never sell a one-cup pot. But I have to have them there just for the comparison, just so that people will feel that this is a store that has everything, that has all the choices they can possibly get, they don't need to go anywhere else for it. I've seen a lot of coffee stores make this mistake, having only two sizes of something. It just doesn't give you the confidence in the store.

"I do rotating displays on the expensive items every other week. I try to create the kind of display that will make customers stop and look, but not so much that the background will overpower the items you are selling. You can't have too many plants, you can't have things that will distract from your merchandise.

"And you can't have a no-don't-touch atmosphere. You don't want things looking too pretty because people will be afraid to touch them, they'll feel inhibited. Most important of all, you can't have any bare walls. There was a place in San Francisco that opened and the woman just didn't have enough money to buy another cabinet, so she had one wall, the prime wall for display, just blank. Mr. Peet came in and said, 'Oh, that's a lovely wall; are you selling walls?'"

THE FUTURE OF SMALL BUSINESS

Since the dawn of economic time, a person with the right idea at the right time and any degree of competence could make a go of small business. Today, even in our shaky economy, with giant corporations getting more and more of the consumer's dollars and with chain stores driving independents out of business, small businesses can and do survive and thrive. Businesses attentive to local and neighborhood needs and businesses attentive to customers' personal needs will always have an edge over large, faceless corporations.

Small business owners themselves can help, by patronizing other small and locally owned businesses. Not only does it help the small business environment in general, it keeps the money in town, to be re-spent again in town. What's more, you might meet other local business owners, and exchange help and ideas.

Small business is an ever changing world—not just the laws, but the entire concept of how to be successful as the world continues to change around us. No business can stand still.

I invite you to write me if I can be of further help to you.

Bernard Kamoroff
c/o Bell Springs Publishing
Box 1240, Willits, Calif. 95490
kamoroff@bellsprings.com

UPDATE SHEET

Each January, I prepare a one-page Update Sheet for *Small Time Operator*. The Update Sheet lists changes in tax laws and other government regulations, referenced to the corresponding pages in the book.

If you would like a copy of the Update Sheet, send a self-addressed, stamped #10 (business size) envelope and $1.00 to: Small Time Operator Update, Box 1240, Willits, CA 95490.

With the Update Sheet, you can keep your edition of *Small Time Operator* up to date, year after year.

Section Seven
THE LEDGERS

If you were able to examine a hundred different businesses you would probably see a hundred different bookkeeping systems. Every business has its own needs and its own idea how the ledgers should be set up. Some business owners enjoy bookkeeping and like to keep elaborate ledgers. Many owners hate the paper-work and keep books to the barest minimum.

I designed these ledgers to be of use to the greatest number of small businesses, particularly new businesses with no bookkeeping experience. There is nothing elaborate about them. They are basic, but complete. You can use these ledgers as is or change them to fit your needs. I encourage you to experiment with your bookkeeping, to alter the ledgers in any way that will make them more useful to you and your particular business.

These ledgers are samples to use as you want. You are welcome to photocopy them for your personal use. Or you can buy blank ledgers from any office supply store, and set them up using these ledger as a model.

If you use a computer to do bookkeeping, these ledgers can be used as a prototype. When first using a computer, I suggest you keep duplicate hand posted ledgers for at least a month, just to be sure your computer program is error-free and producing correct information.

Your ledgers should be a permanent record. Keep them for as long as you own the business. They will help you prove your figures if you are ever audited. Comparing months and eventually comparing years will help you plan for the future. Lenders, investors and possible future buyers will want to see your old ledgers.

INCOME LEDGER Month of ——————————

1	2	3			4		5		6		7	
DATE	SALES PERIOD	TAXABLE SALES			SALES TAX		NON-TAXABLE SALES				TOTAL SALES	
1												
2												
3												
4												
5												
6												
7												
8												
9												
10												
11												
12												
13												
14												
15												
16												
17												
18												
19												
20												
21												
22												
23												
24												
25												
26												
27												
28												
29												
30												
31												
	TOTALS FOR MONTH											

INCOME LEDGER — Year-End Summary

1	2 TOTALS FOR MONTH OF	3 TAXABLE SALES	4 SALES TAX	5 NON-TAXABLE SALES	6	7 TOTAL SALES
	January					
	February					
	March					
	April					
	May					
	June					
	July					
	August					
	September					
	October					
	November					
	December					
	TOTAL FOR YEAR					

EXPENDITURE LEDGER

DATE	CHECK NO.	PAYEE	TOTAL	1 INVEN-TORY	2 SUPPLIES, POSTAGE, ETC.	3 OUTSIDE CONTRACTORS

4	5	6	7	8	9	10	11
EMPLOYEE PAYROLL	ADVERTISING	RENT	UTILITIES	TAXES & LICENSES		MISC.	NON-DEDUCT.

YEAR-END EXPENDITURE SUMMARY

			TOTAL	1 INVEN-TORY	2 SUPPLIES, POSTAGE, ETC.	3 OUTSIDE CONTRACTORS
		January total				
		February total				
		March total				
		April total				
		May total				
		June total				
		July total				
		August total				
		September total				
		October total				
		November total				
		December total				
		Unpaid bills (Acct's. Payable):				
		TOTALS FOR YEAR				
		ADDITIONAL EXPENSES:				
		Return Checks (from your "Bad Debts" folder)				
		Uncollectible Accounts (from your "Bad Debts" folder)				
		Auto expense (if you take the standard mileage rate) Mileage for year _____				
		Depreciation (from Depreciation Worksheet. Col. 9, 11, 13, 15 or 17)				

4	5	6	7	8	9	10	11
EMPLOYEE PAYROLL	ADVERTISING	RENT	UTILITIES	TAXES & LICENSES		MISC.	NON-DEDUCT.

EQUIPMENT LEDGER AND DEPRECIATION WORKSHEETS

1	2	3	4	5	6	7	8	9	
DATE	DESCRIPTION	METH.	WRITE OFF PERIOD	NEW OR USED	%	COST	BAL. TO BE DEPR.	DEPR. Year:_____	

10	11	12	13	14	15	16	17	18
BAL. TO BE DEPR.	DEPR. Year:_____	BAL. TO BE DEPR.	DEPR. Year:_____	BAL. TO BE DEPR.	DEPR. Year:_____	BAL. TO BE DEPR.	DEPR. Year:_____	BAL. TO BE DEPR.

PAYROLL LEDGER

Name _____

Address _____

Social Security _____

Pay Rate _____

1	2	3	4	5	6	7	8	9	10	11	12	13
PAYCHECK DATE	CHECK NO.	PAY PERIOD	HOURS REG	O/T	GROSS	F.I.T.	SOCIAL SECURITY	MEDI-CARE	STATE INCOME	OTHER WITHHOLDING		NET PAY

PARTNERS CAPITAL LEDGER

1	2	3	4	5	6	7
DATE	DESCRIPTION	ACTIVITY	BALANCE	ACTIVITY	BALANCE	TOTAL BALANCE

PETTY CASH LEDGER

Period _____   Page _____ of _____

DATE	DESCRIPTION	AMT.	BAL.
	Beginning Balance		
		TOTAL	

Check Number _____   Posted to Ledger _____

INVENTORY RECORD

Item _____   Supplier _____

DATE ORDERED	QUANTITY ORDERED	DATE REC'D.	QUANTITY REC'D.	QUANTITY SOLD	BALANCE ON-HAND

CREDIT LEDGER

1	2	3	4	5	6
SALE DATE	CUSTOMER	INV. NO.	TOTAL SALE AMOUNT	DATE PAID	MEMO

INDEX

More Help for Your Business...

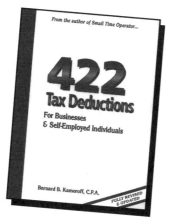

Support Your Local Bookstore

Small Time Operator is available in bookstores across the country. If you are unable to locate it, or any of our other titles, please order directly from us.

Our Guarantee:

All Bell Springs books and software are fully guaranteed. If you are not satisfied for any reason, return the items for a full cash refund, no questions asked.

Need more information?

If you want to know more about any of our titles, don't hesitate to call. We know these books well. Call toll-free: **800-515-8050.**

Telephone and fax orders:

In a hurry? We usually ship the same day. Call toll-free **800-515-8050**, or fax your order to **707-459-8614**. We accept all major credit and debit cards.

Quantity Orders

We offer substantial discounts on bulk sales to organizations, schools, professionals, and businesses. Call our Special Accounts Dept. at **707-459-6372.**

- -

BELL SPRINGS PUBLISHING
Mail Order Sales Dept.
Box 1240, Willits, California 95490

___ #01	Small Time Operator	**$17.95**	_____
___ #02	422 Tax Deductions	**$17.95**	_____
___ #03	Small Time Operator Software	**$29.95**	_____
___ #04	Marketing Without Advertising	**$18.95**	_____
___ #05	Selling Arts & Crafts	**$14.95**	_____
___ #06	Getting Into Mail Order	**$14.95**	_____
___ #07	Negotiating Purchase or Sale	**$18.95**	_____
___ #08	Golden Entrepreneuring	**$16.95**	_____

Book Total $_____

California residents add 7.25% sales tax   _____

Shipping $ **4.00**

Total: check, money order or credit card $_____

Name_____

Address_____

City _____ State _____ Zip _____

Credit Card or Debit Card Orders: VISA ___   MasterCard ___   AmEx ___   Discover ___

Card # _____ Exp. Date _____

Signature_____